Bibliografische Information der Deutschen Nationalbibliothek

Die Deutsche Nationalbibliothek verzeichnet diese Publikation in der
Deutschen Nationalbibliografie; detaillierte bibliografische Daten sind
im Internet über http://dnb.d-nb.de abrufbar.

ISBN 978-3-8325-2239-1

Logos Verlag Berlin GmbH
Comeniushof, Gubener Str. 47,
10243 Berlin
Tel.: +49 030 42 85 10 90
Fax: +49 030 42 85 10 92
INTERNET: http://www.logos-verlag.de

Wolfgang Lohmann

On Language Processors
and
Software Maintenance

Dissertation
zur
Erlangung des akademischen Grades
Doktor-Ingenieur (Dr.-Ing.)
der Fakultät für Informatik und Elektrotechnik
der Universität Rostock

The present work has been accepted by the Faculty of Computer Science and Electrical Engineering at University of Rostock in May 2009 as dissertation to achieve the academic degree Doktor-Ingenieur (Dr.-Ing.).

Referees:	Prof. Dr. rer. nat. Dr. Ing. habil. Günter Riedewald (supervisor) University of Rostock, Germany
	Prof. Dr.-Ing. Ralf Lämmel University of Koblenz-Landau, Germany
	Professor Dr. Marjan Mernik University of Maribor, Slovenia

Submission:	27th October 2008
Defence:	17th April 2009

Abstract

Software maintenance factories are infrastructures that generate tools for software main-tenance from language descriptions and additional information. Besides the maintenance of language specifications, software language evolution requires maintenance of software written in that language as well as maintenance of software that transforms software writ-ten in the evolving language. We argue that a software maintenance factory needs special maintenance. It should provide support for maintenance of language descriptions, derived tools, and the maintenance factory itself. As language processors can form the core of such technology, we investigate their improvement. This is done in three areas:

Maintenance: We investigate the consequences of software language evolution. A gram-mar change can have an effect on the words of the language and can require an adap-tation of documents containing the words. A special case is the format evolution of data and a necessary adaptation of the data existing. We study this problem for for-mat evolution for DTDs. While the words of the language remain the same after the refactoring of a context-free grammar, semantic rules have to be adapted in an attribute grammar. We study the consequences of left-recursion removal to attribute grammars and justify that the semantic rules can be automatically adapted while preserving the semantics. Declarative transformation rules can transform programs that are available as abstract syntax trees. When an underlying grammar is extended, existing transformation rules need to be adapted. To study the problem we introduce layout preservation to an existing language processor and demonstrate that transfor-mation rules can be automatically adapted. By defining an aspect-oriented model for Prolog we support modularity of language descriptions based on logic gram-mars, and consequently, that of derived language processors, which makes them better maintainable, replaceable, and configurable.

Technical improvement: By defining basic roles of program extension we provide a way for more disciplined meta-programming for declarative programs including lan-guage descriptions. Using language technology we introduce layout preservation in existing language processors for maintenance. We analyse transformation rules regarding their layout preservation behaviour. Besides using the analyse to for auto-matic decisions on layout preservation, it can advice the coder of a transformation rule to change the specification style to make layout preservation more likely.

Usability for the user: Disciplined meta-programming increases the usability, as it al-lows to define reusable and better understandable recipes of meta-programs. We discuss that the left recursion removal with automatic migration of semantic rules can help to preserve readability of grammars in use. We show that complexity of argument positions in transformation rules can be hidden by applying the approach of grammar extension and automatically migrating the transformation rules. We provide an object-oriented combination model for transformations. Based on it, a workbench for visual interactive explorative transformational programming has been implemented with grammars and transformations as first class citizens.

Kewords: Software Language Engineering, Software Language Evolution, Grammarware, Software Evolution, Software Maintenance, Program Transformation, Language Processors, Meta-Programming, Declarative Programming, Aspect-Oriented Programming, Language Definition, Source to Source Transformation

CR Classification: D.1.6 [Logic Programming], D.1.7 [Visual Programming], D.2.1 [Requirements/Specifications], D.2.6 [Programming Environments], D.2.13 [Reusable Software], D.3.3 [Language Constructs and Features], D.3.4 [Processors], F.3.3 [Studies of Program Constructs], F.4.2 [Grammars and Other Rewriting Systems]

Zusammenfassung

Ein Konstruktionssystem für die Softwarewartung ist eine Infrastruktur, die aus Sprachbeschreibungen und zusätzlicher Information Werkzeuge generiert. Neben der Wartung von Sprachbeschreibungen erfordert die Evolution von Softwaresprachen sowohl die Wartung der in dieser Sprache geschriebenen Software als auch die Wartung der Software, welche in dieser Sprache geschriebene Software transformiert. Wir argumentieren, dass so ein Konstruktionssystem spezielle Wartung erfordert. Es sollte außerdem Unterstützung für die Wartung von Sprachbeschreibungen, für die davon abgeleiteten Werkzeuge und für das Konstruktionssystem selber bieten. Da Sprachprozessoren den Kern solcher Technologie darstellen, untersuchen wir deren Verbesserung auf drei Gebieten:

Wartung dieser Werkzeuge: Wir untersuchen die Folgen der Evolution von Softwaresprachen. Eine Grammatikänderung kann Auswirkungen auf die Wörter der Sprache haben und die Anpassung der Dokumente erfordern, welche diese Wörter enthalten. Ein Spezialfall ist die Evolution von Datenformaten und die dann erforderliche Anpassung der existierenden Daten. Wir untersuchen das Problem anhand der Formatevolution von XML Dokumenten. Während die Wörter der Sprache bei einem Refaktoring einer kontextfreien Grammatik gleich bleiben, müssen semantische Regeln in einer attributierten Grammatik angepasst werden. Wir untersuchen die Folgen der Entfernung von Linksrekursion in attributierten Grammatiken auf die semantischen Regeln. Wir beweisen, dass diese Regeln automatisch semantik-erhaltend angepasst werden können. Deklarative Regeln können Transformationen von Programmen beschreiben, die als abstrakte Syntaxbäume vorliegen. Wird eine zugrundeliegende Grammatik erweitert, müssen diese Regeln angepasst werden. Um dieses Problem zu untersuchen, erweitern wir bestehende Sprachprozessoren, so dass sie Layouterhaltung unterstützen. Wir zeigen, dass die bestehenden Transformationsregeln automatisch angepasst werden können. Wir definieren ein aspekt-orientiertes Modell für Prolog. Dadurch unterstützen wir die Modularisierung von Sprachbeschreibungen basierend auf logischen Grammatiken und folglich auch die Modularisierung von daraus abgeleiteten Sprachprozessoren, was diese besser wartbar, austauschbar und konfigurierbar macht.

Verbesserung der Werkzeuge hinsichtlich der Ausdruckskraft: Durch die Definition von Basisoperatoren für die Erweiterung von logischen Programmen bieten wir einen Weg für verbessertes diszipliniertes Metaprogrammieren auf deklarativen Programmen einschließlich Sprachbeschreibungen. Wir erweitern die Sprachprozessoren für die Softwarewartung mit Hilfe von Sprachtechnologie, so dass sie layouterhaltend transformieren. Wir analysieren Transformationsregeln hinsichtlich ihres Einflusses auf die Layouterhaltung bei Transformationen. Neben der Verwendung für die automatische Anpassung von Transformationsregeln zur Unterstützung von Layouterhaltung kann diese Analyse dem Ersteller einer Transformationsregel auf einen Stil verweisen, der die Layouterhaltung verbessert.

Usability für den Nutzer: Diszipliniertes Metaprogrammieren erhöht die Usability, da dadurch wiederverwendbare und besser verständliche Rezepte von Metaprogrammen definiert werden können. Wir diskutieren, wie die Entfernung von Linksrekursion in attributierten Grammatiken hilft, die Lesbarkeit der verwendeten Grammatik zu erhalten. Wir zeigen, dass die Komplexität von Argumentpositionen in Transformationsregeln durch den Ansatz der Grammatikerweiterung und der automatischen Anpassung von Transformationsregeln versteckt werden kann. Wir geben ein objekt-orientiertes Modell zur Kombination von Transformationen an. Darauf aufbauend ist ein Arbeitsplatz zur visuellen interaktiven explorativen Programmieren mit heterogenen Transformationen implementiert, bei dem Grammatiken und Transformationen als Objekte erster Ordnung behandelt werden.

Acknowledgement

Research is rarely an individual performance in an empty space. I would like to thank everybody who has helped me in several ways.

First of all, I would like to thank my advisor Prof. Günter Riedewald for his guidance. He was always available when I needed him. He was very patient and provided me with many advice and much freedom regarding both, the choice of research topics and the style of working. He shaped my view of a university of a place for research *and teaching*. His dedication to teaching was always a guide for me.

Next, I am very grateful to Prof. Ralf Lämmel who I consider to be an extraordinary researcher and who continuously influenced my research interests. He also opened opportunities for research visits, which were very important for my development. Thanks for many discussions, for repeatingly motivating me, and for introducing me to red Bordeaux.

I have visited two places repeatedly for research stays, which formed the foundation of my research topic. First, I would like to thank the Programming Research Group at University of Amsterdam and CWI Amsterdam, and particularly Paul Klint, who provided me the opportunity of the research visits at UvA and CWI, and Chris Verhoef for the opportunity of the research visit at Vrije University Amsterdam. Jurgen Vinju was very helpful regarding all technical questions. Second, I would like to thank Marjan Mernik and his colleagues for very kind hospitality during three research visits in Maribor. Marjan Mernik also introduced me to the field of Aspect-Oriented Programming. We had many fruitful discussions. Thanks to Damijan Rebernak for his help with the Lisa web service.

Also, I would like to thank my former colleagues in Rostock for their comments and discussions; especially Jörg Harm and Elke Tetzner for sharing the office with me, and Prof. Forbrig for his kind of humor. I would like to emphasise my thanks to Anke Dittmar for her view on the world I share and for being a researcher who does not forget that it is the human who should be the centre of our attention.

My thesis has profited from discussions and comments at workshops and conferences. I would like to thank Mark van den Brand, Jim Cordy, Meike Klettke, Günter Kniesel, Damijan Rebernak, Eelco Visser, Joost Visser, the anonymous reviewers of LOPSTR'99, CSMR'03, LDTA'04, Object-Oriented Technologies '06, LOPSTR'06, TOOLS'07, IET Software Special Issue on SE '08. Some former students contributed in some way to my work, especially Benjamin Mesing, Markus Stoy, Guido Wachsmuth, and Thomas Zühlke.

Thanks to Axel Arnold, Heiko Kopp, Lothar Ludwig, Yves Maurischat, Georg Petry, Arches of The Lands of Evermore, for their work in the MUD. Much of the thesis has been influenced by the maintenance activities we have performed together.

Much of my energy and support I got from many others. Thanks to my best friends Jörn Oldag and Henning Güldner. I am very grateful for the discussions and wine we had together, not to speak of financial support. I would like to thank Randolf Schultz for many delicious salads and the daily companionship at lunch (as well for many technical discussions). Thanks to Carsten Eichholz for philosophical discussions and for showing me that there can always be another point of view at the world and both views, though contrary, can still be valid. Thanks to Uwe "mein Zahnarzt" Poser, who saved my set of teeth, and Jens Neumann. I am very grateful for the motivation I got from Peggy Kronen.

Finally, thanks to my brothers, who participated endless political discussions, and my parents, especially my mother, who made my study and this thesis possible in the first place.

As a final remark, I would like to mention that this kind of work often is done on the expense of the family or a partner. It is important for me to acknowledge that Maryline Roussette probably suffered and sacrificed more than me through and after all these years to let me complete the thesis. For this, and for her love, I bow to her and say I am really sorry that things turned out this way.

One night with full moon

Futoa

Full moon. It is there. Round.
Through the night.
Scary, the sound.
Right.

Jedsjala zuto fromask
Huo tao brask
Emid eowu
Taloa penado

Magic. It develops. Strong.
It's just enough.
Nearly. How long?
Tough.

Tequo polo zonka bong
Yoma dola rong

Oria dra gna so
Piso wa fraso
Demi rua eh
Zunda brodame

Some Work. It is hard. Fine.
All. Well done.
Saved. In time.
Gone.

Tequo polo zonka bong
Yoma dola rong

Bardsja yo-ima te
Fora rula nee
Demi vao ska
Oton Tunskala

Tequo polo zonka bon
Yoma dola rong

(From the Library of Tunskala, by Wolfgang Lohmann: A poem and a song of Tunskala that are somehow related to the thesis... it may serve as an apologise for all remaining errors in the thesis, technical as well as english.)

Contents

List of Figures   **xvii**

1 Introduction   **1**
  1.1 Summary   1
  1.2 Bird's eye view - The larger Context : Software Evolution   3
    1.2.1 Software Maintenance   3
    1.2.2 Co-evolution   7
  1.3 Middle View: an Instance of the Co-evolution Problem   9
    1.3.1 Software Maintenance Factories 10
    1.3.2 Language Processors 11
  1.4 Evolution in Maintenance Tools - Experience and Research Questions . . 13
    1.4.1 Change of Language Description 13
    1.4.2 Migration of Source Code due to Grammar Change 14
    1.4.3 Migration of Rewrite Rules due to Grammar Change 14
    1.4.4 Adaptation of Language Descriptions to improve Maintenance Tools 15
    1.4.5 Modularisation of Language Descriptions and Derived Tools . . . 15
    1.4.6 Usability in Transformational Programming 16
  1.5 Overview of the Chapters 16
  1.6 Origins of the Chapters 18

2 Roles of Program Extension   **21**
  2.1 Introduction 21
  2.2 The Underlying Meta-programming Framework 23
    2.2.1 The Effect Space 24
    2.2.2 Object Programs 25
    2.2.3 Types at the Object Level 27
    2.2.4 Addressing Fragments 28
  2.3 Extending Computational Behaviour 29
    2.3.1 Semantics-preservation 29
    2.3.2 A Core Calculus 30
    2.3.3 Completion of the Core Calculus 32
    2.3.4 Techniques 35
  2.4 Related Work 37
  2.5 Concluding Remarks 39

3 Format Evolution   **41**
  3.1 Introduction 41
  3.2 The Approach in a Nutshell 43

3.2.1   Restructuring 43
3.2.2   Enrichment 44
3.2.3   Attributes to Elements Conversion 45
3.2.4   Transformation Technology 45
3.3   Properties of Transformations 46
3.3.1   Well-formedness 46
3.3.2   Validity 47
3.3.3   Totality and Partiality 47
3.3.4   Structure Preservation 48
3.4   Refactoring 49
3.4.1   Renaming 49
3.4.2   Introduction and Elimination 50
3.4.3   Folding and Unfolding 51
3.4.4   Elements vs. Attributes 52
3.5   Construction and Destruction 54
3.5.1   Generalisation and Restriction of Expressions 54
3.5.2   First Intermezzo: Replacing Content Particles 55
3.5.3   Second Intermezzo: Matching at the XML Level 56
3.5.4   Structure Enrichment and Removal 56
3.5.5   Attributes 57
3.6   Related Work 58
3.7   Concluding Remarks 60

4   Semantics-preserving Migration of Semantic Rules during Left Recursion Removal in Attribute Grammars   63
4.1   Introduction 63
4.2   Notions of Attribute Grammars 64
4.3   Left Recursion Removal in an Example AG 66
4.4   Transformation Schemes for Left Recursion Removal in Multi-pass Attribute Grammars 68
4.4.1   S-attributed Grammars 68
4.4.2   Transformation for IAG 72
4.4.3   Multi-pass Attribute Grammars 74
4.5   Practical Experiences 75
4.6   Related Work 76
4.7   Concluding Remarks 78

5   Towards Automatical Migration of Transformation Rules after Grammar Extension   79
5.1   Introduction and Running Example 79
5.1.1   Two Problems with Maintenance Tools 80
5.1.2   Aim and Result 82
5.1.3   Remainder of the Chapter 83
5.2   Layout in Software Maintenance 83

	5.2.1	The Need for Layout Preservation	83
	5.2.2	Layout in Abstract Syntax	84
5.3		Introducing Layout Preservation to Existing Transformation Systems	84
	5.3.1	Grammar Extension and Transformation Rules	84
	5.3.2	Generalised Use of the Approach	85
5.4		Implementation	87
	5.4.1	Notations and Used Tool	87
	5.4.2	Generating an Internal Representation	88
	5.4.3	Extending the Base Grammar	88
	5.4.4	Migration of Transformation Rules	90
	5.4.5	The Migration Relation	91
5.5		Discussion and Related Work	94
5.6		Concluding Remarks	95

6 Automatic Layout Preservation in Declarative First Order Rewriting   97
6.1		Introduction	97
	6.1.1	Common Approach to treat Layout	98
	6.1.2	Problem Description	98
6.2		Simplifying Assumptions	99
6.3		Notions	100
6.4		Case Discrimination over Argument Positions	101
	6.4.1	Input Position on LHS	102
	6.4.2	Input Position on RHS	103
	6.4.3	Output Position on RHS	105
	6.4.4	Output Position on LHS	106
	6.4.5	Remarks	107
6.5		Related Work	108
6.6		Concluding Remarks	109

7 Aspect-Oriented Prolog in a Language Processing Context   113
7.1		Introduction	113
	7.1.1	Motivation: Modularisation for Logic Grammars	113
	7.1.2	Overview on Key Concepts in the Chapter	115
	7.1.3	Remainder of the Chapter	117
7.2		Aspects in Grammars for Language Processors - a Motivating Example	117
	7.2.1	Grammar Example and a Derived Parser	117
	7.2.2	Scanner Integration is a Concern	118
	7.2.3	AST Construction while Parsing is a Concern	119
	7.2.4	Program Analysis is a Concern	120
	7.2.5	Program Transformation Based on a Generic Aspect traverse/1	121
	7.2.6	A Note on Description Size	122
7.3		A Simple Running Example	123
	7.3.1	Computations on Lists	123
	7.3.2	Aspect-Oriented Description of sumlist	123

7.4 Representing Concepts of AOP in Prolog - Level 1 125
    7.4.1 Control Flow in Prolog and Join points 125
    7.4.2 Pointcuts and Pointcut Descriptions 126
    7.4.3 Pointcut Context 127
    7.4.4 Advice 129
    7.4.5 Aspects 130
    7.4.6 Weaver 131
    7.4.7 A Note on the Implementation 132
7.5 The Aspect Library - Level 2 133
    7.5.1 Stepwise Enhancement, Skeletons, and Techniques 133
    7.5.2 Generalised Techniques 134
    7.5.3 Formalising Techniques as Generic Aspects: Calculate 134
7.6 A DSL - Level 3 136
7.7 Related Work 138
7.8 Concluding Remarks 143

8 A Lightweight Infrastructure to support Experimenting with Heterogeneous Transformations **145**
8.1 Introduction 145
    8.1.1 Experiments with Transformation Nets 145
    8.1.2 Using .NET 146
    8.1.3 Resulting Prototype 146
8.2 Trane Concept 147
8.3 Object-Oriented Model 148
    8.3.1 First Level: Combination Infrastructure 148
    8.3.2 Second Level: Interactivity and Views 150
    8.3.3 Providing a New Box 151
    8.3.4 Computation Strategy 151
8.4 Variants of Boxes 152
    8.4.1 Web Services 152
    8.4.2 Hierarchical Transformations 152
    8.4.3 Use of Native Libraries 152
    8.4.4 XSLT Boxes 154
    8.4.5 Command Line Tools 155
    8.4.6 Dynamic Compilation and Integration 156
    8.4.7 F# and Other Languages 156
8.5 Related Work 157
8.6 Concluding Remarks 158

9 Concluding Remarks **161**
9.1 Summary 161
9.2 Achievements 162
9.3 Outlook 165

A Left Recursion Removal   **169**
  A.1 Algorithm for Simple Multi-pass AG 169
  A.2 The Practical View 171
    A.2.1 An AG-like Notation in Prolog 171
    A.2.2 Prototypes 173
    A.2.3 Scalability 174

Bibliography   **175**

Index   **197**

Contents

List of Figures

1.1 Selected challenges in software evolution from [MWD⁺05] 4
1.2 Selected research challenges from the Grammarware Agenda [KLV05a]
and contributing chapters of the thesis 10
1.3 Chapters vs. questions 16
1.4 Contents of the chapters 16

2.1 The effect space 24
2.2 Interface of the abstract data type for object programs 26
2.3 Interface of the Abstract Data Type for Addressing 29
2.4 The core calculus 31
2.5 Monadic foldr/map on lists 32
2.6 Lifting by *mmap* 33
2.7 The completed calculus 34
2.8 Technique for Accumulation 36
2.9 A notion of projections of programs 38

3.1 Induced XML document migration 42
3.2 A DTD for music albums 43
3.3 A music album as XML document 44
3.4 The identity transformation in XSLT 46
3.5 Form restructuring 51
3.6 Two inconvenient implementations of the fold problem from Section 3.2.1 59

4.1 An example use of the approach 65
4.2 Left recursion removal for context-free grammars 67
4.3 Simple expression definition (left) with left recursion removed (right) . . 67
4.4 Attributed syntax tree for 1+2*3 (left) and without left recursion (right) 68
4.5 Expression with removed left recursion and migrated semantic rules . . . 68
4.6 Transformations of an S-attribute grammar, * representing inherited (on
left side) and synthesised (on right side) attributes of a nonterminal . . . 69
4.7 Syntax trees for the derivation of $\beta\alpha^n$ 71
4.8 Transformations of an I-attribute grammar, * representing inherited (on
left side) and synthesised (on right side) attributes of a nonterminal . . . 73
4.9 Input (left) and output (right) of the prototype 75
4.10 Context-free extract from a yacc specification for expression definition . 76
4.11 Reuse of the original grammar for small maintenance transformations . . 77

5.1 Loop optimisation 80
5.2 A grammar fragment 80

5.3   Rules to extract the assignment of a loop invariant variable   81
5.4   Counting assignments of a variable   81
5.5   Extension by explicit layout   82
5.6   Migrated rules for layout extension   82
5.7   Result without layout preservation   84
5.8   Adaptation of grammar, abstract syntax and rewrite rules   85
5.9   Relations between the grammar, the extended grammar, the abstract syntax
      and migrated abstract syntax, the rewrite rules, and the migrated rewrite rules 86
5.10 Interesting parts of a tree structure   86
5.11 Grammar of LLL-Grammars   87
5.12 Description of the transformation   88
5.13 Resulting logic grammar rule   89
5.14 Some locations for term construction   90
5.15 Migration relation: top level   91
5.16 Configuring the weaving and heuristics for layout preservation   92
5.17 Weaving nonterminals into terms   93

7.1   Extended port model of the IF/Prolog-Tracer. The outer goal box contains
      two clause boxes. Possible control flows are visualised by arrows. 116
7.2   A logic grammar is the starting point for derived language processors. . . 117
7.3   Result: Keywords and lexeme classes need to be scanned. 118
7.4   Result: Parsing, AST construction, and determination of free variables. . . 118
7.5   The pointcut `lexeme` describes positions to scan lexeme classes. 119
7.6   Weaving scanner integration into the grammar using a specialised parser
      aspect. 119
7.7   Description of AST construction for `let`-Expressions using the generic
      aspect `build` from the library (`build/3` implements the build-technique
      using AOP). 120
7.8   Generic build and its pointcuts are instantiated to describe the construction
      of program analysis for unused variables. 121
7.9   Aspect edl: Describing removal of dead lets based on a generic aspect
      traverse/1 similar to parser/1. 122
7.10 Computations on a list skeleton 124
7.11 Pointcut and advice of aspect `sumlist` to sum up the elements of a list . 124
7.12 Parallel, parent, and left context of a goal G_i in a clause c 128
7.13 Result of weaving the `sumlist` aspect to `list/1` of Figure 7.10 131
7.14 Generic Aspect `rename/2` for renaming predicates 131
7.15 Transformations implementing advice 132
7.16 The `calculate`-technique can be described as a generic aspect 135
7.17 `sumlist` can be described based on `calculate` and `rename` 137
7.18 Grammar snippet for the DSL 137
7.19 Mapping of Swell to Laola by example 139

8.1   Trane in action 147

8.2   Class model of Trane 149
8.3   A web service box 153
8.4   A plain hierarchy box 154
8.5   DLL Import 155
8.6   Providing direct Prolog access 155
8.7   Apply XSLT script to input 156
8.8   Wrapping command line tools 157

A.1   Simulation of computation of an attribute by function application   171
A.2   Delayed evaluation of attribute values 172
A.3   Example of Knuth: Converting binary to decimal numbers 172
A.4   Output of the TXL prototype for the Knuth example 173

List of Figures

Chapter 1

Introduction

1.1 Summary

To save costs, time and avoid errors, *language processors* are used to (semi-)automate *software maintenance* tasks. We refer to implemented maintenance tasks as *transformations*. Software language evolution as a special case of software maintenance requires the maintenance of both, the software written in that language and the software that transforms software written in the evolving language.

Software maintenance factories (SMF) are infrastructures to generate, adapt and manage maintenance tools. We study how to improve the SMF by increasing support for automatic *maintenance* of created software maintenance tools, better support for meta-programming and improved *usability* for the user of a factory. As language processors form the heart of such technology, our research is related to the emerging discipline of software language engineering (SLE). *"[SLE] is the application of a systematic, disciplined, quantifiable approach to the development, use, and maintenance"* of *"all sorts of artificial languages used in software development including general purpose programming languages, domain-specific languages, modeling and metamodeling languages, data models, and ontologies."* It *"is concerned with all phases of the lifecycle of software languages; these include the design, implementation, documentation, testing, deployment, evolution, recovery, and retirement of languages. Of special interest are tools, techniques, methods and formalisms that support these activities. In particular, tools are often based on or even automatically generated from a formal description of the language. Hence, of special interest is the treatment of language descriptions as software artefacts, akin to programs - while paying attention to the special status of language descriptions, subject to tailored engineering principles and methods for modularisation, refactoring, refinement, composition, versioning, co-evolution, and analysis."* [CFP08].

Maintenance for maintenance tools. We use the term *language technology* to address tools, techniques, methods and formalisms that support these mentioned activities.

Besides the usual maintenance of software, software maintenance factories need special kind of maintenance. Firstly, the language description libraries (of the SMF) have to be maintained, new language descriptions have to be supplied, language descriptions have to be converted, language desriptions have to be reused and adapted for new dialects of a language, extracted languages from sources have to be maintained, etc. For this kind of task, one needs an SMF for languages (SMFL). Secondly, changes in the language descriptions require a re-generation of tool components, the adaptation of several *generated* components, or the adaptation of *user supplied* information for generated components. Information about the change in the language description is available in the language description maintenance process, i.e., in the SMFL and the applied transformation. Therefore, SMFL should be part of SMF to allow the adaptation of generated tools as well as user supplied information. Thirdly, the SMF should provide the tools to maintain the SMF itself. While SMF use *software language technology for software maintenance* the improvement and maintenance of SMF means *maintenance for language technology*, which again can be applied to maintain language technology itself.

Contents. We investigate construction, maintenance, and reuse of language processors and disciplined meta-programming applicable for manipulations of language descriptions and tools. We investigate the consequences of evolution in language descriptions to a) software written in that language, and b) language processors derived from these language descriptions as well as problems in those language processors arising during their evolution. We study how some of the maintenance transformations can be derived automatically. We also show how language technology and evolution can be used to increase the quality of maintenance tools, not only their design and maintainability but also their output. Automatically derived meta- and meta-meta-programs play a role for improvements of readability of language descriptions and modularity of tools, too. Thus, aspects like *usability* [1] and *explorative prototyping* are included.

The remainder of the introduction. The following Section 1.2 introduces the wider *context* of the thesis, which is concerned with *software evolution*. The notion of *co-evolution* and resulting problems are discussed motivating the maintenance for generation processes, and as a consequence, for maintenance transformations. Section 1.3 shortly introduces an *instance of the co-evolution problem*. In the subsequent Section 1.4 we develop *research questions* as result from experiences in refactoring and from work with language descriptions and their maintenance resp. related tools. Section 1.5 gives an *overview* of the remaining chapters in the thesis, and thus provides the guide through the thesis. Section 1.6 completes the introduction with the *origins* of the core chapters as the thesis is a cumulative work based on published papers.

---

[1]Usability: The extent to which a product can be used by specified users to achieve specified goals with effectiveness, efficiency and satisfaction in a specified context of use [ISO98]

1.2 Bird's eye view - The larger Context : Software Evolution

> *"The ability to change and evolve software easily, quickly and reliably is a 'grand challenge' within software engineering."*
> K. H. Bennett, V. T. Rajlich [BR00]

1.2.1 Software Maintenance

Software engineering is the systematic approach to design, construction and maintenance of software. While design and construction aim for the creation of software, the *mission of software maintenance* is to preserve its value, including to organise and perform activities that ensure to keep it running, remove bugs, adapt it to changed technical or user requirements, adapt documentations, and even adapt processes.

Software maintenance is underestimated in regards to the amount of time and effort that is needed for it [RC06], although is has been estimated to be 60-80% of the overall cost ([KV98, MDDB$^+$03]).

Instead, emphasise is put on new design and construction techniques, for example, a) to raise the level of abstraction on which software is developed (e.g., Model Driven Engineering - MDE [Sch06, Gro]), b) to quickly produce several variants of software (e.g., Generative Programming - GP [CE00]), or c) new concepts are introduced to reduce the weak points of older concepts (e.g., Object-Oriented Programming - OOP, for reuse or different kind of modelling; Aspect-Oriented Programming - AOP [KLM$^+$97b], to modularise crosscutting concerns).

However, new techniques are often introduced without looking at the effect to what happens to the software when it has to be changed [BR00]. No matter how good design and construction are, experience shows that software in use always needs change, it needs to evolve. This has been formulated in the first law of *software evolution* by Lehman [Leh74, Leh97]: *"Continuing Change: A[..] program that is used must be continually adapted else it becomes progressively less satisfactory."* [Leh97]. Even worse, many changes actually required are those that the original designers cannot even conceive of [BR00].

In Figure 1.1, we summarised actual challenges in software evolution relevant to the thesis, which have been determined by an international group of researchers during the International Workshop on Principles of Software Evolution 2005 [MWD$^+$05].

Sometimes the term software evolution is used as a substitute for software maintenance [BR00]. We rather agree with [RC06] to *"consider evolution as the process by which programs change shape"* including, in our opinion, all activities in the software engineering. Software maintenance is part of this process.

Software maintenance was considered a separate phase after delivery of the software (which is reflected in the original definitions *" modification of a software product after delivery to correct faults, to improve performance or other attributes, or to adapt the product to a changed environment."* [ANS] and *" The software product undergoes modification to code and associated documentation due to a problem or the need for improvement. The objective is to modify the existing software while preserving its integrity."* [ISO]. How-

---

1. Preserving and improving SW quality (provide tools and techniques that preserve or even improve the quality characteristics of a SW system)

2. A common software evolution platform (issue of exploratory prototyping)

3. Support for model evolution (SW evolution techniques should be raised to a higher level of abstraction, in order to accommodate not only evolution of programs, but also evolution of higher-level artefacts such as analysis and design models, SW architectures, requirement specifications, and so on.)

4. Support for co-evolution (keeping evolution of related artefacts in sync)

5. Formal support for evolution (existing formal methods provide poor support for evolving specifications)

6. Support for multi-language systems (techniques, that are language-parametric, language independent, language generic)

7. Need for better versioning systems (new ways of recording the evolution of SW that overcome shortcomings of the current state-of-the-art tools)

8. Integrating data from various sources

Figure 1.1   Selected challenges in software evolution from [MWD+05]

ever, in our opinion maintenance is woven through the whole lifecycle of software, as stated in [Pig96]: *"Maintenance should begin coincident with the decision to plan a new system."*

Source Manipulation.   In the context of this thesis that part of maintenance is interesting which is concerned with the (possibly automated) editing aspect, e.g., with removing bugs, API evolution or restructuring.

Object to manipulation in maintenance are sources, i.e., the material from which the (executable) software is constructed. From a technical point of view, there is only a small difference (mainly the degree of abstraction) between program texts, models, or specifications. This means, similar maintenance problems occur in source-based techniques in software engineering. (Documentation plays a special role due to the more informal and semi-structured nature.) We use the term *source* to emphasise that more general artefacts are object to maintenance than simply source-code of a general purpose programming language.

There are several areas which work with source-based techniques (cf. [Vin05]), for example

- Programming language definition (language tools are generated from formally defined syntax and semantics),

- Compiler construction (translators are built from high level programming languages to lower level programming languages or machine instructions),

- Software maintenance and evolution (the software is adapted in a stepwise manner to the needs of the user) and

- Software renovation (analysing source code of legacy software systems in order to retrieve their high-level design, then subsequently adapt the derived abstractions the functionality after which an improved system will be derived).

But there are also techniques to increase productivity and as a side effect to "reduce maintenance" such as

- Model Driven Engineering (develop applications on a high level descriptive and technology independent format, for example, using UML. From these, platform dependent source code is generated) and

- Generative Programming (model similar software systems such that using a concise requirements specification: customised software can be automatically constructed).

These parts of software (the sources, source code) we name *brittleware*. Even small changes quickly result in breaking the compilation or execution of the software, or worse, it leads to producing wrong results. Consider, for example, the change of a non-local variable. The "brittleness" is due to the ***complex dependencies*** between items in the software. An important principle is *separations of concerns*, often cited in the context of AOP. Essentially, it tries to reduce and concentrate the dependencies between different items to defined interfaces in the software development phase, so that changing tasks, understanding, etc. are easier.

Many tasks typical for maintenance are necessary even while developing the software. A good example is refactoring, which has had much attention during the last decade and will escort/assist us through the thesis.

Refactoring as main(tenance) example. *"Refactoring is [..] changing a software system in such a way that it does not alter the external behaviour of the code yet it improves its internal structure"* [FBB+99]. Refactoring has been done ever since writing programs, but it was not until 1991, when Opdyke examined the topic from a more scientific point of view [Opd92], and 1999, when Fowler wrote [FBB+99] that the greater audience became aware of a more systematic way of restructuring. The achievement of Opdyke was to formally describe a list of refactorings relevant in C++ programs and also give pre- and postconditions that, when met, ensure that the modification does not change the observable behaviour. The credit of Fowler was to create a list of recipes (for programs written in Java) that was less formal, easy to understand, and easy to apply by programmers.

An example of refactoring is *Extract Method* (cf. [FBB+99]): a set of declarations and method calls in the body of some method are replaced with a single call of a method whose body is formed by the replaced declarations and method calls. This corresponds to *fold*-operation known from program transformations [PP96].

The pre- and postconditions as given by Opdyke and the recipes of Fowler (and many others by now) actually ensure that the **dependencies are not destroyed**. This is additionally supported by the consistent use of unit testing [Bec94]. Refactoring and unit testing also play a central role in the method of *Extreme programming* that puts change (of software) as a welcome fact expressed by the slogan *"embrace the change"* [Bec00].

Besides improving the design of existing code, refactoring can be and has been applied to achieve other aims. While in the beginning of this trend refactoring has been applied on object-oriented programming languages mainly, it (and similar manipulations) has now been investigated and partially automated for programs of several languages including modelling languages, e.g., for UML models, XML documents, and more.

Refactoring for declarative languages has been investigated. For the thesis, the application to Prolog is interesting, e.g., by a master thesis directed by us [Ste03] or in [SS04]. Also important for the thesis are the articles on evolution of rule based systems [Läm04b] and on grammar adaptations [Läm01]. However, the authors in [KLV05a] claim that there is still much work to be done.

Automated changes. Many changes to be applied are similar in nature, which resulted, for example, in a catalog of refactorings. Many changes have to be done repeatedly at several places in the source. Manual editing is not only inefficient, i.e., it does not scale up for larger applications. It is also boring, demotivating, and error-prone work. As much of it as possible should be automated. Scripts with tools based on regular expressions are gladly used, e.g., scripts based on the famous `find`, `grep`, `awk` and `sed` known from Unix. But these scripts are very restricted. For example, source manipulations depending on conditions are nearly impossible. They have their advantage, however: a simple global *search and replace* is very easy to describe, and what is more, it is mostly *layout preserving*. Layout preserving transformations are very important as they produce results with only the changes necessary. The source code looks as similar to the original as possible. In a reduced version, at least the comments in the source are preserved.

For more sophisticated tools, it is required to parse the source, analyse it, perform the manipulation, and write it out as source again. This is typically called source-to-source transformation or more general, a meta-program. We call the construction of meta-programs meta-programming.

These tools are often specialised on *one language* and dedicated to *one task* such as refactoring tools for Smalltalk [RBJ97] or Java [KG98, WWWd]. More general tools such as Eclipse [WWWb] and IntelliJ IDEA [WWWc] are configurable for several languages.

Systems for meta-programming. Especially the use of declarative languages and rule based systems allows for tools that are more language parametric and allow the maintenance programmer to (meta-)program new transformations.

Examples for such systems are DMS [BP97], TAMPR [BHW97], TXL [CDMS02] and Stratego/XT [Vis01, JVV01, BKVV06]. We refer to [WWWa] for a more extensive list of rewriting systems. We especially emphasise the MetaEnvironment with ASF+SDF [Kli93], as this is our archetype of a meta-programming system that is open to extension and provides a graphical user interface. Finally, Prolog [SS97] is our example for a declarative language applied for meta-programming. This language will escort us through most of the examples in the thesis as object language and meta-programming language.

These systems are applicable very flexibly. However, one disadvantage (which is interesting for our thesis) is the often insufficient support for layout preservation. We will go in for it in Chapters 5 and 6. Another drawback is that unrestricted meta-programming is difficult to manage. Note, meta-programs are programs, too, and have to be maintained as well. A good example for the problem is the maintenance of Prolog transformations which manipulate Prolog sources. Meta-program and object-program are amalgamated. Moreover, the meta-language and the object-language are the same, which makes it difficult to distinguish the different levels in a program. This is in contrast of, for example, TyRuBa [dV98], where the logic meta-language combines strings containing Java-program fragments. Also, Prolog is extremely flexible regarding term manipulation. Here, too, restrictions are desirable to allow a systematic approach to (*disciplined*) *meta-programming* and to support the development of *meta-programming recipes* to increase understanding and reusability. We will consider this problem in Chapters 2 and 7. Note, automating the maintenance of the meta-level leads to *meta-meta-programs*.

1.2.2 Co-evolution

The application of source-based techniques discussed above implies that there are several views on the software constructed. We call these views layers as they provide a different degree of abstraction (e.g., model vs. model implementation), or a different degree of extension in the derivation of software from software artefacts (e.g., grammar vs. parser). Note, the manipulations like refactoring often addressed are performed *at one layer*, e.g., at model layer or at implementation language layer. Due to the dependencies between these layers the evolution of software is mirrored on several layers. In the thesis, we are interested how changes on one layer affect *more than one layer*. We use *"[..] the term co-evolution implying that managing evolution requires the synchronisation between different layers (or views) in the software development process."* [DDVMW00]. If software evolution on more than one layer can be described each by a transformation one speaks of coupled transformations [Läm04a], co-transformations [CH06], or two-level transformation [COV06].

Derived software needs maintenance. Co-evolution is not perceived if all what is changed are the sources of a generation process. For example, a parser reflects the modifications in a grammar as long as the parser is derived from the grammar. Similarly, when a model is changed the corresponding implementation is simply generated again. Co-evolution is a challenge, however, when there is no direct transformation available. Here, *changes at more than one layer* are necessary. For example, D'Hondt et al. [DDVMW00, Tou02, TM03] examine co-evolution of documentation of designs to implementation, and give methods to identify inconsistencies.

Also, it can be necessary to modify the generated results. This leads to two problems. First, extensions / refinements (e.g., framework completetion code, cf. [AC06]) of the generated results need to be preserved when the generation process is initiated again due to modifications on a higher layer. For example, a YACC specification can be generated from some other form of reference grammar, e.g., from some existing code base or a specification of the grammar during the development of a language. As soon as further code is added, changes of the original grammar lead to conflicts in the implementation.

Second, it is desired that changes in the lower layer are propagated to the higher level, e.g., the model reflects the extensions made at generated results. Propagating changes between the layers (e.g., from models to code and vice versa) is called *Round trip engineering* and is examined, for example, by Czernacki et al. [AC06, AC08]. Bidirectional model transformations to keep several layers consistent are investigated, for example, in [EEE+07, Ste07].

Co-evolution between software and software language. Software maintenance is usually considered to be caused by reasons such as change of technical, political or user desired requirements, or the repair to remove bugs. However, another important reason for maintenance of software is that software languages evolve, too [Fav05, PJ07]. Here, the co-evolution happens between the language and words of the language, if existing sources have to be adapted [VV08]). The development of domain-specific language shows this clearly [PJ07]. Software language evolution is related to format evolution (cf. [COV06]). We investigate the format evolution for XML documents in Chapter 3.

Generation processes need maintenance. Additionally, the generation process (e.g., a meta-program) itself underlies evolution because the transformations are software and probably have their bugs, too. This does not necessarily correspond to a co-evolution of sources. Ideally, it has no direct consequences to the sources used for generation. This corresponds to the (internal) evolution in language processors. Furthermore, the generation process can be subject to improvement and might require adaptations on other layers (targets of the generation) when the target format is changed.

Maintenance of a generation process is also enforced, when the format of the input, i.e., the language evolves (e.g., the development of UML, versions 1.3 - 2.1.2 [OMG]), or the formats into which the source is generated evolve, for example, the deployment platforms in MDD [AK03] or XMI (XML Metadata Interchange) [OMG08], to store UML-diagrams. Applying (automated) maintenance on the generation process is meta-meta-programming, i.e., manipulating a transformation as first order citizen.

> *"Who maintains the maintenance tools?"*
>
> Plato[Pla]
> freely adapted

Maintenance transformations need maintenance. Transformations that map software to a new version are potentially reusable. Examples are implementations of refactorings or converters from an old to a new language version. This immediately leads to the need to maintain this software.

Thus, meta-programs should be readable, too. Restricting the way they are defined supports understandability. A disciplined way to create such programs is required, as the use of meta-programming quickly leads to confusion, especially, if different levels are mixed. We repeatedly refer to meta-programs written in Prolog for manipulating Prolog programs. Another example is ASF+SDF [Deu96], where concrete syntax for specification is used. For example, variable names can confuse the reader as it might not be clear immediately, whether the name denotes a part of the object program or whether the name denotes a variable of the specification.

Observation. It is necessary to find the dependencies between the layers discussed and to examine their kind. This helps to create improved support for evolution. The thesis examines a small part of co-evolution in a language setting. We try to automate part of the transformations required to ensure adaptation and consistency. Also, we try to derive part of these transformations automatically. We provide ways for disciplined meta-programming (Chapters 2 and 7) and contribute to usability of maintenance tools.

1.3 Middle View: an Instance of the Co-evolution Problem

In the previous section we have discussed that language technology is applied to support maintenance. Language technology is also the base for the generation process in source based techniques.

As mentioned, the generation process needs maintenance. When the format of the input changes, both, the sources and the generation process need to be treated. This corresponds more generally to evolution of language descriptions while keeping derived tools (or tools partially derived and manually completed) in sync. Maintenance of language descriptions and derived tools therefore also underlie the problem of co-evolution (cf. [PJ07]). We also argued that the maintenance transformations evolve and therefore need maintenance. Thus, we are interested in consequences of evolution in language descriptions and in derived tools investigate how we can automate necessary changes.

Since grammars play a central role, we list selected research challenges for grammars from [KLV05a] in Figure 1.2 together with the relevant chapter; we summarise in Figure 1.4, where the thesis contributes.

As we are talking about maintenance, we will use language processors for maintenance as object to maintenance as special application. This simultaneously allows for the support of maintenance of maintenance tools. For example, in Chapters 5 and 6 transformation rules (e.g., to describe a refactoring) are automatically extended to improve quality of the maintenance tool for both, its output and its usability. The detailed context is the improvement of software maintenance factories (SMF) with the management of language processors being at their heart.

---

1. A collection of grammarware properties (e.g., what is/ are distance between grammars (4, 5), perservation properties (2), grammar slices (7), grammar modules (7))

2. An interoperational web of grammar forms (mappings between different notations of grammars (8))

3. A framework for grammar transformations (transformations accross grammar notation, data and grammar integration by grammar transformation (3), reuse pure grammar transformations in the context of customisation for grammar use cases (4), grammar refactoring(4) and enhancement (5))

4. Co-evolution of grammar-dependent software (3, 4, 5)

5. Parsing technology revisited (e.g., migration between parsing styles (4), engineering aspects of parser development (7))

6. Modular grammarware development (generic aspects for grammar-dependent functionality (7))

7. Grammarware life cycling (e.g., evolution and customisation (3, 4, 5))

8. Comprehensive grammarware tooling (interactive and batchmode transformations (8), co-evolution of grammar-dependent programs (3, 4, 5))

Figure 1.2   Selected research challenges from the Grammarware Agenda [KLV05a] and contributing chapters of the thesis

1.3.1 Software Maintenance Factories

A software maintenance factory (SMF) (e.g., [SV99]) is an infrastructure that generates tools from language descriptions and additional information. These tools can be used, configured and extended by the maintenance teams so that they can develop assembly lines for automated maintenance. Parts of the tool chains are created manually based on generated components, e.g., transformations that map between a certain kind of abstract syntax trees (AST). Several language descriptions to generate tools from are collected libraries of the factory. Reusable meta-programs, i.e., generation tools to create new tools and reusable tools, are also collected in libraries.

Software maintenance factories need special maintenance.   We have discussed that language based tools are affected by evolution, and consequently they should also be subject to maintenance. Besides the "common" maintenance tasks of software there are dependencies between the generated language processor and the software language causing a stronger maintenance effort. The generated language processor as well as the generation process of the SMF itself has to be adapted.

Especially, adaptations of the language descriptions do occur, e.g., to provide a tool for a further variant of the language ([LV01a]). Some transformation rules written for a certain language are not applicable for a similar language dialect, or are unusable after a language change. Also, languages themselves are object to evolution [Fav05, PJ07]. Also, transformation tools derived do no longer work together with other tools in the library. Hence, maintenance is required for language dependent components. Furthermore, changes should be propagated through to the constructed assembly lines. As a consequence, SMF underlie an evolution, too.

SMF for language descriptions are needed. To generate the maintenance tools, language descriptions are needed. These are collected by the SMF in a library. Maintaining the generation for these tools requires that language artefacts, too, have to be maintained as they evolve. Also, sometimes in maintenance languages have to be extracted from existing code and documents. Many language descriptions are not described formally enough, leave room for interpretation or are available in an unsuitable format, which requires modification to allow technical use. For example, several tools cannot work with left recursion. In Chapter 4 we study how left recursion in attribute grammars can be removed automatically and at the same time preserving the semantics.

These tasks can be supported by specialised software maintenance factories – software maintenance factories for languages (SMFL) – because language descriptions can be considered as programs of special DSLs such as EBNF.

SMFL should be part of SMF. It seems a special SMF for languages is needed. However, once maintenance tools (and then tool chains) have been constructed, every change of a language description also has consequences to these tools in a tool chain.

Maintenance of these tools should be coupled to maintenance of language descriptions, because in the change of the language the knowlege is hidden of what has to be changed in derived tools, according to the co-evolution problem. Also, it may be that the language description is developed to just another version of the language. Additionally, evolving language descriptions, especially in the area of language prototyping, might require the evolution of programs already existing for that language. For their adaptation, the SMF should provide tools as far as possible, which again could be derived partially from the change in language descriptions. Hence, we argue, the SMFL should be part of each SMF. Moreover, an SMF should contain tools for self-maintenance and extension.

1.3.2 Language Processors

The tools managed by an SMF can be considered as specialised language processors. We focus on language processors that are specified based on rule-based systems and declarative languages.

The main property of these language processors in this context is their simplicity compared to a fully implemented compiler. They can be quickly provided, are well-suited for experiments and are simple enough for quick modifications, and thus they allow an exploration of the solution space. Parsing needs to be just fast enough for experiments on

11

small examples. Declarative languages are well-suited for these tasks as they allow an easy mapping between syntax trees, and thus they simplify a specification of the transformation. The speed of the tool is secondary. It is more important to increase the productivity of the maintenance programmer, i.e., to enable him to quickly create a tool for his task. Some transformations are applied once only. It is rather important to get the language processor and small examples quickly to work.

For software maintenance, the distance between source and target language is small or the languages are the same. Base parsers and unparsers can be derived from grammars, if these are present in a suitable format. The transformations are simply mappings between terms.

Language processors in our context often consist of mainly three components: a parser, one or more transformations and an unparser. Parser and unparsers are usually generated based on a grammar. Transformations are written manually or partially generated using libraries of transformations and program fragments. The language processors can use part of the infrastructure of the generating environment, e.g., libraries of grammar or program fragments.

Prolog for language processors. Prolog is the main vehicle for our experiments with some exceptions. It is very suitable for language processing and related problems [Rie91, Paa91, LR01, CH87, War80, BP89, SK94]. Due to its facilities for symbolic term manipulation, Prolog is particularly suited for the phases of language processing which can be performed at the level of abstract representations. It is well established that logic programs are well-suited to describe analysis, evaluation and transformation of abstract representations. Additionally, Prolog programs are structured grammar-like. This simplifies representations of grammars including attribute grammars. Thus, language processing can be mapped easily to Prolog.

(At least) two tools exploited this in our working group. LDL (Language Development Laboratory) [Rie92, HLR97] makes use of grammars of syntactical functions (GSF) and supports modularisation into language fragments. Laptob (Language processing toolbox) [LR01], the successor of LDL, focuses on logic grammars to obtain a more lightweight approach to achieve prototype interpreters.

Logic grammars. It is very easy to derive language processors from logic grammars [LR01]. A logic grammar (as described in [LR01]) is a Prolog program where predicates represent nonterminals and terminals are represented by strings or are constructs especially marked by operators. When these operators are interpreted as predicates consuming lexemes, Prolog's evaluation mechanism immediately provides a recursive descent parser with backtracking already included. Logic grammars are interesting because transformations on grammars are conventional meta-programs on Prolog programs, which is natural in Prolog. In contrast to definite clause grammars [PW80] their external and internal representation do not differ. This simplifies treatment of grammars in several transformation steps. Logic grammars can easily be extended with semantics by adding variables and other predicates which, when deriving a prototype interpreter, perform several kinds of analysis or other tasks in a language processor. This resembles defining a language using attribute grammars. A logic grammar can then be considered as a special kind of attribute grammar. The strong relationship between Prolog and attribute grammars has been discussed in [DM93, RL88, DM85].

The tool Laptob mentioned provides additional libraries that contain meta-programs on Prolog programs to manipulate this kind of grammars as well as several general traversals on heterogeneous data structures such as fold to collect/compute data. It has been the base for most of the experiments for the thesis.

1.4 Worm's-eye View: Evolution in Maintenance Tools - Experience and Research Questions

We show starting from the standard example of refactoring where problems arise.

The SMF presented in [SV99] has been implemented in the ASF+SDF MetaEnvironment [Kli93]. Tools based on the MetaEnvironment (ME) can be connected to the toolbus [BK96], which allows tools to communicate with each other based on a process algebra, or they are specified using SDF (Syntax Definition Formalism) and ASF (Algebraic Specification Formalism) [Deu96]. While with SDF the syntax of a language can be specified, ASF is used to describe rewrite rules in form of conditional equations to specify the semantics. Specifying programs using these formalisms means writing language descriptions from which language processors are generated.

In year 2000, we used ASF+SDF (SDF2 [Vis97b]) to perform a case study for creating transformation support for refactoring on Java programs. (The MetaEnvironment was under rewrite that time, which underlines the need for maintenance of these tools). While [FBB+99] describes refactoring for Java in an informal way, we wanted to specify operations more formally together with necessary preconditions similar to those given by [Opd92] for C++ to allow a more automatic modification of source code and avoid introduction of bugs due to editing errors or conditions overseen. We used an existing Java-grammar in SDF.

The practical experiment was supposed to get us aquainted with refactoring and term rewriting, and did not lead to published results. However, we encountered a number of problems that suggested research questions for a coherence work on language processing and software maintenance.

1.4.1 Change of Language Description

Grammar part The grammar we reused was incomplete and also it contained errors. This included undefined Java constructs, too restrictive grammar rules, and too liberal grammar rules. Also, we cleaned up (refactored) the grammar on some positions to simplify the specification task, hence we did language-preserving as well as language-modifiying changes. The adaptations of the grammar have been done manually.

Semantics part While developing different refactoring specifications, we had to *change larger portions of the equations* for several reasons. First, the underlying compiler was under reconstruction. Our specification revealed bugs. Their removal and other changes in the compiler required adaptations in our specification. Secondly, we modified the specification while we learnt more a) about the Java semantics and could describe conditions more elegantly, b) we learnt more about ASF and could be more expressive in the specification. Thirdly, grammar changes required several equations directly depending on the syntactic structure. Next, we identified patterns that could be reused in more equations and applied manual refactoring to the specification, which was very error-prone. Finally, we had to rewrite parts which contained errors due to misunderstanding.

From a declarative perspective, the language descriptions consisting of grammar rules and rewrite rules are declarative programs.

Research Question 1 (**Evolution Support** for Declarative Programs): How can we support evolution for declarative formalisms for describing grammars or rewrite rules in a more disciplined way while preserving certain properties of programs?

1.4.2 Migration of Source Code due to Grammar Change

Grammars are subject to change in the development of domain-specific languages. As a consequence, words for the language generated by the grammar (i.e., programs for that language) have to be adapted (cf. [PJ07]). We study the special case of format evolution of XML documents, which need a migration after the DTD has been changed. It would be nice, if this forced migration could be done automatically. Can such a tool exist?

Research Question 2 (**Program Migration**): Can structural evolution in a grammar induce necessary migrations of program texts to meet the new grammar?

1.4.3 Migration of Rewrite Rules due to Grammar Change

Rewrite rules/ transformation rules directly depend on syntactic structures, which depend on the grammar. As mentioned in Section 1.4.1, the grammar was subject to structural evolution. It required the already written specifications (rewrite rules) to be migrated to work with the modified grammar.

Research Question 3 (**Rule Migration**): Is there structural evolution in a grammar, where specifications can be migrated automatically?

1.4.4 Adaptation of Language Descriptions to improve Maintenance Tools

The problems above are related with co-evolution.

Later, we realised another problem that also required the adaptation of the grammar. Refactorings as described by [FBB+99] or [Opd92] do not consider comments and layout in source texts, which is no problem if the migration is done manually. Tools based on rewrite rules with abstract syntax can either neglect the layout and skip it or have to find a technical solution. One way is to add layout nonterminals to the grammar. If a parser is derived, parsing adds layout information to the abstract syntax tree, and thus it gives the rewriter access to layout. However, the treatment of layout is distracting during the actual specification task. Also, there can be many reusable transformations specified already.

Research Question 4 (Introduction of **Layout Preservation**): Can language technology help with introduction of layout preservation? More specifically: Can support for layout preservation be integrated in existing transformation tools? Can existing transformation rules be adapted automatically? Can this be made transparent to the user?

Adding layout preservation support to existing transformation tools by extending the grammar requires an adaptation of transformation rules to work on a changed grammar. To perform this adaptation automatically requires an analysis of these rules to extend them with meaningful behaviour.

Research Question 5 (Analysis of **Transformation Rules**): How does the form of a transformation rule control its migration?

1.4.5 Modularisation of Language Descriptions and Derived Tools

Modularisation is one way to increase maintainability. For language based tools, modularity can appear on the level of language descriptions or in the implementation of the tools. Besides the common hierarchical modularisation, aspects (as in AOP [KLM+97b]) can be of use here, too.

The layout preservation problem can be considered as aspect in the grammar G, in the abstract syntax and in patterns of transformation rules that describe manipulation of programs of G. The layout aspect in transformation rules should be hidden from the programmer so he can concentrate on the important content of the transformation.

We also demonstrate how AOP is integrated in Prolog, and thus it allows several kinds of aspects. This is demonstrated by specifying components of a language processor as aspect.

Research Question 6 (**Modularisation** in Language Description): Can AOP improve modularisation in language descriptions and modularisation of derived tools?

1.4.6 Usability in Transformational Programming

Many transformation rules carry many arguments which are not of interest in a certain context. It would help to hide unnecessary argument positions. For example, layout information carried in an AST obfuscates the "interesting" part. Also, technical needs force the use of grammars that are often unreadable or they have rules that differ from those in the reference manual making them more difficult to understand and to compare whether the rules are correct. A typical example is the left recursion removal when the tool of choice uses of top-down parsing. Many transformations are developed in a rather explorative way. A good transformation development tool should allow exploration of alternative implementations.

Also, though the changes in a language description, the refactorings in a grammar or on transformation programs, in the abstract syntax and the programs are on different levels, the maintenance tasks are rather similar. Thus, these maintenance tasks use should also be supported similarly. Many different transformation programs exist written in different languages. It would be nice if these transformations could be reused together in a common setting.

Research Question 7 (**Usability**): How can the usability of transformation tools be improved? More specifically: Can language technology support better usability? Can existing transformation tools be combined in a transparent, visual and easy way? How can performing experiments with transformations be supported?

1.5 Overview of the Chapters

The Chapters 2-8 address the given research questions. As the thesis is organised in a cumulative way based on published papers the chapters address several questions. Figure 1.3 lists the research questions with the chapters that contribute to it. Figure 1.4 gives an overview on the chapters. The order of the chapters are organised as follows.

Question	Chapters
1 (Evolution Support)	2,7, 8
2 (Program Migration)	3
3 (Rule Migration)	4,5,6
4 (Layout Preservation)	5, 6
5 (Transformation Rules)	6
6 (Modularity)	7
7 (Usability)	8,4,5,7

Chapter	Questions	Publication	Grammarware
2	1	[LRL00]	1, 3
3	2	[LL01]	3, 4, 5, 7, 8
4	3,7	[LRS04]	1, 3, 4, 7, 8
5	3,4,7	[LR03b]	1, 3, 4, 7, 8
6	3,4,5	[LR03a]	7
7	1,6,7	[LRW08]	1, 5, 6,7
8	1,7	[LRZ06]	2, 8

Figure 1.3   Chapters vs. questions   **Figure 1.4**   Contents of the chapters

Chapter 2. In the chapter we focus on the support for *systematic manipulation of programs* written in a (first order) declarative formalism. We present an approach based on concepts of program transformation and meta-program technology. Basic roles for extending program behaviour are identified: adding parameters, applying substitutions, renaming symbols, inserting literals in bodies of clauses, adding definitions for predicate symbols. A framework for meta-programming is defined that ensures the construction of well-formed object programs. Object programs are logic programs. This forms a basis for evolution of language processors that build on declarative transformations. Using the framework we formalise the basic roles by functional meta-programs. We give an example demonstrating that high-level abstractions of common adaptations of programs can be defined to support stepwise enhancement as known in logic programming [JS94]. The defined roles allow disciplined meta-programming.

Chapter 3. A grammar change can have an *effect on the words* of the language generated by the grammar and require an adaptation of documents containing the words. A special case is the format evolution of data and a necessary adaptation of the data existing. We study this problem for format evolution of XML-based formats. Changes in the formats are represented as stepwise transformations on the underlying DTDs (i.e., grammar). The corresponding migration of the XML documents is largely induced by the DTD transformations. This is related to other recent work on format evolution, e.g., [COV06, Kle07].

Chapter 4. While the words of the language remain the same after a *grammar refactoring*, semantic rules might have to be adapted. In the chapter we study the consequences of left recursion removal to semantic rules in attribute grammars. We justify that the semantic rules can be automatically adapted.

Chapter 5. In this chapter we are interested in consequences of a *grammar extension* on transformation rules. To study the problem we extend the grammar with nonterminals and terminals representing layout to introduce layout preservation for declarative transformation rules. To avoid that existing transformation rules break with the extended abstract program representations derived from the grammar and input programs, those transformation rules are migrated accordingly. This migration is derived automatically.

To hide the new complexity of patterns (for new rules to be written in future, too), the migration is done as a subsequent pass. This requires automatic decisions on which layout is to be preserved. Heuristics are used to decide on the mapping of layout. We argue that the approach is applicable to hide complexity of argument positions in other areas as well.

Chapter 6. Automatic migration of transformation rules (meta-programs) according to a grammar extension requires an *analysis of transformation rules* (meta-programs) necessary to derive a required meta-meta-program.

This chapter systematically examines the cases of transformation rules wrt. the layout preservation problem to decide how the migration should be performed. For that purpose we ask, to what extent the layout preservation problem can be solved. The analysis forms the basis for assumptions that the style in which transformation rules are programmed determines the quality of layout preservation.

Chapter 7. In the chapter we study *aspects in language descriptions* (crosscutting concerns, cf. AOP [KLM+97b]). The previous chapter addressed the aspect of layout in grammars and aspect of layout preservation in transformation rules. Here, we demonstrate that several concerns in a language processor such as parsing, analysis, transformations can be specified as aspects of a logic grammar. A logic aspect-oriented language is developed, which is integrated into Prolog in a systematic way. Thus, we support a modularisation in language descriptions that is not restricted to hierarchical decomposition. This modularisation also increases modularity of language based tools.

Chapter 8. We develop an interactive *workbench for visual transformational programming*. Grammars and programs are available as first class data. We give an object-oriented transformation model that forms the base for an combination infra-structure. It allows combination of transformations available in different formats (e.g., command line tools, native libraries such as SWI-Prolog, hierarchical transformations) and languages (e.g., XSLT, C#, F#, Yacc, Stratego, Prolog). In the example a compiler hosted in Maribor as a web service is used within a locally defined transformation pipeline. On a second level, interactivity and views are added allowing explorative compositions of transformations.

Chapter 9. The last chapter summarises the thesis and gives an overview over the achieved results of the thesis. Then it finishes with an outlook.

1.6 Origins of the Chapters

The thesis is designed as a cumulative thesis. Chapters are previously published papers. The changes consist in formatting and removing of typos, as well as replacing references to own articles with references to corresponding chapters of the thesis. The papers are collaborate work. Parts we have not contributed to are pointed out with an acknowledgement.

Chapter 2, "Roles of Program Extension", is collaborative work with Ralf Lämmel. It was published at LOPSTR'99 [LRL00]. Acknowledgement: The core calculus and the specification of the `accumulate`-technique has been done by Ralf Lämmel alone.

Chapter 3, "Format Evolution", is collaborative work with Ralf Lämmel, too. It was published in the Proceedings of the 7th International Conference on Reverse Engineering for InformationSystems (RETIS 2001) [LL01].

Chapter 4, "Semantics-preserving Migration of Semantic Rules during Left Recursion Removal in Attribute Grammars", is collaborative work with Günter Riedewald and Markus Stoy and has been published in ENTCS 110C [LRS04]. An earlier version was accepted for 4th Workshop on Language Descriptions, Tools and Applications (LDTA 2004). Section 4.4 comes from an later revision. It replaces its counter parts from [LRS04]. It contains a more readable and corrected proof.

Chapter 5, "Towards Automatical Migration of Transformation Rules after Grammar Extension", is collaborative work with Günter Riedewald and published in Proceedings of 7th European Conference on Software Maintenance and Reengineering [LR03b].

Chapter 6, "Automatic Layout Preservation in Declarative First Order Rewriting" has been taken from the technical report "Layout Preservation for non-trivial Traversal Schemes in Declarative First Order Rewriting". It is collaborative work with Günter Riedewald and published in Rostocker Informatik-Berichte 28 [LR03a].

Chapter 7, "Aspect-Oriented Prolog in a Language Processing Context", is collaborative work with Günter Riedewald and Guido Wachsmuth. It is published in the journal IET Software 2008 [LRW08]. Acknowledgement: The initial idea to implement aspect-oriented programming in Prolog we got from Ralf Lämmel during a research stay at CWI Amsterdam. The original idea to use the context as addressing and communication concept is by Guido Wachsmuth. The `calculate`-technique has also been specified by Guido Wachsmuth.

Chapter 8, "A Lightweight Infrastructure to support Experimenting with Heterogeneous Transformations", is collaborative work with Günter Riedewald and Thomas Zühlke. It was published in the Proceedings of 3rd International Conference on .NET Technologies [LRZ06].

Chapter 2

Roles of Program Extension

A formal and effective approach to the extension of the computational behaviour of logic programs is presented. The approach builds upon the following concepts. The extension of computational behaviour is modelled by semantics-preserving program transformations. Several basic roles involved in such transformations are identified. Every transformation defined solely in terms of the basic roles will be semantics-preserving by definition. Functional meta-programs on logic object programs are used to specify the basic roles and to derive programming techniques in the style of stepwise enhancement. Thus, the process of extending the computational behaviour of logic programs is regarded as disciplined meta-programming.

2.1 Introduction

This chapter is about adding functionality to declarative programs. We present a rigorous approach which relies on program transformation concepts and meta-programming technology. Transformations are used to model the enhancement of programs, i.e., the extension by computational behaviour. The approach is spelled out in this chapter for logic programs (definite clause programs), but it is also applicable to several other declarative languages such as attribute grammars and algebraic specifications as discussed to some extent in [Läm99b, Läm99a, LR99]. The chapter identifies the following basic roles involved in semantics-preserving transformations facilitating the extension of computational behaviour:

- adding parameters,

- applying substitutions,

- renaming symbols,

- inserting literals in bodies of clauses,

- adding definitions for predicate symbols.

The basic roles will be defined in terms of functional meta-programs. They also will be illustrated by deriving programming techniques in the style of stepwise enhancement [SS97, Lak89, KMS96].

Example 1. The following example has been adopted from [Jai95]. Let us start with a very simple program for traversing *AND-OR* trees: [1]

$traverse(\downarrow \text{tree}(\text{OP}, \text{NODE}, \text{TREE}^\star_{\text{child}})) \Leftarrow traverse\_list(\downarrow \text{TREE}^\star_{\text{child}}).$
$traverse\_list(\downarrow [\,]).$
$traverse\_list(\downarrow [\text{TREE}|\text{TREE}^\star]) \Leftarrow traverse(\downarrow \text{TREE}), traverse\_list(\downarrow \text{TREE}^\star).$

An enhancement of this simple program is the following version which additionally computes labels for each node. A node is labelled with true or false according to the conventions of an *AND-OR* tree, i.e., all *AND* leaf-nodes are considered as successful and all *OR* leave-nodes are considered as failed:

$label(\downarrow \text{tree}(\text{OP}, \text{NODE}, \boxed{\text{TREE}^\star_{\text{child}}}) \boxed{, \uparrow \text{LABEL}}) \Leftarrow$
$\boxed{init\_label(\downarrow \text{OP}, \uparrow \text{LABEL}_{init}),}$
$label\_list(\downarrow \text{TREE}^\star_{\text{child}} \boxed{, \downarrow \text{OP}, \downarrow \text{LABEL}_{init}, \uparrow \text{LABEL}}).$
$label\_list(\downarrow [\,] \boxed{, \downarrow \text{OP}, \downarrow \text{LABEL}, \uparrow \text{LABEL}}).$
$label\_list(\downarrow [\text{TREE}|\text{TREE}^\star] \boxed{, \downarrow \text{OP}, \downarrow \text{LABEL}_{in}, \uparrow \text{LABEL}_{out}}) \Leftarrow$
$label(\downarrow \text{TREE}) \boxed{, \uparrow \text{LABEL}}),$
$\boxed{and\_or(\downarrow \text{OP}, \downarrow \text{LABLE}_{in}, \downarrow \text{LABEL}, \uparrow \text{LABEL}_{temp}),}$
$label\_list(\downarrow \text{TREE}^\star \boxed{, \downarrow \text{OP}, \downarrow \text{LABEL}_{temp}, \uparrow \text{LABEL}_{out}}).$

> $init\_label (\downarrow \text{and}, \uparrow \text{true}).$
> $init\_label (\downarrow \text{or}, \uparrow \text{false}).$

> $and\_or (\downarrow \text{and}, \downarrow \text{false}, \downarrow \text{false}, \uparrow \text{false}).$
> $and\_or (\downarrow \text{and}, \downarrow \text{false}, \downarrow \text{true}, \uparrow \text{false}).$
> ...

The label computed, for example, for the *AND-OR* tree

$\text{tree}(\text{and}, n_1, [\text{tree}(\text{and}, n_2, [\,]), \text{tree}(\text{or}, n_3, [\,])])$

is false, where, n_1, n_2 and n_3 are some values at the nodes. Note that the boxed clauses, literals and parameters had to be projected away in order to derive the basic program from the enhanced program. Moreover, renaming is involved in the sense that the symbols *traverse* and *traverse_list* used in the basic program are called *label* and *label_list* resp. in the enhanced version.

The rest of the chapter is structured as follows.

- In Section 2.2, a general meta-programming framework for specifying and executing program transformations is developed. The framework is not yet tuned towards

---

[1] The arrows ↑ and ↓ are used in the logic programs in this chapter to indicate the mode of the positions (input versus output).

the particular kind of semantics-preserving transformations we have in mind. Transformations are represented as functional programs in this framework. There is an abstract data type for object programs, i.e., logic programs.

- Section 2.3 is the central part of the chapter. First, the basic roles listed above are investigated more carefully with emphasis on semantics-preservation. Second, the basic roles are specified in the meta-programming framework from the previous section. Third, the operators are shown to be useful to derive common programming techniques such as accumulators.

- In Section 2.5, related work is discussed, results are summarised and some topics for future work are indicated.

2.2 The Underlying Meta-programming Framework

The meta-programming framework used to specify program transformations in this chapter can be characterised as follows:

- Program transformations are regarded as functions and finally represented as *pure functional programs* in *Haskell.* [2]

- *Monads* [Mog91, Wad92, Esp95] are used to model two effects involved in meta-programs, namely errors and a state for generating fresh symbols and other entities.

- Meta-programs do not operate on concrete representations of object programs. Construction and destruction of object programs are supported by a corresponding abstract data type. Thereby, well-formedness / well-typedness can be enforced for constructed object programs.

- Parameter positions are associated with *modes* and *types*. These annotations can be used in order to enforce a certain type system of the object language. Modes and types are also used to control meta-programs. This role is also sensible for untyped object languages.

- While modes and types support more conceptual addressing methods, internally unambiguous *selectors* are used at several levels of addressing.

To the best of our knowledge, this setting is unique. Some of the characteristics are explained in detail in the subsequent subsections. The framework is discussed in more detail in [Loh99].

---

[2]We assume familiarity with functional programming (in *Haskell*), in particular with curried functions, standard higher-order functions like *map* and *foldr*, and monads. We do not rely on lazy evaluation. Other typed functional languages, e.g., languages from the *SML* family, would be applicable, too.

2.2.1 The Effect Space

In our setting, meta-programs need to cope with two global effects, that is to say propagating errors and generating fresh symbols, variables and others.

Errors It is an inherent property of program transformations to be partially defined. Usually, transformations are only applicable if certain preconditions are satisfied. If a precondition for a meta-program is not satisfied, it should fail. Meta-programs are functions. Thus, the functions used in a meta-program return an error value to encode failure.

States It is also very common for program transformations to require fresh entities, e.g., fresh variables in Example 1. Thus, we need to keep track of entities in use and we need a scheme to generate fresh entities.

Assuming a pure style of functional meta-programming, monads [Mog91, Wad92, Esp95] seem to be most appropriate to deal with effects. Consequently, the functions in the meta-programming framework are supposed to be computed in an effect space; refer to Figure 2.1 [3] for an illustration and a definition of the type constructors of the relevant monads. The error monad $\mathcal{E}$ is adopted to deal with errors and especially strict error handling (propagation). The state monad $\mathcal{S}$ hides states used for the generation of fresh symbols, variables and others. $\mathcal{ES}$ denotes the composed monad. [4] $\mathcal{M}$ is used in the text whenever an explanation applies to an arbitrary monad.

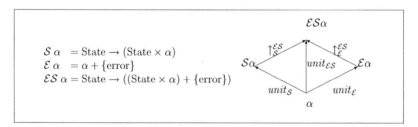

$$\mathcal{S}\,\alpha \;= \text{State} \rightarrow (\text{State} \times \alpha)$$
$$\mathcal{E}\,\alpha \;= \alpha + \{\text{error}\}$$
$$\mathcal{ES}\,\alpha = \text{State} \rightarrow ((\text{State} \times \alpha) + \{\text{error}\})$$

Figure 2.1   The effect space

For convenience, we recall some facts on monads. A monad can be regarded as a triple $\langle \mathcal{M}, \mathit{unit}_{\mathcal{M}}, \ggg=_{\mathcal{M}} \rangle$, where $\mathcal{M}$ is a type constructor, and $\mathit{unit}_{\mathcal{M}}$ (sometimes also called *return*) and $\ggg=_{\mathcal{M}}$ (usually called *bind*) are polymorphic functions with the following types:

---

[3]We only use *Haskell*-notation in *Hakell*-code. Otherwise, we use mathematical notation: $\times$ for products; $+$ for disjoint unions; * and $^+$ for list types; $\mathcal{P}$ for power sets; $\langle$ and $\rangle$ to enclose tuples and sequences; $\pi_1, \pi_2, \ldots,$ for projections operators, i.e., $\pi_i \langle d_1, \ldots, d_n \rangle = d_i$; $\#s$ for the length of the sequence s; $+\!\!+$ for list concatenation.

[4]Monad transformers could be used in order to derived $\mathcal{ES}$ in a more modular way.

$$unit_{\mathcal{M}} : \alpha \rightarrow \mathcal{M}\,\alpha$$
$$\gg=_{\mathcal{M}} : \mathcal{M}\,\alpha \rightarrow (\alpha \rightarrow \mathcal{M}\,\beta) \rightarrow \mathcal{M}\,\beta$$

The type constructor $\mathcal{M}$ models "computations" for a certain effect. It takes a type – the type of "values" – and returns the corresponding type of computations. $unit_{\mathcal{M}}$ lifts a simple value to a computation in $\mathcal{M}$. The infix operator $\gg=_{\mathcal{M}}$ is used to sequence computations and to pass intermediate results. $unit_{\mathcal{M}}$ and $\gg=_{\mathcal{M}}$ have to obey the common monad laws. In the effect space in Figure 2.1, the functions $\uparrow_{\mathcal{S}}^{\mathcal{ES}}$ and $\uparrow_{\mathcal{E}}^{\mathcal{ES}}$ are used to lift computations in $\mathcal{S}$ resp. $\mathcal{E}$ to $\mathcal{ES}$. The definitions are straightforward; refer to [Mog91, Wad92, Esp95] for similar definitions.

2.2.2 Object Programs

Logic programs are regarded as object programs in the meta-programming framework. Actually, the terminology used below will occasionally deviate from logic programming terminology because the framework is more generic in the sense that it also supports other declarative languages as discussed in [Läm99b, Loh99]. Object programs are modelled by an abstract data type whose interface is defined in Figure 2.2.

The structure of object programs can be best understood by looking at the types of the constructor functions in Figure 2.2.[5] A complete program consists of a number of definitions, that is to say groups of rules. The rules in such a group are meant to define one "operator" corresponding to the definite clauses for a certain predicate symbol in logic programming. A rule consists of a kind of tag, a LHS (left-hand side; the head in a definite clause) and a RHS (right-hand side; the body in a definite clause). A LHS is just a literal, whereas a RHS is a list of literals each qualified with a selector to facilitate addressing. A literal, in turn, is a parameterised operator (say, predicate symbol). Each parameter of a literal is associated with a selector and a mode. Finally, parameters are either variables or compound terms and they are associated with a type.

Example 2. The initial program in Example 1 consists of two definitions, one for *traverse* and another for *traverse_list*. The definition of *traverse_list* consists of two rules. There are only parameters with the mode $\downarrow$. The program is not explicitly annotated with selectors.

It is an important observation that most constructor functions in Figure 2.2 are computations in $\mathcal{E}$, i.e., it is assumed that the construction of object program fragments might fail. That is indeed necessary because the framework has to prevent meta-programs from constructing and observing improper object program fragments as constrained by straightforward notions of well-formedness and well-typedness. The attempt to construct an ill-typed logic program must result in an error. The *fresh*-constructors in Figure 2.2 are computations rather in $\mathcal{S}$ than in $\mathcal{E}$. These constructors serve for the generation of certain kinds of entities.

---

[5]We should mention that some uses of * or $^+$ versus $\mathcal{P}$ are debatable. We prefer lists rather than power sets for minor implementational reasons.

Sorts of object program fragments

Program	– complete programs
Definition	– groups of rules
Rule	– tagged rules consisting of LHS and RHS
Literal	– parameterised operators
Parameter	– variables and compound parameters
Variable	– variables
Term	– compound parameters
Operator	– symbols used in literals
Constructor	– symbols used in terms
Selector	– selectors for addressing
Type	– object type expressions
Mode	$= \downarrow, \uparrow, \ldots$ – parameter modes

Functions to construct object programs

$$
\begin{aligned}
\textit{program} \quad &: \text{Definition}^\star \to \mathcal{E} \text{ Program} \\
\textit{definition} \quad &: \text{Rule}^+ \to \mathcal{E}\text{Definition} \\
\textit{rule} \quad &: \text{Selector} \to \text{Literal} \to (\text{Selector} \times \text{Literal})^\star \to \mathcal{E} \text{ Rule} \\
\textit{literal} \quad &: \text{Operator} \to (\text{Selector} \times \text{Mode} \times \text{Parameter})^\star \to \mathcal{E} \text{ Literal} \\
\textit{term} \quad &: \text{Constructor} \to (\text{Selector} \times \text{Parameter})^\star \to \text{Type} \to \mathcal{E} \text{ Parameter} \\
\textit{fresh}_{Variable} &: \text{Type} \to \mathcal{S} \text{ Parameter} \\
\textit{fresh}_\alpha \quad &: \mathcal{S} \ \alpha \text{ for } \alpha = \text{Selector}, \text{Operator}, \text{Constructor}
\end{aligned}
$$

Functions to destruct object programs

$$
\begin{aligned}
\textit{definitions} \quad &: \text{Program} \to \text{Definition}^\star \\
\textit{defines} \quad &: \text{Definition} \to \text{Operator} \\
\textit{rules} \quad &: \text{Definition} \to \text{Rule}^+ \\
\textit{tag} \quad &: \text{Rule} \to \text{Selector} \\
\textit{lhs} \quad &: \text{Rule} \to \text{Literal} \\
\textit{rhs} \quad &: \text{Rule} \to (\text{Selector} \times \text{Literal})^\star \\
\textit{operator} \quad &: \text{Literal} \to \text{Operator} \\
\textit{parameterization} &: \text{Literal} \to (\text{Selector} \times \text{Mode} \times \text{Parameter})^\star \\
\textit{typeOf} \quad &: \text{Parameter} \to \text{Type} \\
\textit{descend} \quad &: (\text{Variable} \to \alpha) \to (\text{Constructor} \to \\
& \quad (\text{Selector} \times \text{Parameter})^\star \to \alpha) \to \text{Parameter} \to \alpha
\end{aligned}
$$

Figure 2.2   Interface of the abstract data type for object programs

Example 3. Consider a list of definitions. To qualify it as a proper program, the constructor *program* has to be used. The application of the constructor might fail for two reasons. Either the types of the symbols involved in the different definitions are not compatible, or there are two or more definitions for the same symbol.

There are no effects involved in the destruction of object programs. The destructor functions should be self-explanatory by their types. *descend* is a kind of case construct on parameters. Two functions need to be supplied to *descend*, one to handle variables, another one for compound parameters.

Consequently, program transformations are modelled as functions of type Trafo = Program $\rightarrow$ $\mathcal{ES}$ Program. By now, the utility of monads should also be clear. They enforce some discipline of meta-programming, and they facilitate reasoning about meta-programs. Without encapsulating the error effect, the strict propagation of errors could not be guaranteed. Without encapsulating the state effect, freshness of entities could hardly be ensured. Besides, meta-programs get tangled if they had to deal with the effects explicitly.

2.2.3 Types at the Object Level

Types (including modes of parameter positions) at the object level are relevant in the meta-programming framework in two important ways:

1. Types are regarded as annotations of object programs useful to provide more information about the sorts of data and the data flow. Types can be used to address, for example, parameter positions. This conceptual role of types is used to control meta-programs.

2. If the object language is typed, e.g., Gödel [HL94], the type system should be respected by the meta-programming framework in the sense that well-typedness is enforced. For untyped languages like Prolog, still a kind of "conceptual" well-typedness in the sense of 1. should be enforced.

The notion of typing we use corresponds, essentially, to many-sorted (like in Gödel [HL94] directional [BM97] types. Note, however, that the framework is not restricted to typed logic programs as explained above. Technically, a type of a program or some fragment is just a collection of profiles for the symbols in the program as modelled by Sigma:

$$\text{Sigma} = \mathcal{P}(\text{Operator} \times (\text{Selector} \times \text{Mode} \times \text{Type})^\star)$$
$$\times \mathcal{P}(\text{Constructor} \times (\text{Selector} \times \text{Type})^\star \times \text{Type})$$

It is assumed that overloading is not supported, i.e., $\forall \Sigma \in \text{Sigma} : \forall p, p' \in \pi_i(\Sigma) :$ $\pi_1(p) = \pi_1(p') \Rightarrow p = p'$, where $i = 1, 2$. $\mathcal{TYPE}(P) \in \text{Sigma}$ denotes the type of a program $P \in \text{Program}$. It is easily defined by traversing P and accumulating the profiles of the operators and constructors.

Example 4. Using some standard notation for profiles, the predicate symbols for the enhanced program in Example 1 are of the following types:

label   : TREE $\rightarrow$ LABEL
label_list : TREE* $\times$ OP $\times$ LABEL $\rightarrow$ LABEL

$init\_label : OP \rightarrow LABEL$
$and\_or \quad : OP \times LABEL \times LABEL \rightarrow LABEL$

Based on modes, parameter positions can be subdivided into *applied* and *defining* positions. LHS positions with mode ↑ and RHS positions with mode ↓ are called applied positions; complementary for defining positions. The intuition behind these terms is that variables on applied positions are expected to be "computed" in terms of variables on defining positions. These terms are actually used in much the same way in extended attribute grammars [WM77]. The concept of applied and defining positions is relevant for metaprogramming, for example, if certain positions need to be computed from other positions according to some scheme like accumulation or reduction.

2.2.4 Addressing Fragments

It is clear that fragments of object programs need to be addressed during meta-programming. We should discuss all the various ways to address fragments. At the top level, a certain definition in a program can be addressed by the symbol on the LHS which have all the rules in a definition in common. At the next level, a certain rule in a definition can be addressed by its tag. At the level of a rule, first, either the LHS or the RHS has to be selected. For RHS, a certain literal can be addressed using a selector. Finally, a possibly nested parameter position can be addressed by a non-empty selector sequence. Consequently, it is maybe more convenient to use modes and types instead of selectors.

Example 5. Let us consider the first rule in the enhanced program in Example 1. The additional computational behaviour as manifested by new parameter positions of *label* and *label_list*, and the new literal *init_label(. . .)* refers to some variables of the initial program. Thus, a transformation performing the enhancement would have to address these variables. Using an ad hoc notation for references, the variable *OP*, for example, can be addressed by LHS → ↓ TREE → tree.OP, i.e., first, the LHS of the rule is addressed, then the input position of type TREE s selected, and, finally, the nested parameter of type OP rooted by the constructor *tree* is selected.

It is debatable whether there should be different kinds of selectors (rule tags, selectors for RHS literals, etc.). Of course, it is a basic well-formedness requirement that selectors are pairwise distinct at any level of addressing. Moreover, selectors also contribute to "conceptual" well-typedness in a straightforward sense. The selectors used for the parameter positions of literals, for example, have to be the same for all literals with a certain symbol in a program. Note also that object programs do not necessarily need to define selectors explicitly. Selectors might be generated automatically during the construction of the internal representation so that they can be observed by meta-programs traversing object programs.

The interface of a corresponding abstract data type for addressing is shown in part in Figure 2.3. The central type is Reference modelling references to a literal within a rule and in turn to a parameter in a literal. *deref* returns the parameter according to a reference.

deref	: Reference $\rightarrow$ Rule $\rightarrow$ $\mathcal{E}$ Parameter	– dereferencing
references	: Rule $\rightarrow$ Reference*	– return all references
lhsOrRhs	: $\alpha \rightarrow$ (Selector $\rightarrow \alpha$) $\rightarrow$ Reference $\rightarrow \alpha$	– handle LHS/RHS reference
operator	: Reference $\rightarrow$ Operator	– referenced operator
typeOf	: Reference $\rightarrow$ Type	– type of the reference
refersToAP	: Reference $\rightarrow$ Bool	– applied position
refersToDP	: Reference $\rightarrow$ Bool	– defined position
leq	: Reference $\rightarrow$ Reference $\rightarrow$ Rule $\rightarrow \mathcal{E}$ Bool– $\leq$ on Reference
rightmost	: Reference* $\rightarrow$ Rule $\rightarrow \mathcal{E}$ Reference	– maximum on Reference

Figure 2.3 Interface of the Abstract Data Type for Addressing

When a meta-program has to iterate on the parameters of a rule, all the references can be accumulated with *references*. The function *lhsOrRhs* provides a case construct on references to process LHS resp. RHS references differently. References have a type, which can be selected with *typeOf*. The remaining functions in Figure 2.3 deal with data flow issues. *refersToAP* and *refersToDP* check if a given reference refers to an applied or a defining position. The operation *leq* defines a left-to-right order on Reference. LHS input positions are the smallest positions. The order of the RHS respects the order of the literals where the input positions of a literal are smaller than the output positions of the same literal. The LHS output positions are the greatest positions. This order is useful in order to enforce a certain data flow from left to right (or vice versa), e.g., in accumulation.

2.3 Extending Computational Behaviour

In Subsection 2.3.1, the basic roles listed in the introduction will be reviewed w.r.t. semantics-preservation. In Subsection 2.3.2, a core calculus supporting these roles is defined in the meta-programming framework. In Subsection 2.3.3, the core calculus is completed to get transformation operators operating at the level of complete object programs. Finally, it is illustrated in Subsection 2.3.4 that the developed calculus is useful to derive common programming techniques.

2.3.1 Semantics-preservation

When extending a program, a crucial question is whether the computational behaviour is preserved. Kirschbaum, Sterlin and Jain have shown in [KSJ93] that program maps, which capture most transformations derivable in our framework, preserve the computational behaviour of a logic program, if it is assumed that behaviour is manifested by the (SLD-) computations of the program. In contrast, we will discuss here in an informal way why the roles identified by us are semantics-preserving. Given a logic program P and an enhancement P', the discussion of the correctness of the transformation will be based on the proof-tree semantics for P and P'.[6] We should point out that we have correctness but not completeness, i.e., each proof tree for P' can be projected onto a proof tree of P, but not vice versa.

Adding parameters Correctness holds because the new parameters in P' can also be projected away in its proof trees. Completeness does not hold in general because the new parameters might constrain variables from P too much or the unification involved in unfolding fails in the new parameter positions. Several schemes to add parameters can be proved to imply completeness.

Applying substitutions Correctness holds because the substitution can also be applied to proof trees of P. Completeness does not hold because a substitution might instantiate variables, and thereby certain unfolding steps are not possible any longer.

Renaming symbols It is clear that a proper renaming is performed consistently. It is very common to require that a renaming does not confuse symbols. In this case, correctness and completeness follows trivially. We also consider renamings, where the parameters of an open program might be confused with each other or with symbols already defined by the program. This is a sensible design decision for open programs.

Inserting literals Proof trees in P' will contain additional subtrees which can be projected away to obtain P. Completeness cannot be ensured because a proof subtree for a new literal might not exist, or variables of P might be constrained by all possible subtrees for the new literal too much.

Adding definitions The extension of a definition for a symbol by new rules needs to be forbidden. Providing definitions for a symbol s previously not defined by P is correct. There are two cases. If s has not been used in P, then the proof-tree semantics for P and P' are equivalent. Otherwise, P is an open program with parameter s. Providing a definition is sensible.

2.3.2 A Core Calculus

In defining transformation operators corresponding to the basic roles, less complex types of object program fragments are preferably chosen, and the state effect is ignored whenever possible. Renaming predicates, for example, can essentially be defined at the literal level, and indeed the state effect is not relevant for renaming. The resulting core calculus is completed in the next subsection by lifting all the operators to the type $\text{Trafo} = \text{Program} \rightarrow \mathcal{ES}\text{Program}$ in a simple and natural way.

The definition of the core calculus is presented in Figure 2.4. States are only involved in adding parameters ($\underline{\text{add}}_0$). Note that it is not possible to abstract from errors at all because all operators construct object program fragments, i.e., the operators are inherently

---

[6]Our arguments for the correctness of the roles do not rely on certain technical conditions assumed for the rigorous proof in [KSJ93].

partial. Adding parameters ($\underline{add}_0$) and renaming operators ($\underline{rename}_0$) can be defined at the Literal level. Substitution ($\underline{substitute}_0$) can even be defined at the Parameter level. On the other hand, inserting literals ($\underline{insert}_0$) must be defined at the Rule level and the definition of operators ($\underline{define}_0$) has even to be defined at the top level, i.e., at the Program level.

$\underline{add}_0$: Operator $\rightarrow$ Selector $\rightarrow$ Mode $\rightarrow$ Type $\rightarrow$ Literal $\rightarrow$ $\mathcal{ES}$ Literal
$\underline{substitute}_0$: Substitution $\rightarrow$ Parameter $\rightarrow$ $\mathcal{E}$ Parameter
$\underline{rename}_0$: Operator $\rightarrow$ Operator $\rightarrow$ Literal $\rightarrow$ $\mathcal{E}$ Literal
$\underline{insert}_0$: Reference $\rightarrow$ Selector $\rightarrow$ Operator $\rightarrow$ Rule $\rightarrow$ $\mathcal{E}$ Rule
$\underline{define}_0$: Definition $\rightarrow$ Program $\rightarrow$ $\mathcal{E}$ Program

$\underline{add}_0$ *op sel m t lit* $=$
  if $(operator\ lit) \neq op$
    then $unit_{\mathcal{ES}}\ lit$
    else $\uparrow_{\mathcal{S}}^{\mathcal{ES}} (fresh_{\mathsf{Variable}}\ t) \ggeq_{\mathcal{ES}} \lambda p \rightarrow$
        $\uparrow_{\mathcal{E}}^{\mathcal{ES}} (literal\ (operator\ lit)\ ((parameterization\ lit) \mathbin{+\!\!+} [(sel, m, p)]))$

$\underline{substitute}_0$ *subst p* $=$ *descend sv st p*
  where
    $sv\ v\ =\ apply\ subst\ v\ (typeOf\ p)$
    $st\ sym\ paras\ =\ mmap\ f\ paras \ggeq_{\mathcal{E}} \lambda paras' \rightarrow term\ sym\ paras'\ (typeOf\ p)$
    $f\ (sel, p)\ =\ \underline{substitute}_0\ subst\ p \ggeq_{\mathcal{E}} \lambda p' \rightarrow unit_{\mathcal{E}}(sel, p')$

$\underline{rename}_0$ *op op' lit* $=$
  $literal\ (\textbf{if}\ (operator\ lit) \neq op\ \textbf{then}\ (operator\ lit)\ \textbf{else}\ op')\ (parameterization\ lit)$

$\underline{insert}_0$ *ref sel op r* $=$
  $deref\ ref\ r \ggeq_{\mathcal{E}} \lambda\_ \rightarrow$
  $literal\ op\ [] \ggeq_{\mathcal{E}} \lambda lit_0 \rightarrow$
  $rule\ (tag\ r)\ (lhs\ r)\ (f\ (sel, lit_0))$
  where
    $f\ new = lhsOrRhs\ il\ ir\ ref$
      where
        $il = \textbf{if}\ refersToAP\ ref\ \textbf{then}\ new\ :\ (rhs\ r)\ \textbf{else}\ (rhs\ r) \mathbin{+\!\!+} [new]$
        $irsel' = g(rhsr)$
        where
          $g(qlit@(sel'', lit) : qlits) =$
            $\textbf{if}\ and[sel' == sel'', (operator\ ref) == (operator\ lit)]$
              $\textbf{then}\ \textbf{if}\ refersToAP\ ref\ \textbf{then}\ [new, qlit] \mathbin{+\!\!+} qlits\ \textbf{else}\ [qlit, new] \mathbin{+\!\!+} qlits$
            $\textbf{else}\ qlit : (g\ qlits)$

$\underline{define}_0$ *d p* $= program\ (definitions\ p \mathbin{+\!\!+} [d])$

Figure 2.4   The core calculus

$$mfoldr : (\alpha \to \beta \to \mathcal{M}\beta) \to \beta \to \alpha^\star \to \mathcal{M}\,\beta$$
$$mfoldr\ f\ e\ l = foldr\ g\ (unit_{\mathcal{M}}\ e)\ l$$
where
$$g\ x\ c = c\ \ggeq_{\mathcal{M}}\ \lambda\,v \to f\ x\ v$$
$$mmap : (\alpha \to \mathcal{M}\beta) \to \alpha^\star \to \mathcal{M}\,\beta^\star$$
$$mmap\ f = mfoldr\ g\ []$$
where
$$g\ x\ l = f\ x\ \ggeq_{\mathcal{M}}\ \lambda x' \to unit_{\mathcal{M}}\ (x' : l)$$

Figure 2.5   Monadic foldr/map on lists

There is the following rationale for the definition of $\underline{add_0}$ intended to add positions to literals. If the given literal *lit* has an operator which is different from *op*, the whole literal is preserved. Otherwise, first a fresh variable of type *t* is generated. Then, the given literal is reconstructed preserving the operator and extending the list of parameters by the new parameter associating it with the given selector *sel* and mode *m*. Generating fresh variables is performed in the state monad $\mathcal{S}$, whereas fragment construction is performed in the error monad $\mathcal{E}$. To compose these computations, they are lifted to $\mathcal{ES}$ by $\uparrow_{\mathcal{S}}^{\mathcal{ES}}$ and $\uparrow_{\mathcal{E}}^{\mathcal{ES}}$.

The definition of $\underline{substitute_0}$ uses the function *descend* to destruct parameters. Consequently, there are two cases corresponding to the functions *sv* and *st*. Variables are replaced by the term according to the supplied substitution *subst*. The auxiliary function *apply* performs the required table lookup and it behaves like identity if there is no entry for *v*. The monadic map for lists defined in Figure 2.5 is used for the traversal of nested parameters.

We should comment on the design of the $\underline{insert_0}$ operator. For reasons of orthogonality, the inserted literal carries an empty list of parameters because parameters can be added subsequently by $\underline{add_0}$. There should be some way to define the actual target position on the RHS of a rule. Note that the order of the RHS literals may be significant for the data-flow or control-flow in the object program, or for the performance of subsequent transformations. References are a suitable abstract means of specifying a RHS position. The idea is that the literal is inserted *next* to the literal referred to by the reference passed to $\underline{insert_0}$, also using the concept of applied and defining positions.

2.3.3 Completion of the Core Calculus

The core calculus is completed by lifting the operators from the previous subsection to Trafo. Lifting means here that a function defined on a certain fragment type α is lifted to a more complex type α' and finally to Program – the type of the complete object programs. To model that kind of lifting, generalised and monadic *maps* [MJ95] are useful. [7] The meta-programming framework provides monadic maps for all the fragment types of object programs. The symbol *mmap* is overloaded to denote all monadic map functions, including

---

[7]The adventive *generalised* means other types than just α and $\alpha^\star$ are associated. The adjective *monadic* means that computations in a monad can be involved, i.e., a function $f : \tau \to \mathcal{M}\sigma$ (rather than $f : \tau \to \sigma$) is lifted to a function $f' : \tau' \to \mathcal{M}\sigma'$ (rather than $f' : \tau' \to \sigma'$).

the common monadic map for lists as defined in Figure 2.5. In Figure 2.6, all the types related to each other by *mmap* are illustrated. The figure also defines an instance of *mmap*, namely the instance for lifting functions on literals to functions on rules.

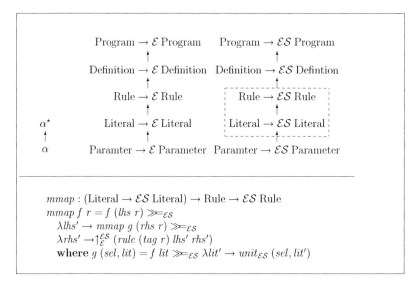

$$mmap : (\text{Literal} \to \mathcal{ES}\ \text{Literal}) \to \text{Rule} \to \mathcal{ES}\ \text{Rule}$$
$$mmap\ f\ r = f\ (lhs\ r) \ggg_{\mathcal{ES}}$$
$$\lambda lhs' \to mmap\ g\ (rhs\ r) \ggg_{\mathcal{ES}}$$
$$\lambda rhs' \to \uparrow^{\mathcal{ES}}_{\mathcal{E}}\ (rule\ (tag\ r)\ lhs'\ rhs')$$
$$\textbf{where}\ g\ (sel, lit) = f\ lit \ggg_{\mathcal{ES}} \lambda lit' \to unit_{\mathcal{ES}}\ (sel, lit')$$

Figure 2.6 Lifting by *mmap*

Figure 2.7 lifts the basic transformation operators in Figure 2.4 up to Trafo. The specification of <u>add</u>, <u>rename</u>, and <u>define</u> should be self-explanatory since only *mmap* and the operation $\uparrow^{\mathcal{ES}}_{\mathcal{E}}$ lifting computations in $\mathcal{E}$ to $\mathcal{ES}$ are involved. The specification of <u>substitute</u> is slightly more complex. The actual substitution to be performed is not passed to <u>substitute</u> as a parameter but more indirectly as a function from Rule to $\mathcal{ES}$ Substitution. This is a sensible design because there is no sense in applying a single substitution to all rules in a program. The specification of <u>insert</u> exploits a similar trick. The first parameter is a boolean function intented to control if for a given rule a literal has to be included, e.g., based on the rule's tag.

Example 6. The enhanced program in Example 1 is derived in the following atomic steps. For readability, we use a semi-formal style. We omit the steps which are specific to the second and the third rule.

1. Rename *traverse* resp. *traverse_list* to *label* resp. *label_list*.

2. Add an output position of type LABEL to *label*.

3. Add an input position of type OP to *label_list*.

$$
\begin{array}{ll}
\underline{\text{add}} & : \text{Operator} \rightarrow \text{Selector} \rightarrow \text{Mode} \rightarrow \text{Type} \rightarrow \text{Trafo} \\
\underline{\text{substitute}} & : (\text{Rule} \rightarrow \mathcal{ES}\ \text{Substitution}) \rightarrow \text{Trafo} \\
\underline{\text{rename}} & : \text{Operator} \rightarrow \text{Operator} \rightarrow \text{Trafo} \\
\underline{\text{insert}} & : (\text{Rule} \rightarrow \mathcal{ES}\ \text{Bool}) \rightarrow \text{Reference} \rightarrow \text{Selector} \rightarrow \text{Operator} \rightarrow \text{Trafo} \\
\underline{\text{define}} & : \text{Definition} \rightarrow \text{Trafo}
\end{array}
$$

$\underline{\text{add}}\ op\ sel\ m\ t = mmap\ (mmap\ (mmap\ (\underline{\text{add}}_0\ op\ sel\ m\ t)))$
$\underline{\text{substitute}}\ f = mmap\ (mmap\ g)$
  where
    $g\ r = f\ r \ggg_\mathcal{E} \lambda subst \rightarrow mmap\ (mmap\ (\lambda p \rightarrow \uparrow_\mathcal{E}^{\mathcal{ES}}\ (\underline{\text{substitute}}_0\ subst\ p)))\ r$
$\underline{\text{rename}}\ op_1\ op_2\ p = \uparrow_\mathcal{E}^{\mathcal{ES}}\ (mmap\ (mmap\ (mmap\ (\underline{\text{rename}}_0\ op_1\ op_2)))\ p)$
$\underline{\text{insert}}\ f\ ref\ sel\ op = mmap\ (mmap\ g)$
  where
    $g\ r = f\ r \ggg_\mathcal{E} \lambda b \rightarrow$
      if b **then** $\uparrow_\mathcal{E}^{\mathcal{ES}}\ (\underline{\text{insert}}_0\ ref\ sel\ op\ r)$
              else $unit_{\mathcal{ES}}\ r$
$\underline{\text{define}}\ d\ p = \uparrow_\mathcal{E}^{\mathcal{ES}}\ (\underline{\text{define}}_0\ d\ p)$

Figure 2.7   The completed calculus

4. Add an input position of type LABEL to *label_list*.

5. Add an output position of type LABEL to *label_list*.

6. Focus on the first rule

   a) Insert *init_label* before *label_list*'s input position of type LABEL.

   b) Add an input position of type OP to *init_label*.

   c) Add an output position of type LABEL to *init_label*.

   d) Apply a substitution unifying the positions for the variable OP.

   e) Apply a substitution unifying the positions for the variable LABEL_{init}.

   f) Apply a substitution unifying the positions for the variable LABEL.

7. Focus on the second rule ...

8. Focus on the third rule ...

9. Add the definitions for *init_label* and *and_or*.

It is relatively easy to see that the defined operators actually implement the intended roles. We do not attempt a proper verification here, but a few arguments regarding the correctness of the implementations should be provided. Let us consider, for example, the operator $\underline{\text{add}}$:

- The output program has the same shape as the input program (number of definitions, number of rules in a definition, tags of rules, number of RHS literals, selectors on

RHSs) because it is obtained by just transforming at the Literal level. This property is implied by simple properties of *mmap*.

- The operator of each literal is preserved. This is implied by standard laws of destruction and construction.

- The list of parameters of a literal is either completely preserved or extended by another parameter as implied again by laws of destruction and construction.

From the above arguments it follows that <u>add</u> only extends the relevant parameter lists without changing any other part of the input program. For <u>substitute</u> and <u>rename</u> one has to show that the simple concepts substitution and consistent renaming resp. are actually specified. The correctness of <u>define</u> follows from the fact that all definitions from the input program are preserved in the output program. We skip the discussion of <u>insert</u>.

2.3.4 Techniques

The operators defined above are useful to derive high-level abstractions of common adaptations of programs – techniques in the terminology of stepwise enhancement [SS97, Lak89, KMS96], e.g., the *accumulate* technique can be derived from <u>add</u> and <u>substitute</u>, whereas *calculate* techniques also require <u>insert</u>.

Figure 2.8 presents the operator <u>l2r</u> capturing certain data flow oriented techniques. One important way to use the operator is to simulate the *accumulate* technique. Note that <u>l2r</u> is more flexible. The operator unifies parameters of a given type in a way to establish a dataflow from left to right. To introduce an accumulator with <u>l2r</u>, first all relevant symbols had to be extended by two parameter positions of the given type, one of mode $\downarrow$, another of mode $\uparrow$. The operator <u>l2r</u> is based on the operator <u>copy</u> also shown in Figure 2.8. <u>copy</u> inserts a "copy rule" (using attribute grammar jargon) by means of <u>substitute</u>. Its first argument is – as in the case of <u>insert</u> – a function to decide which rule should be adapted. The remaining two arguments refer to the parameters which should be unified. *solve* is assumed to compute the most general unifier for a list of equations on parameters according to Robinson's algorithm.

Example 7. We cannot use <u>l2r</u> for the enhancement in Example 1 because an *accumulate-calculate* rather than a pure *calculate* technique would be needed. To illustrate <u>l2r</u>, an enhancement of the initial program to support an accumulator is derived:

$$traverse(\downarrow tree(OP, NODE, TREE^*_{child}) \boxed{, \downarrow ACC_0, \uparrow ACC_1}) \Leftarrow$$
$$traverse\_list(\downarrow TREE^*_{child} \boxed{, \downarrow ACC_0, \uparrow ACC_1}).$$
$$traverse\_list(\downarrow [] \boxed{, \downarrow ACC, \uparrow ACC}).$$
$$traverse\_list(\downarrow [TREE|TREE^*] \boxed{, \downarrow ACC_0, \uparrow ACC_2}) \Leftarrow$$
$$traverse(\downarrow TREE \boxed{, \downarrow ACC_0, \uparrow ACC_1}),$$
$$traverse\_list(\downarrow TREE^* \boxed{, \downarrow ACC_1, \uparrow ACC_2}).$$

$\underline{\text{l2r}}$: Type → Trafo
$\underline{\text{l2r}}\ t\ p = \uparrow_{\mathcal{E}}^{\mathcal{ES}}\ (mfoldr\ f\ e\ (definitions\ p)) \ggg_{\mathcal{ES}} \lambda trafo \rightarrow trafo\ p$
where
$\quad --$identity
$\quad e : $ Trafo
$\quad e = \lambda p\ unit_{\mathcal{ES}}\ p$
$\quad --$transform definitions
$\quad f : $ Definition → Trafo → $\mathcal{E}$ Trafo
$\quad f\ d\ e = mfoldr\ g\ e\ (rules\ d)$
$\quad\quad --$transform rules
$\quad g : $ Rule → Trafo → $\mathcal{E}$ Trafo
$\quad g\ r\ e = mfoldr\ h\ e\ to$
$\quad$**where**
$\quad\quad --$accumulate all relevant references
$\quad\quad from = [x|x \in references\ r, typeOf\ x == t, refers\,ToDP\ x]$
$\quad\quad to = [x|x \in references\ r, typeOf\ x == t, refers\,ToAP\ x]$
$\quad\quad --$iterate applied references
$\quad\quad h : $ Reference → Trafo → $\mathcal{E}$ Trafo
$\quad\quad h\ x\ e = mfoldr\ before\ []\ from \ggg_{\mathcal{E}} \lambda from' \rightarrow$
$\quad\quad\quad\quad\quad\quad\quad rightmost\ from'\ r \ggg_{\mathcal{E}} \lambda y \rightarrow$
$\quad\quad\quad\quad\quad\quad\quad unit_{\mathcal{E}}\ (\lambda p \rightarrow e\ p\ \ggg_{\mathcal{ES}} \underline{\text{copy}}\ (\lambda r' \rightarrow unit_{\mathcal{ES}}\ (tag\ r == tag\ r'))\ y\ x)$
$\quad\quad$**where**
$\quad\quad\quad --$find all defining references smaller than x
$\quad\quad\quad before : $ Reference → Reference* → $\mathcal{E}$ Reference*
$\quad\quad\quad before\ y\ ys = leq\ y\ x\ r \ggg_{\mathcal{E}} \lambda b \rightarrow unit_{\mathcal{E}}\ (\textbf{if}\ b\ \textbf{then}\ (y : ys)\ \textbf{else}\ ys)$
$\quad\underline{\text{copy}} : $ (Rule → $\mathcal{ES}$ Bool) → Reference → Reference → Trafo
$\quad\underline{\text{copy}}\ cond\ ref\ ref' = \underline{\text{substitute}}\ f$
$\quad$**where**
$\quad\quad f\ r = cond\ r \ggg_{\mathcal{ES}} \lambda b \rightarrow$
$\quad\quad\quad \textbf{if}\ b\ \textbf{then}\ \uparrow_{\mathcal{E}}^{\mathcal{ES}}\ (deref\ ref\ r \ggg_{\mathcal{E}} \lambda p \rightarrow deref\ ref'\ r \ggg_{\mathcal{E}} \lambda p' \rightarrow solve\ [(p, p')])$
$\quad\quad\quad \textbf{else}\ unit_{\mathcal{ES}}\ empty$

Figure 2.8 Technique for Accumulation

This enhancement is derived by adding the parameter positions of type ACC with the operator $\underline{\text{add}}$ and performing $\underline{\text{l2r}}$ ACC afterwards.

In [Läm99b, LR99], the Lämmel et al. consider other techniques based on similar operator suites, e.g., a reduction technique, where the intermediate results computed by some predicates are combined in a pairwise manner. The technology developed in [Läm99b] is also sufficient to support the kind of higher-order reconstruction of stepwise enhancement proposed in [NS98]. A proper catalogue of techniques covering all the common techniques in stepwise enhancement is a subject for further work.

2.4 Related Work

In this section, related work will be discussed to some extend with emphasis on stepwise enhancement.

Research in the field of program transformation for logic programs traditionally focusses on optimisation rather than support for reusability and extensibility. Fold/unfold strategies provide the basic mechanism; refer, e.g., to [PP96, RF98]. It is a common point of view to regard techniques in stepwise enhancement [SS97, Lak89, KMS96] as transformations but this is the first place which presents an effective calculus to describe the corresponding transformations (cf. [LRL00]).

Related notions for relations on programs have been defined in the stepwise enhancement community [PS90, KSJ93, Jai95]. Our roles can be captured by a kind of projection notion which is similar to the program maps in [KSJ93] and symbol mappings in [Jai95]. The former preserve computational behaviour. However, substitution is involved neither in program maps nor in symbol mappings. Another important difference is that modes, selectors, and types are used in our setting. Symbol mappings are slightly more general than program maps because many-1 rather than 1-1 predicate symbol mappings are used. Many-1 symbol mappings may not preserve computational behaviour when symbols get unified. Our role of renaming facilitates unification in a safe way. Unification is only possible for the symbols which are not defined by a program, i.e., parameters of an open program can be unified. It is easy to see that our renaming operator does not support general (i.e., unsafe) many-1 symbol mappings, since a corresponding unification of symbols results in a non-well-formed object program with multiple definitions for one symbol and thus in an error. In [PS90], a more general notion of enhancement is sketched. It includes modulations and mutations, i.e., programs equivalent under fold/unfold transformations, and programs obtained by structural alterations of the control flow. However, [PS90] formalises only extensions in the sense of program maps [KSJ93].

The Figure 2.9 depicts the definition of a projection notion underlying the roles in the chapter. The idea is that for all transformation operators defined in the chapter, an input program P and the corresponding output program P' are related according to the projection notion. Stepwise enhancement has been integrated with programming environments [Lak89, BRV+94, Rob96]. Such environments focus on tool support for applying techniques whereas our framework is intended as a soli basis for defining and executing techniques. It is a subject for future work to develop a transformational programming environment based on the framework. In [WBBL99], Whittle et al. describe an ML editor based on the proof-as-programs idea. Programs are created incrementally using a collection of correctness-preserving editing commands. Such an approach might also be sensible for our roles and techniques derived from them.

In [BMPT90], Brogi et al. describe a related meta-programming framework. The approach is based on a special language LML which can be regarded as another approach to integrate functional and logic programming in a certain way. LML also is intended for the construction of knowledge based systems. Logic programming is supported by means of a data type of theories at the level of functional programming. Our intentions are different. We just want to provide a solid framework for general and typeful meta-

---

The class of transformations covered by the chapter can be captured by a kind of projection notion as follows. A *projection P* of a program *P'*, denoted by $P \rhd P'$, is a program where some of the functionality of *P'*, i.e., some of its definitions, RHS literals, parameters, have been projected away. Moreover, substitution, renaming and permutation my be involved. The relation $\rhd$ is formalised in the meta-programming framework as follows. Given $P, P' \in Program$, $P \rhd P'$ if $\exists \sigma : Operator \rightarrow Operator$:

1. $\forall p \in \pi_1 \, \mathcal{TYPE}(P) : \exists p' \in \pi_1 \, \mathcal{TYPE}(P') : \sigma(\pi_1 \, p) = \pi_1 \, p' \wedge \pi_2 \, p \subseteq \pi_2 \, p'$

2. $\pi_2 \, \mathcal{TYPE}(P) \subseteq \pi_2 \, \mathcal{TYPE}(P')$

3. $\forall d \in definitions \, P : \exists d' \in definitions \, P'$:

   a) $\sigma(defines \, d) = defines \, d'$ and $\#(rules \, d) = \#(rules \, d')$

   b) $\forall r \in rules \, d : \exists r' \in rules \, d'$:
      $\exists \theta : Variable \rightarrow Parameter : \exists w_1, \ldots, w_n \in \{1, \ldots, n'\}$:

      i. $tag \, r = tag \, r'$
      ii. $\sigma(operator \, l_0) = operator \, l'_0$
      iii. $\theta(parameterization \, l_0) \subseteq parameterization \, l'_0$
      iv. $w_1 < \cdots < w_n$
      v. $s_i = s'_{w_i}$ for $i = 1, \ldots, n$
      vi. $\sigma(operator \, l_i) = operator \, l'_{w_i}$ for $i = 1, \ldots, n$
      vii. $\theta(parameterization \, l_i) \subseteq parameterization \, l'_{w_i}$ for $i = 1, \ldots, n$
      where
      - $lhs \, r = l_0, rhs \, r = \langle \langle s_1, l_1 \rangle, \ldots, \langle s_n, l_n \rangle \rangle$,
      - $lhs \, r' = l'_0, rhs \, r' = \langle \langle s'_1, l'_1 \rangle, \ldots, \langle s'_{n'}, l'_{n'} \rangle \rangle$.

We assume that $\subseteq$ is defined on sequences by regarding dem as sets.
The definition can be read as follows. σ is a function which renames (or substitutes) operators. (1.) constrains types of operators by saying that the types of *P'* should cover the types of *P*, where an operator in *P'* might have more positions than the corresponding operator in *P*. (2.) says that the constructors of *P'* should cover the constructors of *P*. (3.) formalises the actual projection on rules. *P'* might provide more definitions than *P*. θ is a substitution. Tags and LHS operators (modulo renaming) must be the same for the matching rules from *P* and *P'*. The rule in *P'* might have more literals on the RHS. The literals originating from *P* are indexed by the w_i. The relative order of the literals from *P* must be preserved in *P'* (refer to 3.iv.). Regarding related literals, the literal in *P'* might have more parameters than in *P*. Substitution is involved in relating the parameters (refer to 3.vii.).
The definition is restricted in the sense that constructors and selectors cannot be renamed, and permutation and projection is not performed for nested parameters. It is straightforward to remove these restrictions.

Figure 2.9   A notion of projections of programs

programming. Our approach is entirely different from multi-stage programming [TS97], where code and functions on code facilitate different binding times but not enhancement of given object programs. The selection of *Haskell* to implement the framework is in line with Bowers [Bow98]. Typed and modular functional languages like *Haskell* provide an excellent basis for meta-programming.

Our work on extending computational behaviour is related to modularity, composition and decomposition. Modularity concepts such as [BMPT94] are well-suited for functional decomposition but they do not facilitate the introduction of additional functionality if it had to be weaved into the program in a systematic way as facilitated by the developed transformation operators. There are notions of composition which go beyond the limit of modularity in the common sense, e.g., Sterling et al. suggest in [SJK93a] the composition of programs having some basic skeleton in common. Related proposals can be found elsewhere based on terms like superposition, partitioning and tupling. This perspective on composition merely emphasises that we can compose different extensions of the same underlying program by a kind of descriptional composition. In contrast, the chapter is concerned with the actual specification of extensions.

There are certain techniques in the sense of stepwise enhancement which have some counterpart in actual attribute grammar specification languages. Such constructs are studied in [LR99].

2.5 Concluding Remarks

We give the main results of the chapter, before we conlude it with a perspective for future work.

Results. This chapter addressed the following questions and provided the following answers:

1. What are the *basic roles* needed for the development of transformations to extend the computational behaviour of programs. We identified five roles, e.g., adding parameters and performing substitutions. These roles can be specified in separation and they can effectively be used to derive interesting program transformations.

2. How can the basic roles and the derived techniques be *formalised* and *implemented*? We developed a formal and operational framework supporting functional (and thus *declarative*) meta-programming. The framework employs a number of powerful concepts such as monads, abstract data types and generalised maps. The actual language *Haskell* has been chosen to implement the framework.

We believe that the result from research in stepwise enhancement in general, and our new results on extending computational behaviour in particular, provide a solid ground for contributions to a more formal and technical understanding of notions in mainstream programming like adaptive and aspect-oriented programming. In [Läm99a], Lämmel presents a proposal for declarative aspect-oriented programming including a form of weaving by means of meta-programming.

Future Work. The class of semantics-preserving transformations should be enriched to cover modularisations and mutations as suggested (but not formalised) in [PS90].

The static analysis of meta-programs has to be improved based on further formal properties of transformations. We should be able, for example, to provide sufficient criteria for a transformation to be defined, or to associate a transformation with a kind of type constructor modelling the effect of the transformation regarding object types. It is a demanding experiment to investigate the utility of dependent types [Aug99, XP99] in order to model such properties in the meta-programming framework.

A speculative topic for future work concerns the generalisation of the chosen object language. There is some evidence that other rather different languages (e.g., higher-order functional languages, object-oriented languages) and formalisms (e.g., syntax definition formalisms) are sensible for similar roles of transformation. There are relate notions like superposition and refinement in several frameworks. Any contribution to the unification of some of these concepts had to be regarded as a progress in programming theory.

Chapter 3

Format Evolution

A systematic approach to the adaptation of XML documents and their Dtds is developed. The approach facilitates the evolution of XML-based formats. There are two essential ideas. Firstly, changes in the formats of documents are represented as stepwise transformations on the underlying DTDs. Secondly, the corresponding migration of the XML data is largely induced by the DTD transformations. The presentation focuses on concepts of format evolution, namely roles of corresponding transformations, properties of the transformations, and expressiveness to implement the transformations.

3.1 Introduction

The XML-age. XML (cf. [W3C00a]) is more and more used as interchange format in distributed, client-server, intra- and internet applications. It also finds its way to specific application domains to serve as storage and exchange format, e.g., for abstract syntax trees or intermediate representations in language processing. XML is usually employed back-to-back with DTDs (document type definitions; cf. [W3C00a]) in order to constrain the XML documents according to a specific format. In a non-trivial application architecture of the XML-age, various components cooperate based on various interchange formats (i.e., DTDs) serving as contracts between the components. The underlying data might be stored in a database (presumably according to some relational or object-oriented database schema). XML data is obtained via database queries. XML data might also be managed in a database or in a file system in a more native manner. The components of the application query the database, access XML files, or they obtain the (XML) data from other components. The data to be presented to the user as spreadsheets, active web-pages, reports etc. is also encoded as XML data.

Evolution of XML/DTD In many application contexts of XML, the formats regulated by the underlying DTDs are repeatedly changed, either due to maintenance requirements, or due to refactoring, or due to independent evolution of one of the components. Also, if different components need to interact, often the corresponding interfaces need to be matched up—especially if the interaction was not anticipated (cf. [BKK+01]). In the present chapter, we show that the systematic evolution of DTDs can usually be represented by a number of atomic transformation steps which in turn induce a transformation for XML document migration. The resulting *evolution by transformation* approach is outlined in Figure 3.1. XML document transformation is an established concept. We are rather interested in the intertwined treatment of format change and document migration. Such a treatment contributes to *format and document reengineering*. The overall approach is not too much dependent on XML/DTD. The concepts should also be of value for other technical settings of format evolution, e.g., for proprietary formats, or for the setting of SGML (cf. [SGM86]). The approach is also applicable to XML schema languages other than DTD, e.g., XML Schema (cf. [W3C00b, W3C01a, W3C01b]) or DSD (cf. [KMS00]).

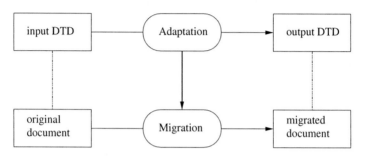

Figure 3.1 Induced XML document migration

Databases and XML. We should point out that our approach to format evolution is only sensible if the DTDs and XML documents at hand are the primary artefacts, that is, if XML is used as interchange or storage format in the first place. By contrast, if the XML data originates from database queries, and the underlying DTD corresponds to a (relational or an object-oriented) database schema (cf. [SSB+00]), then the database schema and the database instance are the primary artefacts. Consequently, we had to focus on a (database) schema evolution as opposed to a (DTD) format evolution. There is a large body of research on database re- and reverse engineering dealing with the problem of schema evolution and instance mapping (cf. [HTJC94]). As an aside, if XML data is solely *managed* in a database according to some mapping (cf. [KM00]), we still consider DTDs and XML documents as the primary artefacts.

Structure of the Chapter. In Section 3.2, we present our approach in a nutshell, that is, we examine a few scenarios of transforming DTDs, and we indicate in what sense the DTD transformation steps induce a migration for XML documents. In Section 3.3, we define some terms to reason about DTD and XML transformations. In the subsequent two sections, we systematically examine roles of format evolution, that is, transformations for DTDs and XML documents. There are two groups: In Section 3.4, transformations for refactoring are studied. In Section 3.5, structure-extending and -reducing transformations are studied. The assumption underlying our approach is that the evolution of a format can be represented as a number of transformation steps according to the identified roles. The chapter is concluded in Section 3.7 including a discussion of related work.

Disclaimer. As we are mainly interested in the study of a migration induced by the DTD transformations, we only cover a (nevertheless substantial) fragment of the full expressiveness of XML and DTDs. As for the element type declarations, we only cover the form that children are precisely specified (as opposed to the options ANY or MIXED), and the form #PCDATA (which is a specific instance of MIXED). Also, we do not consider entity declarations at all. Furthermore, we only consider the attribute type CDATA, and enumerated types. In fact, the treatment of other attribute types is not straightforward. The treatment of IDs and IDREFs, for example, requires to deal explicitly with references in a document.

3.2 The Approach in a Nutshell

We will explain the rationale for our approach to format evolution by a few illustrative transformations on a simple sample DTD, and a corresponding XML document. Figure 3.2 shows a DTD for music albums, whereas Figure 3.3 shows an XML document with a particular album. The example has been adopted from [WR99].

```
<!ELEMENT album (title, artist, recording?,
                 catalogno*, player+, track*, notes)>
<!ELEMENT title (#PCDATA)>
<!ELEMENT artist (#PCDATA)>
<!ELEMENT recording EMPTY>
   <!ATTLIST recording date CDATA #IMPLIED  place CDATA #IMPLIED>
<!ELEMENT catalogno EMPTY>
   <!ATTLIST catalogno label CDATA #REQUIRED   number CDATA #REQUIRED
             format (CD | LP | MiniDisc) #IMPLIED
             releasedate CDATA #IMPLIED       country CDATA #IMPLIED>
<!ELEMENT player EMPTY>
   <!ATTLIST player name CDATA #REQUIRED  instrument CDATA #REQUIRED>
<!ELEMENT track EMPTY>
   <!ATTLIST track title CDATA #REQUIRED   credit CDATA #IMPLIED
                   timing CDATA #IMPLIED>
<!ELEMENT notes (#PCDATA | albumref | trackref)*>
   <!ATTLIST notes author CDATA #IMPLIED>
<!ELEMENT albumref (#PCDATA)>
   <!ATTLIST albumref link CDATA #REQUIRED>
<!ELEMENT trackref (#PCDATA)>
<!ATTLIST trackref link CDATA #IMPLIED>
```

Figure 3.2   A DTD for music albums

3.2.1 Restructuring

Let us assume that the structure of the album element type is going to be somewhat richer than originally declared in Figure 3.2. In particular, there will be further personnel than

```
<?xml version='1.0'?>
<!DOCTYPE album SYSTEM "album.dtd">
<album>
  <title>Time Out</title>
  <artist>Dave Brubeck Quartet</artist>
  <recording date="June-August 1959" place="NYC"/>
  <catalogno label='Columbia' number='CL 1397' format='mono'/>
  <catalogno label='Columbia' number='CPK 1181'
             format='LP' country='Korea'/>
  <player name='Dave Brubeck' instrument='piano'/>
  <player name='Eugene Wright' instrument='bass'/>
  <player name='Joe Morello' instrument='drums'/>
  <track title='Blue Rondo &agrave; la Turk'
         credit='Brubeck' timing='6m42s'/>
  <track title='Strange Meadow Lark' credit='Brubeck' timing='7m20s'/>
  <track title='Take Five' credit='Desmond' timing='5m24s'/>
  <track title='Three To Get Ready' credit='Brubeck' timing='5m21s'/>
  <notes>
    <trackref link='#3'>Take Five</trackref> is a famous jazz track of
    that period. See also
    <albumref link='cbs-tfo'>Time Further Out</albumref>.
  </notes>
</album>
```

Figure 3.3 A music album as XML document

just players. To prepare for that enrichment, we *fold* player+ to obtain an element type personnel. The relevant fragment of the adapted DTD is the following:

```
<!ELEMENT album (title, artist, recording?, catalogno*,
                 personnel, track*, notes)>
<!ELEMENT personnel (player+)>
```

At the data level, that is, for XML documents, the element tags for personnel have to be inserted accordingly. Thus, we get the following:

```
<personnel>
  <player name='Dave Brubeck' instrument='piano'/>
  <player name='Eugene Wright' instrument='bass'/>
  <player name='Joe Morello' instrument='drums'/>
</personnel>
```

The important thing to notice here is that the XML transformation is *induced* by the DTD transformation: Performing a fold at the DTD level, the necessary migration of XML data to witness folding is (completely) determined.

3.2.2 Enrichment

Let us carry on with the evolution. We want to add some structural component to the element type personnel, namely we want to support an optional manager. Thus, we get the following extended definition of personnel, and a definition of manager:

```
<!ELEMENT personnel (player+, manager?)>
<!ELEMENT manager EMPTY>
    <!ATTLIST manager name CDATA #REQUIRED>
```

Actually, this transformation consists of two steps, namely the introduction of `manager`, and the enrichment of the structure of `personnel` to include an optional manager. The introduction step does not affect the XML level because all original element types are preserved. As for the enrichment step, a decision is due. Do we insert actual managers or not? Since the manager is optional, we can decide to leave the field for `manager` blank. Thus, we can say that the XML transformation induced by the enrichment of `personnel` is the identity mapping.

3.2.3 Attributes to Elements Conversion

As a final example, let us consider the problem of turning attributes into elements. Consider, e.g., the element type declaration for `recording` in Figure 3.2. A `recording` element does not have children but it might carry attributes. Suppose we want to change the status of the attributes `date` and `place` to become element types. Thus, we want to derive the following DTD:

```
<!ELEMENT recording (date?, place?)>
<!ELEMENT date (#PCDATA)>
<!ELEMENT place (#PCDATA)>
```

The induced XML transformation is somewhat involved. `CDATA` needs to be coerced to `#PCDATA`. Attribute lists have to be converted to elements. The migrated `recording` element is the following:

```
<recording>
    <date>June-August 1959</date>
    <place>NYC</place>
</recording>
```

This concludes our introductory list of examples. The purpose of the chapter is to systematically study the roles involved in DTD transformations, and the induced XML transformations.

3.2.4 Transformation Technology

The most obvious language candidate for XML transformation is XSLT (cf. [W3C99b]). In fact, throughout the chapter, we will use XSLT to illustrate some of the XML transformations which we employ for format evolution. Lacking an obvious candidate for DTD transformations, the transformations at the DTD level are described verbally. If we resorted to XML-based XML schema representations (as opposed to DTDs) such as XML Schema (cf. [W3C00b, W3C01a, W3C01b]), we can also use XSLT (or any other XML transformation language) for encoding the schema transformations.

```
<?xml version="1.0"?>
<xsl:stylesheet version="1.0"
    xmlns:xsl="http://www.w3.org/1999/XSL/Transform">
<xsl:template match="*|@*|comment()|processing-instruction()|text()">
<xsl:copy>
<xsl:apply-templates
    select="*|@*|comment()|processing-instruction()|text()"/>
</xsl:copy>
</xsl:template>
</xsl:stylesheet>
```

Figure 3.4 The identity transformation in XSLT

In Figure 3.4, we describe, for example, an identity function on XML documents in XSLT. The program descends into all elements and reconstructs them identically. The program is useful as a starting point for more meaningful XML transformations which are specific about certain patterns but behave like identity most of the time. The identity function is encoded with a single XSLT template which applies to all elements (cf. `match="*|...")`, all attributes (cf. `match="...|@*|...")` and others (i.e., comments, processing instructions, and text). Tags are copied (cf. `<xsl:copy>`). The template recursively descends into all children (cf. `<xsl:apply-templates ...>`).

Despite the popularity of XSLT, our experiments clearly indicated that XSLT is not really convenient for some transformations involved in format evolution. We will detail this experience in Section 3.7. We will also discuss other languages for XML transformation in Section 3.7.

3.3 Properties of Transformations

We need a few terms to reason about the transformations for format evolution. Transformations are functions, often partial ones. We are concerned with two levels: DTD transformations are (partial) functions on DTD—the domain of all DTDs. XML transformations are (partial) functions on XML— the domain of all XML documents. For every DTD transformation f we intend to supply an induced XML transformation $\bar{f}$. Let us consider required or convenient properties of f and $\bar{f}$.

3.3.1 Well-formedness

All DTDs we process have to be well-formed. By well-formedness we mean that the DTDs are deterministic / unambiguous (cf. [W3C00a, BK93]). Furthermore, we require a reducedness property in the sense of context-free grammars (cf. [HU80]), that is, all element names used in element type declarations are defined, and they are reachable from the root element, and all alternatives of all declarations are feasible. As for XML documents, the standard regulates what well-formedness means. We restrict XML to the set of all well-formed XML documents. Without further mentioning, all subsequently discussed

DTD and XML transformations are constrained by an implicit postcondition to produce well-formed outputs from well-formed inputs (or to fail otherwise).

3.3.2 Validity

Using XML terminology, an XML document is said to be valid w.r.t. a given DTD if the document is formed according to the DTD. We use the notation $d \vdash x$ to express that an XML document $x \in XML$ is valid w.r.t. a DTD $d \in DTD$. Informally, this means that x can be derived from d starting with the root element of d.[1] A minimum requirement for an induced XML transformation is that validity is preserved, say that the migrated XML data is valid (w.r.t. the adapted DTD):

Definition 1. Let f be a DTD transformation. The induced XML transformation $\overline{f}$ *preserves validity* if for all $d \in DTD$ and $x \in XML$ with $d \vdash x$ it holds if $f(d)$ and $\overline{f}(x)$ are defined, then $f(d) \vdash \overline{f}(x)$.

Example 8. The XML document from Figure 3.3 is valid w.r.t. the DTD in Figure 3.2. Consider the folding step from Section 3.2.1. The migrated XML document with the additional tags for `personnel` is valid w.r.t. the adapted DTD where `player+` has been folded to `personnel`. Note that the original XML document is not valid w.r.t. the adapted DTD.

3.3.3 Totality and Partiality

DTD transformations are inherently partial because of applicability constraints. Of course, a DTD transformation should be feasible, that is, there exist DTDs which the transformation is applicable to. We should be able to describe precisely the applicability constraints for a DTD transformation.

Example 9. Folding is only feasible if the element name introduced by folding (cf. `personnel` in Section 3.2.1) is fresh in the input DTD, and the particle to be folded (cf. `player+` in Section 3.2.1) does indeed occur. Otherwise, there are no preconditions for folding to succeed at the DTD level.

Ideally, we want an induced XML transformation to be total. In a sense, the DTD transformation should be responsible for establishing all preconditions, and then the induced XML transformation should be enabled. In this case, we speak of a total induced XML transformation:

Definition 2. Let f be a DTD transformation. The induced XML transformation $\overline{f}$ is *total* if for all $d \in DTD, x \in XML$ with $d \vdash x$ it holds that $f(d)$ is defined implies $\overline{f}(x)$ is defined.

---

[1]Here, we resort to terminology used for string languages, e.g., languages defined via context-free grammars.

Example 10. We continue with the folding scenario from Example 9. The induced XML transformation is indeed total because the insertion of the additional tags for `personnel` is feasible without further preconditions.

In turns out that some induced XML transformations have to establish preconditions specific to the data level. Consequently, these induced XML transformations are partial since they are supposed to fail if the preconditions are not met by the XML document at hand.

Example 11. Consider, for example, a DTD with a particle "n?" for an optional element. Assume that we want to enforce an obligatory element, that is, we have to replace "n?" by "n". A candidate for the induced XML transformation is the identity mapping. However, for the sake of preserving validity, we have to refuse XML data where the optional element is omitted.

3.3.4 Structure Preservation

Starting at the DTD level of transformation, we would like to be sure that the structure of the input DTD is preserved by the transformation in some reasonable manner. At the XML level of transformation, we also want to be sure that the structure[2] of the documents is preserved in a similar sense. We indeed have to consider structure preservation at both levels: Given a structure-preserving DTD transformation, the structure-preservation for a validity-preserving XML transformation is not implied. There are different ways to formalise that a transformation is "well-behaved". One classical approach— often used in transformational programming (cf. [Par90])—is to identify *semantics-preserving* transformations. For that purpose, one could define the semantics of a DTD as the set of all valid XML documents admitted by the DTD. The problem is that this semantics is too concrete, i.e., there are hardly semantics-preserving transformations in this sense. There is no obvious alternative semantics. Furthermore, it is not clear how to lift semantics-preservation from the DTD level to the XML level. This motivates our simple formalisation of structure preservation based on *reversibility*. This is also a prominent approach in the context of database schema transformations (cf. [BCN92]).

Definition 3. A transformation t is called *structure-preserving*, if t is a bijective function. The transformation t is called *structure-extending*, if t is an injective but not a surjective function. The transformation t is called *structure-reducing*, if t is not an injective function.

Example 12. Folding as exemplified in Section 3.2.1 is injective because there is an inverse at the DTD level, that is, unfolding, and there is also an inverse at the XML level, that is, the additional tags which were inserted to witness folding are simply removed again. Since unfolding is also injective, folding and unfolding are structure-preserving.

In studying the properties of the transformations for format evolution, we do not simply want to check if a transformation is injective or surjective. We also want to explicitly

---

[2]For a uniform terminology, we use the term *structure* at both the DTD and the XML level (as opposed to *content*).

specify the inverse transformations as in the above example. For transformations which are meant to restructure a given DTD, we plan to point out injective inverses. For transformations which are meant to extend the structure at one or both levels, we should be able to point out the inverse transformations which remove the added structure. This also explains how we can discipline structure-reducing transformations. While they cannot be reversed, they should be conceived as inverses of structure-extending transformations.

3.4 Refactoring

We start our catalog of roles for format evolution with transformations for refactoring DTDs. By refactoring we mean structure-preserving transformations intended to improve the structure of DTDs, or to "massage" the structure so that it becomes more suitable for subsequent adaptations. Structure-extending and -reducing transformations are considered in Section 3.5.

3.4.1 Renaming

As a warm-up, we start with renaming which is a fundamental operator applicable to names of abstractions of any language. For DTDs, there are two abstractions which have to be covered, namely elements and attributes. Renaming means to replace the corresponding names consistently. Renaming attribute values is conceivable, too. Replacing text is clearly not to be regarded as proper renaming.

Renaming elements. Suppose the original element name is n, and the new element name is n'. At the DTD level, the following replacements are due. The element type declaration $< !\texttt{ELEMENT}\ n\ e >$ is replaced by $< !\texttt{ELEMENT}\ n'\ e>$ where e serves as place-holder for the definition of n.[3] Within all content particles all occurrences of n have to be located and replaced by n' as well. At the XML level, all tags of the form $< n >$, $< /n >$, and $< n/ >$ (optionally with attributes) have to be updated accordingly.

Renaming attributes. Renaming attributes is only slightly more interesting. One specific property that we have to cope with is a kind of scope rule. Attributes belong to elements. Renaming an attribute (name) a to a' should include the identification of the corresponding element type n. At the DTD level, we have to lookup the attribute list declaration $< !\texttt{ATTLIST}\ n\ l>$, and then we replace a by a' in the list l. At the XML level, similarly, we have to lookup start tags $<n\ l>$ and empty element tags $<n\ l/>$, and then replace a by a' in the list l of name-value pairs.

Example 13. The following XSLT template renames the attribute *link* of the element type $\texttt{albumref}$ to $\texttt{url}$. If we add the template for the identity transformation (cf. Figure 3.4), we will obtain a complete XSLT program.

---

[3]In XML terminology, e is called *content specification*. If e is of the form that *children* are specified for n (as opposed to $\texttt{\#PCDATA}$), then we say that e is built from *content particles*, namely names, choice and sequence lists of content particles, and content particles postfixed with "?", "+", and "*".

```
<xsl:template match="albumref">
<xsl:copy>
  <xsl:attribute name="url">
    <xsl:value-of select="@link"/>
  </xsl:attribute>
  <xsl:apply-templates
    select="*|comment()|processing-instruction()|text()"/>
  <xsl:apply-templates
    select="attribute::*[not(name(.)='link')]"/>
</xsl:copy>
</xsl:template>
```

The template matches with `albumref`. The attribute value associated with `link` is copied using the new name `url` in the name-value pair. All other attributes are copied without changes.

Properties. Renaming admits several universal properties. For renaming elements, these properties can be explained as follows. It is easy to see that renaming is validity-preserving. Renaming is also reversible. Renaming n to n' is undone by renaming n' to n. Thus, renaming is structure-preserving. At the DTD level, renaming is not total because of the precondition that n' must be fresh. The induced XML transformation is total.

3.4.2 Introduction and Elimination

We describe two auxiliary structure-preserving transformations. One can *introduce* element type declarations which are not (yet) used in the DTD altogether. Subsequent adaptations are meant to make use of the new element types. Dually, one can *eliminate* element type declarations which are not used (anymore) in the DTD.

Introduction of element types. There are simple preconditions at the DTD level. The introduced element name must be fresh in the input DTD. The induced XML transformation is the identity mapping without further requirements, since all element type declarations are completely preserved.

Elimination of element types. At the DTD level, an important constraint is that the element type to be eliminated is not used in other declarations. Otherwise, we would create a "non-terminated" DTD. Furthermore, we require that the element type corresponding to the name of the document type is never eliminated (cf. `album` in `<!DOCTYPE album SYSTEM "album.dtd">` in Figure 3.2). Note that the root element of a valid XML document must match the name of the document type. These preconditions are sufficient to ensure that actual XML data cannot exercise the eliminated element types. Hence, the identity mapping is the appropriate induced XML transformation.

Properties. Clearly, the induced identity mappings are in both cases validity-preserving since the DTD transformations do not change reachable element type declarations. The induced transformations are also total. Structure-preservation holds since introduction and elimination are each other inverses.

3.4.3 Folding and Unfolding

Most forms of abstractions in specification formalisms and programming languages admit two important dual concepts, that is, folding and unfolding. Refer, for example, to [PP96], for an in-depth discussion of these concepts in the context of functional and logic programming. Folding and unfolding is particularly useful for restructuring DTDs (and, in general, for grammar formalisms). In an abstract sense, unfolding means to replace the name of an abstraction by the definition of it. Dually, folding means to introduce a new abstraction according to some identified expression, and then to replace the expression by the new name. As for DTDs, folding and unfolding is all about elements.

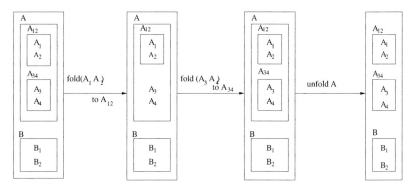

Figure 3.5 Form restructuring

Example 14. In Figure 3.5, folding and unfolding is illustrated in the context of form restructuring. We start from a form (say DTD) with two top level elements A and B corresponding to the two main regions of the form. We want to refactor the structure underlying the region A in a way that two subregions are identified. The first fold step points out the first subregion A_{12} which encloses A_1 and A_2. In the same manner, the second fold step points out the second subregion A_{34} enclosing A_3 and A_4. The unfold step drops the nesting of A_{12} and A_{34} inside A. The final form has now three instead of two main regions. The splitting of the region A was achieved by fold-fold-unfold.

DTD level. Folding consists of two steps: an introduction step for the new element type, and a replacement step to refer to the new element type instead of using its definition. It is conceivable to define unfolding completely dual to folding, that is, after unfolding the corresponding element type would be eliminated. We do not pursue this approach because, usually, unfolding is only done in the focus of a particular occurrence of the considered element type.[4] Thereby, some references to the unfolded element type will remain after unfolding, and thus elimination will not be feasible. Otherwise unfolding behaves completely inverse to folding, that is, the name of an element type is replaced by its definition.

XML level. Folding means to identify XML fragments corresponding to the folded expression, and to surround them accordingly with the tags for the new element. We postpone discussing details of the replacement process at both levels until Section 3.5.2 and Section 3.5.3. Unfolding is dual to folding, i.e., the tags for the unfolded element are removed.

Example 15. The following XSLT template describes unfolding for the element type `personnel`. Again, if we add the template for the identity transformation (cf. Figure 3.4), we will obtain a complete XSLT program.

```
<xsl:template match="personnel">
  <xsl:apply-templates
     select="*|@*|comment()|processing-instruction()|text()"/>
</xsl:template>
```

The template applies to elements of type `personnel`. As in the case of the identity transformation, we descend into all children. However, there is no mentioning of `<xsl:copy>` (as opposed to the template for the identity transformations). Thus, the tags for `personnel` are not copied. This directly implements the idea of unfolding.

Properties. At the DTD level, folding is constrained by the precondition of element type introduction. Furthermore, we should require that there is indeed an occurrence of the expression to be folded away. Dually, unfolding is only meaningful if we focus on at least one occurrence of the corresponding element type. The induced XML transformations for folding and unfolding are total. Folding can be reversed by unfolding (at both levels). To be precise, unfolding and the replacement step involved in folding are each other's inverses at the DTD level. At the XML level, the described insertion or removal of tags resp. to witness folding and unfolding are obligatory to achieve preservation of validity.

3.4.4 Elements vs. Attributes

We only sketch the topic of turning attributes into elements and vice versa. We refer to Section 3.2.3 for an example of the former direction. The following correspondences can be established to deal with element to attribute conversion and vice versa:

- Implied attributes correspond to optional elements.

- Required attributes correspond to obligatory elements.

- The attribute type `CDATA` corresponds to `#PCDATA` content.

---

[4]We assume that all our transformations can be applied in a *focus* as spelled out in [Läm01].

Turning a content particle into an attribute declaration. A selected content particle e is removed from the content specification of the selected element type n. The attribute list declaration for n is extended accordingly. The content particle e has to be of the form "n' " or "n'?" where n' is the name of an element type. There is no straightforward way to deal with choice lists and with the repetition operators "$+$" and "$*$". Furthermore, the content specification of n' should be #PCDATA, since it is not obvious how to turn structured content into an attribute value. The attribute type of n' will be CDATA, and the default declaration for n' (#REQUIRED vs. #IMPLIED) depends on the form of e as pointed out above. Another precondition for the transformation (at the DTD level) is that n' must not yet be used as an attribute name in the attribute list declaration for n.

Turning an attribute declaration into a content particle. A selected attribute declaration a is removed from the attribute list declaration for the selected element type n. We extend the content specification of n by a corresponding particle, the location of which needs to be defined explicitly. The attribute name n' of a serves as the name of the element type in the content particle e to be inserted. The particle e will be of the form "n'?" if n' is an implied attribute, or the form "n'" if n' is a required attribute. There is no obvious way to deal with attribute types for n' other than CDATA.[5] We assume that the introduction of the corresponding element type for n' (with #PCDATA as content specification) is done separately before the attribute to element conversion.

XML level. An element is turned into a name-value pair by regarding #PCDATA content as a CDATA value, and by interpreting the element name as an attribute name; similarly for the other direction. If the element is not present, then we omit the (implied) attribute.

Example 16. The following XSLT template implements an attributes to elements conversion for elements of type recording. In fact, all attribute values are turned into corresponding elements. Therefore, we perform iteration over all attributes (cf. <xsl:for-each select="@*">). The template is again to be completed by the template for identity transformation (cf. Figure 3.4). The code only provides an approximative solution as it ignores the problem that the order of the actual name-value pairs might differ from the order prescribed in the content specification which was derived from the attribute list declaration.

```
<xsl:template match="recording">
 <xsl:copy>
  <xsl:for-each select="@*">
    <xsl:element name = "name(.)">
     <xsl:value-of select="."/>
    </xsl:element>
  </xsl:for-each>
  <xsl:apply-templates/>
 </xsl:copy>
</xsl:template>
```

---

[5]We can cope with enumerated types for attributes the values of which are then represented as #PCDATA however.

3.5 Construction and Destruction

As a matter of fact, format evolution is hardly restricted to pure restructuring. New structure (say content) needs to be included. Dually, existing structure (say content) might become obsolete. Two classes of adaptations are identified for these purposes, namely *construction* and *destruction*. We will discuss corresponding roles back-to-back since the latter behave as the inverses of the former. In format evolution, steps for refactoring, construction, and destruction alternate.

3.5.1 Generalisation and Restriction of Expressions

Generality of content particles. In the process of extending a format, we need to generalise content particles; dually for restricting a format. Contrast that with renaming, folding, and unfolding where we deal with tags only. To reason about generality of content particles we define a partial order "$<$" on content particles:

$$
\begin{aligned}
e_1 &< e_3 & &\text{if } e_1 < e_2 \text{ and } e_2 < e_3 \\
e_1 &\not< e_2 & &\text{if } e_2 < e_1 \\
e &< e? & & \\
\texttt{EMPTY} &< e? & & \\
e^+ &< e^* & & \\
e &< e^+ & & \\
(e_1,\ldots,e_n) &< (e_1',\ldots,e_n') & &\text{if } 1 \leq i \leq n, e_i < e_i', e_j = e_j' \\
& & &\text{for } j = 1,\ldots,n, j \neq i \\
(e_1 \mid \ldots \mid e_n) &< (e_1' \mid \ldots \mid e_n') & &\text{if } 1 \leq i \leq n, e_i < e_i', e_j = e_j' \\
& & &\text{for } j = 1,\ldots,n, j \neq i \\
(e_1 \mid \ldots \mid e_n) &< (e_1' \mid \ldots \mid e_{i-1}' \mid e_i' + 1 \mid \ldots \mid e_n') & &\text{if } 1 \leq i \leq n
\end{aligned}
$$

The first two properties state transitivity and asymmetry. Then, we have a number of properties to deal with optionals, star- and plus-notation. Afterwards, sequence lists (with associative concatenation) are addressed. Finally, we address choice lists. It is said, for example, that a choyice with less branches admits less structure than a choice with more branches. Generality of content particles can be lifted to generality of DTDs. We say that $d \in DTD < d' \in DTD$ if for all $x \in XML, d \vdash x$ implies $d' \vdash x$ but not vice versa.

DTD level. A replacement of a content particle e by another content particle e' is called a (DTD) *generalisation* if $e < e'$. In the opposite case (i.e., $e' < e$), the replacement is called a (DTD) *restriction*. The specification of "$<$" clearly indicates how we can generalise; dually for restriction: A child can be turned into an optional one. $\texttt{EMPTY}$ can be replaced by an optional. From e we might also generalise to plus-lists of e. Finally, we can add alternatives to choice lists.

XML level. Initially, we choose the identity mapping as induced XML transformation for both generalisation and restriction. For the former, no further preconditions are to be ensured since a generalisation simply relaxes the format. For the latter, we have to check that the generality of the original particle is never exercised. Consider, for example, a restriction of "$n+$" to "n". If we encounter an XML document where we have non-trivial lists of elements of type n, we have to refuse the document (for the sake of preservation of validity). This is a serious limitation. Thus, we give up the idea of the identity mapping. Instead, we need to perform an XML transformation to simplify the XML data so that the generality which is removed by the DTD restriction is not exercised anymore. Such a simplifying XML transformation h (say XML restriction) can be characterised via the "$<$" relation: For all $d \in DTD$, there exists some $d' \in DTD$ with $d' < d$ such that for all $x \in XML$ with $d \vdash x$ it holds that $h(x)$ is defined implies $d' \vdash h(x)$. Now, if the d' always corresponds to the adapted DTD according to a DTD restriction, both levels of restriction are properly intertwined. In practice, we will specify the DTD transformation by a focused replacement of one content particle e by a more restrictive one e'. We might also specify the XML restriction h by just a function on content of the form e to content of the form e'. The function operating on XML can be derived by lifting.

Properties. XML generalisations preserve validity because of the way how "$<$" is defined for DTDs. XML generalisations are structure-extending simply because the co-domain of the transformation is not exhausted. The above definition of an XML restriction directly enforces preservation of validity. XML restrictions are structure-reducing simply because XML data exercising the obsolete generality will be mapped to a restricted format.

3.5.2 First Intermezzo: Replacing Content Particles

Replacement at the DTD level is not just relevant for generalisation and restriction where the original and the resulting content particles are related by "$<$". We also encountered replacement in the context of folding where a content particle had to be replaced by the name of a newly introduced element type. Further examples are unfolding and renaming. We want to explain the general concept of replacement in some technical detail.

Replacement can be performed as follows. Given two content particles u and v, we want to lookup the occurrences of u in the input DTD, and we want to replace them by v to derive the output DTD. If there are multiple matches for u, we process them in some order. For certain transformations, we might require unique matches. We assume that replacement is always done in a certain focus, for example, for a certain element type declaration, or for a certain occurrence of the particle u. It is important to notice that the operands u and v can be in general sequence lists of content particles rather than single particles. In the context of a fold, for example, u is potentially a list of content particles to be folded, and v is the new element name. Thus, the lookup problem comes down to associative list pattern matching (cf. [BKN87]) where we try to match part of a list $l = (e_1, \ldots, e_m)$ of content particles from the input DTD against u. The list l might occur at the top level of a content specification for an element type n, or in a nested occurrence, e.g., as an alternative of a choice list. Matching means that we want to find p and q with $1 \leq p \leq q \leq m$ such that $(e_p, \ldots, e_q) = u$. The list l is to be replaced by the concatenation of $(e_1, \ldots, e_{p-1}), v$, and $(e_{q+1}, \ldots, e_m)$.

3.5.3 Second Intermezzo: Matching at the XML Level

There is no (completely) determined way how replacement at the XML level would be induced by a DTD transformation. However, the general matching problem preceding specific replacements (and also tests for preconditions), that is, the problem to find the content fragments corresponding to the focus of a DTD transformation is interconnected to the matching problem (i.e., part of the replacement problem) at the DTD level. There are two cases:

1. The sequence list l matching with the operand u occurred at the top level of the element type declaration for n. We can easily locate the elements of type n by looking for matches with $< n > f < /n >$. Thus, the list l corresponds directly to the fragment f, that is, f is supposed to match the content specification l. We split up the fragment f into $f_p f_u f_q$ according to the associative list pattern matching at the DTD level. The fragment f_u matches u, and the surrounding fragments f_p and f_q correspond to the prefix $(e_1, \ldots, e_{p-1})$ and the postfix $(e_{q+1}, \ldots, e_m)$ of l. Note that there is, of course, no 1-1 correspondence of particles to fragments because some elements might be optional, others might be lists. The kind of matching to determine f_p, f_u, and f_q corresponds to parsing, or—more precisely—to regular expression pattern matching (cf. [HVP00, HP01a]).

2. Matching rather happens at some level of nesting. Thus, we first need to descend into f to navigate to the relevant sequence list. This is again a kind of regular expression pattern matching, i.e., we parse f according the element definition for n, and we select the right parse subtree f' corresponding to l. Then, we proceed as in the 1st case, i.e., we split f' into $f_p f_u f_q$ and so on.

Once matching is done, one can observe f_u, for example, to check a certain precondition. One can also perform an actual replacement, that is, f_u is replaced by content for v in the context $f_p f_u f_q$. In the case of unfolding n', for example, we know that f_u must be of the form $< n' > f'_u < /n' >$, and we simply replace f_u by f'_u, i.e., we omit the tags for n'. In the case of a partial identity transformation complementing a DTD restriction at the XML level (cf. Section 3.5.1), we can ensure the precondition that f_u is covered by the restricted particle by a simple inspection of f_u.

Example 17. Suppose we want to turn an optional manager into an obligatory one, i.e., we need to replace `manager?` by `manager`. The obligation at the XML level is that we make sure that all elements of type `personnel` contain a manager. This basically means that we locate all XML content fragments corresponding to the particle `manager?`, and then we only have to examine the matched fragment not to be empty.

3.5.4 Structure Enrichment and Removal

In a sense, generalisation means to add possible "branches" to the format, vice versa for restriction. There is another mode of construction and destruction, that is, if we want to enrich the content model or to remove part of it by means of inserting or removing content particles.

DTD level. Enrichment can be conceived as a replacement as follows. Given a content particle u (typically a sequence list $(e_1, \ldots, e_m)$), we want to replace it by another content particle v which subsumes u in the following sense. The new particle v is of the form $(e'_1, \ldots, e'_{m'})$ with $m' > m$, and there are $i_1, \ldots, i_m$ such that $1 \leq i_1 < \cdots < i_m \leq m'$[6] and $e_1 = e'_{i_1}, \ldots, e_m = e'_{i_m}$. For removal, the roles of u and v are flipped. This explanation makes immediately clear that enrichment and removal can be implemented by means of the replacement procedure discussed in Section 3.5.2.

XML level. To evolve the XML data, we need to insert or to remove elements corresponding to the additional or removed particles. In the case of removal, the induced XML transformation is merely a projection. Matching is sufficient to select those fragments which should be kept. Insertion is more delicate. For new particles, we have to decide how suitable content is obtained. As for optional elements and star-lists of elements, this is easy since the empty content is valid in this case; refer to Section 3.2.2 for the example dealing with an optional manager. Otherwise, we have to augment the transformation for enrichment to supply suitable content. This problem is somewhat similar to the problem of an XML restriction which had to be provided explicitly to enforce a format (say DTD) restriction.

Properties. At the DTD level, there is a way to conceive enrichment and removal as each other's inverse (and hence they would be structure-preserving). For that purpose, we do not directly consider DTDs but DTDs with a focus. Then, we can define an equivalence on DTDs (with a focus), where $d \equiv d'$ if d and d' only differ in the focused particle. This point of view emphasises that the structure-extending or -reducing behaviour of enrichment and removal essentially happens at the XML level. Removal of content is structure-reducing because projections are not injective. By duality, enrichment cannot be surjective, and hence it is structure-extending.

3.5.5 Attributes

In the same way as we can generalise and restrict choice lists for element type declarations (cf. Section 3.5.1), we can also extend or shrink enumeration types for attributes. There is also a counterpart for structure enrichment and removal discussed above, namely attribute addition and removal.

Example 18. Let us consider a simple scenario in the running example. We want to enable DVD albums. Thus, we need to add another alternative (namely, DVD) to the `format` attribute type in the attribute list declaration for `catalogno`:

---

[6]If we omitted this condition, we consider permutations of sequence lists. For the sake of orthogonality, permutation should constitute a separate operation.

```
<!ELEMENT catalogno EMPTY>
  <!ATTLIST catalogno label CDATA #REQUIRED
            number CDATA #REQUIRED
            format (CD | LP | MiniDisc | DVD) #IMPLIED
            releasedate CDATA
            #IMPLIED country CDATA #IMPLIED>
```

3.6 Related Work

One-level vs. two-level transformation. Previous work on XML transformation considers only the scenario, where a transformational program consumes XML documents of one kind and produces some output—often some XML document again. In the optimal case, this scenario is applied in a typeful manner, that is, both inputs and outputs are required to be valid w.r.t. some DTD, and validity is then enforced dynamically or statically. DTDs are considered as given a-priori. We call this (common) transformation setup *one-level* transformation. Another well-known example of one-level transformation is *refactoring* of object-oriented programs (cf. [Opd92, FBB+99]). By contrast, we are concerned with *two-level transformation* (in the context of format evolution). In our case, transformation starts at the DTD level. The induced XML transformations are not typed by fixed DTDs. Conceptually, the induced XML transformations are generic in the sense that they are feasible for all input DTDs which satisfy the preconditions of the underlying DTD transformation. We refer to [Kle07, COV06] for other recent work concerning XML document migration and two-level transformation.

Limitations of XSLT. XSLT (Version 1.0) is not optimally suited for XML transformations which are *conceptually* based on DTD patterns. Most transformations for format evolution indeed are concerned with XML fragments according to DTD patterns as described in Section 3.5.2 and Section 3.5.3. By contrast, the kind of selection or matching supported by XSLT is based on patterns and axes in the sense of XPath (cf. [W3C99a]). XSLT allows one to constrain types and ancestors of nodes to be matched. One can also constrain the position in the list of children. The conditions in matching and selection may involve various axes to select from different parts of the tree relative to the current node (generally the node that the XSLT template matches). All this expressiveness, however, does not allow us to describe matching according to the patterns (consisting of content particles) occurring in element type declarations. The need for language support to process an XML document according to the DTD patterns in a typeful fashion has already been realised by others. In [HVP00, HP01a], *regular expression pattern matching* is proposed as a language construct.

Example 19. Let us implement the fold step from the beginning of the chapter (cf. Section 3.2.1). The plan would be to perform a match with `player+` (to focus on the lists of players), and to surround the matched players with `<personnel>` and `</personnel>`. By contrast, XSLT matching works element-wise. In Figure 3.6, we show two XSLT encodings for the folding problem. The left program catches the first player, and then

```
<xsl:template match="player">              <xsl:template
 <xsl:choose>                                  match ="player[position()=1]">
  <xsl:when test=                           <xsl:text
   "preceding-sibling::*[1][self::player]"/>    disable-output-escaping="yes">
  <xsl:otherwise>                             <![CDATA[<personnel>]]>
   <personnel>                              </xsl:text>
    <xsl:apply-templates select="."         <xsl:copy>
                    mode="players"/>          <xsl:apply-templates
   </personnel>                                 select="*|@*|..."/>
  </xsl:otherwise>                          </xsl:copy>
 </xsl:choose>                             </xsl:template>
</xsl:template>                            <xsl:template  match =
                                              "player[position()=last()]">
<xsl:template match="player" mode="players"> <xsl:copy>
 <xsl:copy>                                  <xsl:apply-templates
  <xsl:apply-templates select="*|@*|..."/>     select="*|@*|..."/>
 </xsl:copy>                                 </xsl:copy>
 <xsl:apply-templates                       <xsl:text
  select=                                      disable-output-escaping="yes">
    "following-sibling::*[1][self::player]"    <![CDATA[</personnel>]]>
  mode="players"/>                          </xsl:text>
</xsl:template>                             </xsl:template>
```

Figure 3.6 Two inconvenient implementations of the fold problem from Section 3.2.1

switches to a different mode to copy all the players. The additional tags are inserted accordingly (cf. `<personnel>...</personnel>`). In a sense, we parse the list of players. The right program in Figure 3.6 is somewhat simpler but at the expense of a hopelessly untyped approach. The first and the last player are caught by two independent templates. The open and close tags are smuggled in as text (cf. `<![CDATA[<personnel>]]>` and `<![CDATA[</personnel>]]>`).

Any XSLT encoding of replacements which have to do with more complex patterns than single elements requires the simulation of regular expression pattern matching. Such parsers are encoded by means of several templates, auxiliary modes, variables to accumulate substructures, or what have you.

A less fundamental but annoying problem of available XSLT implementations is that valid XML documents are not enforced statically. Given an XSLT script, there is no guarantee that the input document will be properly queried, and that a valid output document will be generated. It is not a fundamental problem. In [MSV00], it is shown that type-checking XML transformations based on a model covering the essentials of XSLT, namely k-pebble tree transducers, is decidable.

Other XML transformation frameworks. There is an abundance of XML query languages applicable for extraction and restructuring XML data. Refer to [BC00] for some comparative analysis of some prominent representatives. We want to point out some language proposals originating from the functional programming field which have something to offer in the context of our specific kind of transformations. The typed functional language XDuce (cf. [HP01b]) is a statically typed programming language in the spirit of mainstream functional languages but specialised to the domain of XML processing. XDuce supports regular expression types and the aforementioned regular expression pattern matching to be applicable to XML-kind types. Another functional language for typeful XML transformation is XMλ (cf. [MS99]). The formula underlying the functional approach is the following: DTDs are types. XML document fragments are values. Valid XML documents are enforced statically by type-checking. XML transformations are DTD-typed functions.

A convenient property underlying the XSLT language model is the genericity which allows us to achieve easily a full traversal of the input document by means of default templates as in the identity transformation (cf. Figure 3.4). One way to recover this genericity in a functional language setting is to resort to an untyped generic XML representation, and to use a suitable combinator library (cf. [WR99]) for manipulation. Another way could be based on (typeful) generic programming (cf. [JJ97, Hin00]).

Database schema evolution. There is a large body of related research addressing the problem of (relational or object-oriented) database schema evolution (cf. [BKKK87]). Schema evolution is useful, for example, in database re- and reverse-engineering (cf. [HTJC94]). The schema transformations themselves can be compared with our format transformations only at a superficial level because of the different formalisms involved (ER model etc. vs. DTD). However, database schema evolution provides another instance of a two-level transformation setup since one usually requires an instance mapping for a schema evolution (cf. [BCN92]). The formal underpinnings of schema transformations have been studied in great detail, e.g., schema equivalence (cf. [Kob86]), or reversibility of transformations (cf. [HTJC94]). There exist formal frameworks for the definition of schema transformations (cf. [MP97]), and different catalogs have been developed (cf. [BKKK87, BP96]). Numerous formalisms have been proposed. One appealing method which also covers the intertwined character of schema transformation and instance mapping is based on graph transformations, say graph grammars (cf. [JZ99]). This formal approach is reasonably accessible because of the use of a graphical notation.

3.7 Concluding Remarks

We summarise the contribution of the chapter. The chapter is concluded with the formulation of a challenge in transformational programming to effectively support the proposed style of format evolution.

Contribution. The chapter illustrates how DTD transformations and induced XML counterparts can be employed to master format evolution problems. The use of transformations supports traceability, and it automates document migration. The roles of format evolution were inspired by previous research on grammar adaptation (cf. [Läm01, LW01]). DTD transformations, in a sense, can be conceived as grammar transformations. In [LW01], the authors describe how to use term rewriting technology to describe grammar transformations rigorously. This approach would also applicable to DTD transformations since DTDs are to some extent grammars. Of course, DTDs are not quite context-free grammars or extended BNFs. We have to cope, for example, with tags, attributes, and references. Also, DTDs and context-free grammars require different semantic treatments. Consider, for example, fold/unfold manipulations. They do not affect the string language generated by a context-free grammar. By contrast, folding/ unfolding a DTD changes the content model. The original contribution of the present chapter is the consideration of XML transformations *induced* by the DTD transformations and the investigation of schema transformations in the application context of XML.

A Challenge. For a *fixed* DTD, the description of both a DTD transformation (for format evolution), and the induced XML transformation is merely a matter of choice of some convenient transformation language. We have examined typeful functional XML transformation languages, term rewriting systems, combinator libraries, and logic programming. However, the *coupled* treatment of DTD transformations and induced XML transformations in a *typeful* and `generic` manner poses a challenge for formal reasoning, type systems, and language design. Consider, for example, a generic fold function which takes the particle to be folded, the name of the element type to be introduced, and which returns two functions, namely a DTD transformation, and a dependently typed XML transformation. How can we describe such a function so that properties like preservation of validity are implied by the type of the function? How can the induced character of the XML transformation be made explicit? We might conceive a DTD transformation as a *type transformation t*. The induced XML transformation in turn had to be regarded as a function where source and target are related via *t*. In [MS99], it is pointed out that, indeed, an important topic for future research are generic document transformations, and generic functional programming (cf. [JJ97, Hin00]) is considered as a promising framework in this respect. As yet, it is not clear how generic programming can be made fit to cope with the kind of type and value transformations relevant in format evolution, especially if we think of a complete coverage of XML.

Chapter 4

Semantics-preserving Migration of Semantic Rules during Left Recursion Removal in Attribute Grammars

Several tools for source-to-source transformation are based on top down parsers. This restricts the user to use grammars without left recursion. Removing left recursion of a given grammar often makes it unreadable, preventing a user from concentrating on the original grammar. Additionally, the question arises, whether the tool implements the semantics of the original language, if it is implemented based on a different grammar than in the original language definition. Moreover, existing implementations of semantics for the original grammar cannot be reused directly.

The chapter contributes to the field of automatic migration of software (here semantic rules) induced by a grammar change. It revises removal of left recursion in the context of grammar adaptations and demonstrates that while removing left recursion at the same time the semantic rules can be migrated automatically. Thus, a programmer can continue to use semantic rules on a left recursive grammar. The problem is explained and justified.

4.1 Introduction

In the chapter we consider the consequences of left recursion removal to semantics associated with grammar rules. Our starting point is the need for grammar engineering after semantic rules have been written for the grammar already. We will demonstrate that during automatic left recursion removal in attribute grammars semantic rules can be migrated automatically.

Grammar engineering. Work with grammars is present in software development as well as in maintenance. Grammars are used to describe structure of data, to derive tools for manipulating those data, or to serve as reference between developers, e.g., a language definition. As other software artefacts, grammars are subject to change, e.g., adaptations to make it usable for parser generation, evolution of grammars (grammar corrections, changes and extensions of the language), grammar recovery from existing tools or documents, and refactoring of grammars (to make them more readable, parts better reusable, e.g., for tools adaptable to several language dialects).

Need for left recursion removal. Removal of left recursion in grammars is an adaptation of the grammar to fit technical demands. Many syntactical structures are expressed naturally using recursion, often both, left and right recursion. However, there are tools like ANTLR, JavaCC, TXL, Prolog-based tools, dealing somehow with recursive descent parser generation, for the ease of combination with semantics [RM85], which would fall into infinite recursion or would require backtracking. Removal of left recursion is known in compiler construction for over 40 years, and mostly considered wrt. to context-free grammars or to development of compilers. However, necessity of left recursion removal arises not only in compiler construction, but also during language development, prototyping, and in software maintenance, especially for adaptations in already used and tested grammars.

Technical challenge. The first problem is that removal of left recursion leads to a badly readable grammar. More elaborated semantic rules are necessary. However, the user wants to work on the most comprehensible grammar, or even the reference grammar, if possible. Often the grammar is rewritten using EBNF, where left recursion turns into iteration, which might result in a problem with semantics in loops. Next, a language definition consists of syntax and semantics definitions. If the syntax is modified due to technical demands, this leads to changed semantics. Is the meaning of a language construct unchanged? Finally, if there are semantic rules for the left recursive grammar already (e.g., given as logic language), how are they affected by the change? Can they be reused or have all to be discarded?

Results and benefits. We argue the semantic meaning associated to grammar symbols of the original grammar can be still reconstructed after automatic left recursion removal. This will be justified for S-attributed and I-attributed grammars. We will discuss, how the approach can be generalised for multi-pass attribute grammars. Programmers benefit from our approach, because they can now work on a grammar similar to the reference grammar, i.e., one possibly containing left recursion. The adaptation of the grammar and the semantic rules can be done automatically and can be implemented as a preprocessor as shown in Figure 4.1. The approach can be combined with the above mentioned tools (e.g., ANTLR, Prolog-based tools).

Remainder of the chapter. Section 4.2 recalls the notions of attribute grammars. Section 4.3 uses the small example of arithmetic expressions to explain the basic idea. The transformation of semantic rules and a justification is giveen in in Section 4.4. Section 4.5 reports on practical experience so far. Section 4.6 points to some related work, before the chapter is summarised in Section 4.7.

4.2 Notions of Attribute Grammars

This section recalls the definition of attribute grammars (AG). The following formal definition is similar to [Alb91]. Semantic conditions, which can restrict the language generated

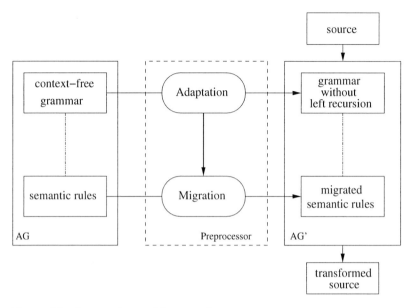

Figure 4.1 An example use of the approach

by the context-free grammar are omitted without loss of generality of our approach. The semantics is as given in [Alb91]. For the origin of attribute grammars the reader is referred to Irons [Iro61] and Knuth [Knu68].

An attribute grammar without semantic conditions is a four-tuple $AG = (G, SD, AD, R)$, where

1. $G = (V_N, V_T, P, S)$ is the base context-free grammar. V_N and V_T are sets of nonterminals and terminals, $V = V_N \cup V_T$ and $V_N \cap V_T = \emptyset$. P is a finite set of production rules, $S \in V_N$ denotes the start symbol, $p \in P$ will be written as $p : X_0^p \to X_1^p \ldots X_{n_p}^p$, where $n_p \geq 0$, $X_0^p \in V_N$ and $X_k^p \in V$ for $1 \leq k \leq n_p$.

2. $SD = (TYPES, FUNCS)$ denotes the semantic domain. $TYPES$ is a finite set and $FUNCS$ a finite set of total functions with $type_1 \times \ldots \times type_n \to type_0$, $n \geq 0$ and $type_i \in TYPES$ $(0 \leq i \leq n)$.

3. $AD = (A_I, A_S, TYPE)$ denotes the attributes. Each symbol $X \in V$ gets finite sets of synthesised and inherited attributes associated, $A_I(X)$ and $A_S(X)$. $A(X) = A_I(X) \cup A_S(X)$ and $A_I(X) \cap A_S(X) = \emptyset$, and $A = \cup_{X \in V} A(X)$ (for A_I and A_S analogously). An attribute a of some symbol X can be written $X.a$, if necessary for distinguishing. For $a \in A$ $TYPE(a) \in TYPES$ is the set of values of a $(TYPE = \cup_{a \in A} TYPE(a))$.

4. $R = \cup_{p \in P} R(p)$ denotes the finite set of semantic rules associated with a production $p \in P$. The production $p : X_0^p \to X_1^p \dots X_{n_p}^p$ has an attribute occurrence $X_k^p.a$, if $a \in A(X_k^p)$. The set of all attribute occurrences of a production p is written as $AO(p)$. It can be divided into two disjoint subsets of defined occurrences $DO(P)$ and used occurrences $UO(p)$, which are defined as follows:

$$DO(p) = \{X_0^p.s \mid s \in A_S(X_0^p)\} \cup \{X_k^p.i \mid i \in A_I(X_k^p) \wedge 1 \leq k \leq n_p\},$$
$$UO(p) = \{X_0^p.i \mid i \in A_I(X_0^p)\} \cup \{X_k^p.s \mid s \in A_S(X_k^p) \wedge 1 \leq k \leq n_p\}.$$

The semantic rules of $R(p)$ define, how values of attribute occurrences in $DO(p)$ can be computed as function of other attribute occurrences of $AO(p)$. The defining rule for attribute occurrence $X_k^p.a$ is of the form

$$X_k^p.a := f_{ka}^p(X_{k_1}^p.a_1, \dots, X_{k_m}^p.a_m)$$

where $X_k^p.a \in DO(p)$, $f_{ka}^p : TYPE(a_1) \times \dots \times TYPE(a_m) \to TYPE(a)$, $f_{ka}^p \in FUNCS$ and $X_{k_i}^p \in AO(p)$ for $1 \leq i \leq m$. The occurrence of $X_k^p.a$ depends on $X_{k_i}^p.a_i$ ($1 \leq i \leq m$). An AG is in normal form, if for each semantic rule additionally holds: $X_{k_i}^p.a_i \in UO(p)$. Each AG can be transformed into normal form. Without loss of generality, we assume our grammar to be in normal form.

There are several subclasses of AG, among those S-attributed grammars (S-AG) and I-attributed grammars (I-AG). For S-AG is $A_I = \emptyset$ and the computation is done bottom up, i.g. the attributes of the root node contain the determined meaning of the program. Analogously, for I-AG is $A_S = \emptyset$, and the computation is top-down. The meaning is in the leaves.

4.3 Left Recursion Removal in an Example AG

We demonstrate the basic idea using the common simple example for left recursive definition of arithmetic expressions. The context-free part of the grammar implements priority of arithmetic operators. Figure 4.2 gives the general algorithm for left recursion removal for context-free grammars (cf., e.g., [Lou97]). This algorithm has to be extended to deal with semantic rules, so that, in our example, expressions are calculated correctly. The left recursive attributed grammar for expressions is given in on the left side of Figure 4.3. The right side shows the context-free grammar with left recursion removed. It is not obvious at a first glance how the semantic rules have to be modified to describe the same meaning. To see how the semantic rules have to be modified, we examine the computation for the expression $1+2*3$. Figure 4.4 depicts the constructed abstract syntax tree together with the computation of the attributes, using the original (left) and transformed (right) grammar. As can be seen on the tree from the transformed grammar, the original tree has been stretched. The given evaluation for the transformed tree presents the basic idea: The computation of synthesised attributes is redirected to inherited attributes (i) of newly introduced nonterminals. From the leaves, the results are copied using synthesised attributes. The intermediate

Input: $G = (V_N, V_T, P, S)$ without ϵ-productions and cycles;
without loss of generality let $V_N = \{A^1, \ldots, A^N\}$
Output: $G' = (V_N', V_T, P', S)$ without left recursion
  for $i := 1$ to N **do**
    {Removal of indirect left recursion}
    for $j := 1$ to $i - 1$ **do**
      replace productions of pattern $A^i \rightarrow A^j\beta$
      by $A^i \rightarrow \alpha_1\beta \mid \ldots \mid \alpha_k\beta$,
      where $A^j \rightarrow \alpha_1 \mid \ldots \mid \alpha_k$ are the current productions of A^j
    end for
    {Removal of direct left recursion}
    replace productions of pattern $A^i \rightarrow A^i\alpha_1 \mid \ldots \mid A^i\alpha_n \mid \beta_1 \mid \ldots \mid \beta_m$
    where no β_k starts with A^i
    by $A^i \rightarrow \beta_1 A^{i'} \mid \ldots \mid \beta_m A^{i'}$ and $A^{i'} \rightarrow \alpha_1 A^{i'} \mid \ldots \mid \alpha_n A^{i'} \mid \epsilon$
    where $A^{i'}$ is a new introduced nonterminal
  end for

Figure 4.2 Left recursion removal for context-free grammars

E_0	$\rightarrow$	$E_1 + T$	$\{E_0.v := E_1.v + T.v\}$	$E \rightarrow TE'$	$\{?\}$
	$\mid$	$E_1 - T$	$\{E_0.v := E_1.v - T.v\}$	$E' \rightarrow +TE'$	$\{?\}$
	$\mid$	T	$\{E_0.v := T.v\}$	$\mid -TE'$	$\{?\}$
T_0	$\rightarrow$	$T_1 * F$	$\{T_0.v := T_1.v * F.v\}$	$\mid \epsilon$	$\{?\}$
	$\mid$	T_1/F	$\{T_0.v := T_1.v/F.v\}$	$T \rightarrow FT'$	$\{?\}$
	$\mid$	F	$\{T_0.v := F.v\}$	$T' \rightarrow *FT'$	$\{?\}$
F	$\rightarrow$	N	$\{F.v := N.v\}$	$\mid /FT'$	$\{?\}$
	$\mid$	(E)	$\{F.v := E.v\}$	$\mid \epsilon$	$\{?\}$
				$F \rightarrow N$	$\{?\}$
				$\mid (E)$	$\{?\}$

Figure 4.3 Simple expression definition (left) with left recursion removed (right)

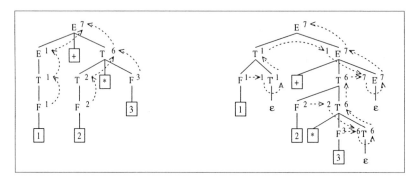

Figure 4.4   Attributed syntax tree for $1+2*3$ (left) and without left recursion (right)

results thus are preserved and combined to the final value with different positions only. The new semantic rules to achieve such behaviour are given in Figure 4.5.

E	$\rightarrow$ TE'	$\{\ E'.i := T.v, E.v := E'.v\ \}$
E'_0	$\rightarrow$ $+TE'_1$	$\{\ E'_1.i := E'_0.i + T.v, E'_0.v := E'_1.v\ \}$
	$\mid$ $-TE'_1$	$\{\ E'_1.i := E'_0.i - T.v, E'_0.v := E'_1.v\ \}$
	$\mid$ ϵ	$\{\ E'.v := E'.i\ \}$
T	$\rightarrow$ FT'	$\{\ T'.i := F.v, T.v := T'.v\ \}$
T'_0	$\rightarrow$ $*FT'_1$	$\{\ T'_1.i := T'_0.i * F.v, T'_0.v := T'_1.v\ \}$
	$\mid$ $/FT'_1$	$\{\ T'_1.i := T'_0.i/F.v, T'_0.v := T'_1.v\ \}$
	$\mid$ ϵ	$\{\ T'.v := T'.i\ \}$
F	$\rightarrow$ N	$\{\ F.v := N.v\ \}$
	$\mid$ (E)	$\{\ F.v := E.v\ \}$

Figure 4.5   Expression with removed left recursion and migrated semantic rules

4.4 Transformation Schemes for Left Recursion Removal in Multi-pass Attribute Grammars

First, we will consider how the algorithm in Figure 4.2 has to be extended for S-AG and discuss the preservation of the attribute values. Next, we do the same for I-AG, before we combine both for a more general case.

4.4.1 S-attributed Grammars

S-attributed grammars are those, where all attribute values are computed from bottom up. Typical examples for practical usage of S-AGs are YACC-specifications.

Transformation algorithm

The section gives the extension to algorithm in Figure 4.2 for left recursion removal for S-attribute grammars. The approach to migrate semantic rules guarantees that the root of the transformed syntax tree contains the same attribute values as the root in the original tree. A justification will be given in the next section. For S-AG, the algorithm for left

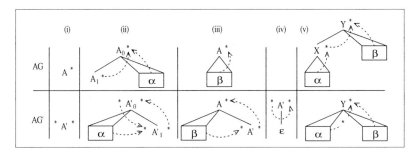

Figure 4.6   Transformations of an S-attribute grammar, * representing inherited (on left side) and synthesised (on right side) attributes of a nonterminal

recursion removal from Figure 4.2 will be extended as follows (cf. Figure 4.6). Suppose $A \rightarrow A\alpha \mid \beta \Longrightarrow A \rightarrow \beta A'$ and $A' \rightarrow \alpha A' \mid \epsilon$:

1. for each nonterminal A' newly introduced during transformation holds:

$$A_S(A') = A_S(A)$$
$$A_I(A') = \{a' \mid a \in A_S(A)\} \quad \text{with} \quad TYPE(a') = TYPE(a) \quad (4.1)$$

A' gets all attributes of A, additionally an inherited attribute with the same type for each synthesised attribute of A.

2. During transformation of production $p : A_0 \rightarrow A_1\alpha$ to $p' : A'_0 \rightarrow \alpha A'_1$ (the index marks different occurrences of the same nonterminal)

$$R(p) = \{A_0.a := f_a(X_1^p.a_1, \ldots, X_{n_a}^p.a_{n_a}) \mid a \in A_S(A)\} \quad \Longrightarrow$$
$$R(p') = \{A'_1.a' := f_a(X_1^{p'}.a_1, \ldots, X_{n_a}^{p'}.a_{n_a}) \mid a' \in A_I(A')\} \cup$$
$$\{A'_0.a := A'_1.a \mid a \in A_S(A)\} \quad (4.2)$$
$$\text{where} \quad X_i^{p'}.a_i = \begin{cases} A'_0.a'_i, & \text{if } X_i^p = A_1 \\ X_i^p.a_i, & \text{otherwise} \end{cases}$$

The actual computation is redirected to the inherited attributes. For synthesised attributes new copy rules are added.

3. For translation of a production $p : A^p \to \beta$ to $p' : A^{p'} \to \beta A'$

$$
\begin{aligned}
R(p) &= \{A^p.a := f_a(X_1.a_1, \dots, X_{n_a}.a_{n_a}) \mid a \in A_S(A)\} \quad \Longrightarrow \\
R(p') &= \{A'.a' := f_a(X_1.a_1, \dots, X_{n_a}.a_{n_a}) \mid a' \in A_I(A)\} \cup \\
&\quad \{A^{p'}.a := A'.a \mid a \in A_S(A)\}
\end{aligned}
\tag{4.3}
$$

Similar, but without replacements of parameters for semantic rules.

4. Adding a new production $p : A' \to \epsilon$ requires

$$
R(p) = \{A'.a := A'.a' \mid a \in A_S(A')\}.
\tag{4.4}
$$

Copy rules are added from each inherited attribute to the corresponding synthesised attribute.

5. During transition of a production $p : Y \to X\beta$ to $p' : Y \to \alpha\beta$ by deploying $q : X \to \alpha$ with

$$
\begin{aligned}
R(q) &= \{X^q.a := f_a^q(\dots) \mid a \in A_S(X)\} \\
R(p) &= \{Y^p.a := f_a^p(X_1^p.a_1, \dots, X_{n_a}^p.a_{n_a}) \mid a \in A_S(Y)\} \quad \Longrightarrow \\
R(p') &= \{Y^{p'}.a := f_a^p(X_1^{p'}.a_1, \dots, X_{n_a}^{p'}.a_{n_a}) \mid a \in A_S(Y)\} \\
&\quad \text{where } X_i^{p'}.a_i = \begin{cases} f_{a_i}^q(\dots), & \text{if } X_i^p = X \\ X_i^p.a_i, & \text{otherwise} \end{cases}
\end{aligned}
\tag{4.5}
$$

Deploying the right hand side of a context-free rule the corresponding right hand side of a semantic rule is deployed parallely. As a consequence, $Y^{p'}.a$ is computed by a nested function application, which is not in line with the form given in Section 4.2. (The nested function application could be folded into semantic rules for the appropriate attribute to remove it.)

To sum up, the algorithm describes the transformation $AG \overset{S}{\mapsto} AG'$ of an S-attributed grammar $AG = (G, SD, AD, R)$ into $AG' = (G', SD, AD', R')$ with $G \overset{G}{\mapsto} G'$ according to the general algorithm for left recursion removal, $AD \overset{S}{\mapsto} AD'$ (4.1), and $R \overset{S}{\mapsto} R'$ (4.2 - 4.5).

Preservation of computed attribute values

Proposition: *For each transformation $AG \overset{S}{\mapsto} AG'$ following Section 4.4.1 holds: For each word derivable from the context-free grammar of AG and AG' all attribute occurrences in the root nodes of the corresponding syntax trees have the same values.*

Moreover, intermediate results are preserved in case of direct left recursion removal, though at different positions in the tree than in the original one.

In general, a left recursive rule is of the form

$A \to A\alpha_1 \mid \dots \mid A\alpha_n \mid \beta_1 \mid \dots \mid \beta_m$. The choice of α_i and β_j does not matter for the argumentation, hence we assume $A \rightarrow A\alpha \mid \beta$ (with $\alpha, \beta \in V^*$). It can be seen that each such rule generates symbol sequences of the form $\beta\alpha^n$ (cf. for example, [ASU86, Lou97]), similarly to the corresponding transformed rules $A \rightarrow \beta A'$ and $A' \rightarrow \alpha A' \mid \epsilon$. Fig. 4.7

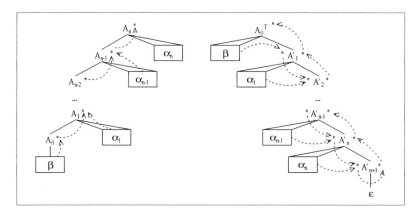

Figure 4.7 Syntax trees for the derivation of $\beta\alpha^n$

shows syntax trees for the derivation $\beta\alpha^n$. Occurrences of the same nonterminal in the syntax tree are numbered top down from n to 0 in the original tree and from 0 to $n + 1$ in the transformed tree. The α_i represent possibly different derivations from α (instead of different alternatives of the rule). Note that in general α_i and β can contain subtrees created by application of left recursive rules. Thus, they would need to be transformed into α_i^T and β^T.

We denote root nodes in the highest level of α (all roots of the forests) by R_α, $R_\alpha.a$ denotes an attribute occurrence at one of these nodes. A_0^T denotes the nonterminal A at the root of the derivation tree of the transformed production. We will show the demonstration in two steps.

Step 1: We assume, the grammar G contains 1 left recursive nonterminal. We choose the largest left recursive subtree without left recursive subtrees in β and α.

For the removal of direct left recursion we have to show that for the transformation depicted in Fig. 4.7 holds

$$\forall n \in \mathbb{N} \, \forall a \in A_S(A) : A_n.a = A_0^T.a \qquad (4.6)$$

We will use induction over depth of derivation trees n.

Base case ($n = 0$):

$$
\begin{aligned}
A_0.a &= f(R_\beta.a_1, \ldots, R_\beta.a_{n_a}) & \text{cf. Def.} \\
A_1'.a' &= f(R_\beta.a_1, \ldots, R_\beta.a_{n_a}) & \text{cf. (4.3)} \\
A_0.a &= A_1'.a' & \forall a \in A_S(A) \\
A_1'.a &= A_1'.a' & \text{cf. (4.4)} \\
A_0^T.a &= A_1'.a' & \text{cf. (4.3)} \\
\hookrightarrow \quad A_0.a &= A_0^T.a & \forall a \in A_S(A)
\end{aligned}
$$

Induction assumption: $\forall a \in A_S(A_n) : A_n.a = A_{n+1}'.a' = A_{n+1}'.a = A_0^T$
Induction step ($n \mapsto n+1, n \leq 0$):

$$
\begin{aligned}
A_{n+1}.a &= f(A_n.a_1, \ldots, A_n.a_{n_a}, R_{\alpha_{n+1}}.b_1, \ldots, R_{\alpha_{n+1}}.b_m) & \text{cf. Def.} \\
A_{n+2}'.a' &= f(A_{n+1}'.a_1', \ldots, A_{n+1}'.a_{n_a}', R_{\alpha_{n+1}}.b_1, \ldots, R_{\alpha_{n+1}}.b_m) & \text{cf. (4.2)} \\
A_n.a_j &= A_{n+1}'.a_j' & \forall j \in \{1, \ldots, n_a\} & \text{ind.assp.} \\
A_{n+1}.a &= A_{n+2}'.a' & \forall a \in A_S(A) \\
A_{n+2}'.a &= A_{n+2}'.a' & \text{cf. (4.4)} \\
A_{n+1}'.a &= A_{n+2}'.a & \text{cf. (4.3)} \\
A_0^T.a &= A_{n+1}'.a & \text{ind.assmpt.} \\
\hookrightarrow \quad A_{n+1}.a &= A_0^T.a & \forall a \in A_S(A)
\end{aligned}
$$

From (4.5) we can conclude that attribute values in the root do not change by deployment of the right hand side of a rule while removing indirect left recursion.

Step 2: No precondition. Due to proof of step 1 it is not necessary to consider left recursion in α_i or β, because the attribute values of α_i and β are equal to the attribute values in the transformed tree.

Hence, the proposition holds.

4.4.2 Transformation for IAG

In I-AGs only inherited attributes are used. They can be treated nearly analogously. The inherited attributes of the root node are copied down in the syntax tree to the node for the ϵ- derivation, where it is copied to a newly introduced synthesised attribute. Using the synthesised attribute, the inherited attributes of the corresponding α_i are computed. I.e., the computation is redirected to synthesised attributes. Similarly, the computation of the synthesised attribute of the next higher node is also based on the actual synthesised attribute.

Transformation algorithm

In detail, the algorithm from Figure 4.2 is extended for IAG as follows (cf. Figure 4.8):

1. for each nonterminal A' newly introduced during transformation holds:

$$
\begin{aligned}
A_I(A') &= A_I(A) \\
A_S(A') &= \{a' \mid a \in A_I(A)\} \quad \text{with} \quad TYPE(a') = TYPE(a) \quad (4.7)
\end{aligned}
$$

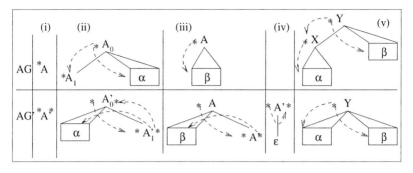

Figure 4.8 Transformations of an I-attribute grammar, * representing inherited (on left side) and synthesised (on right side) attributes of a nonterminal

A' gets all attributes of A, additionally an synthesised attribute with the same type for each inherited attribute.

2. During transformation of production $p : A_0 \rightarrow A_1\alpha$ to $p' : A'_0 \rightarrow \alpha A'_1$

$$
\begin{aligned}
R(p) &= \{X^p.a := f_a(A_0.a_1, \ldots, A_0.a_{n_a}) \mid X^p.a \in DO(p)\} &\implies \\
R(p') &= \{X^{p'}.a := f_a(A'_1.a'_1, \ldots, A'_1.a'_{n_a}) \mid X^p.a \in DO(p)\} \cup \\
&\quad \{A'_1.a := A'_0.a \mid a \in A_I(A')\} &(4.8)
\end{aligned}
$$

$$
\text{where} \quad X^{p'}.a = \begin{cases} A'_0.a', & \text{if } X^p = A_1 \\ X^p.a, & \text{otherwise} \end{cases}
$$

The actual computation is redirected to the synthesised attributes. Inherited attributes are used for value propagation for already computed values only.

3. For translation of a production $p : A^p \rightarrow \beta$ to $p' : A^{p'} \rightarrow \beta A'$

$$
\begin{aligned}
R(p) &= \{X^p.a := f_a(A^p.a_1, \ldots, A^p.a_{n_a}) \mid X^p.a \in DO(p)\} &\implies \\
R(p') &= \{X^{p'}.a := f_a(A'.a'_1, \ldots, A'.a'_{n_a}) \mid X^p.a \in DO(p)\} \cup \\
&\quad \{A'.a := A^{p'}.a \mid a \in A_I(A')\} &(4.9)
\end{aligned}
$$

Replace all attribute occurrences $A.a$ by $A'.a'$. For all inherited attributes a of A add a copy rule from $A.a$ to $A'.a$.

4. While adding $p : A' \rightarrow \epsilon$, also add

$$
R(p) = \{A'.a' := A'.a \mid a' \in A_S(A')\}. \qquad (4.10)
$$

Copy rules are added for each inherited attribute to the corresponding synthesised attribute.

5. During transition of a production $p : Y \to X\beta$ to $p' : Y \to \alpha\beta$ by deploying $q : X \to \alpha$ with

$$
\begin{aligned}
R(q) &= \{A^q.a := f_a^q(X^q.a_1, \ldots, X^q.a_{n_a}) \mid A^q.a \in DO(q)\} \quad \text{and} \\
R(p) &= \{X^p.a := f_{Xa}^p(\ldots) \mid a \in A_I(X)\} \cup \\
&\quad \{B^p.a := f_{Ba}^p(\ldots) \mid B^p.a \in DO(p)\backslash\{X^p.a \mid a \in A_I(X)\}\} \\
&\Longrightarrow \\
R(p') &= \{A^{p'}.a := f_a^q(f_{Xa_1}^p(\ldots), \ldots, f_{Xa_{n_a}}^p(\ldots)) \mid A^q.a \in DO(q)\} \cup \\
&\quad \{B^{p'}.a := f_{Ba}^p(\ldots) \mid B^p.a \in DO(p)\backslash\{X^p.a \mid a \in A_I(X)\}\} \quad (4.11)
\end{aligned}
$$

In semantic rules of q replace attribute occurrences of $X.a$ by their computation in p and add them, while removing the rules to compute attributes of X. (Again, the nested function application could be folded into semantic rules for the appropriate attribute to remove it.)

To sum up, the algorithm describes the transformation $AG \overset{I}{\mapsto} AG'$ of an I-attributed grammar $AG = (G, SD, AD, R)$ into $AG' = (G', SD, AD', R')$ with $G \overset{G}{\mapsto} G'$ according to the general algorithm for left recursion removal, $AD \overset{I}{\mapsto} AD'$ (4.1), and $R \overset{I}{\mapsto} R'$ (4.8 - 4.11).

Preservation of attribute values

Proposition: *For each transformation $AG \overset{I}{\mapsto} AG'$ following Section 4.4.2 holds: For each word derivable from the context-free grammar of AG and AG' all attribute occurrences in the leaves of the corresponding syntax trees have the same values.*

Moreover, intermediate results are preserved in case of direct left recursion removal, though at different positions in the tree than in the original one.

The proof is similar to that of Section 4.4.1. The preservation of attribute values has to be shown by induction over derivation trees. There is a difference, however. The inherited attributes are copied down to the A_{n+1}, where the same ϵ-production is combined with the copy of values to the synthesised attribute. Now, the synthesised attributes of α_i are computed as well as those of the next higher nonterminal. In contrast to the proof of Sect. 4.4.1 the values of the synthesised attributes are not equal on the way up to the root.

4.4.3 Multi-pass Attribute Grammars

In simple multi-pass AGs, each attribute can be computed during a certain pass. We can suppose that each pass is defined by an S-AG or an I-AG. Therefore, the approach can be generalised to simple multi-pass AGs. Because a multi-pass AG can be transformed into an equivalent simple multi-pass AG such AGs can be treated, too.

The extensions of the base algorithm from Sections 4.4.1 and 4.4.2 can now be combined to yield a more general algorithm for multiple-visited attribute grammars. The complete version is extensive and therefore given in the Appendix A.1.

```
                      TXL v10.3 (8.3.03) (c)1988-2003 Queen's University
                      Compiling ag.Txl ...
e(V)  :- e(E), @"+", t(T), V is E+T.   Parsing samples/exp.ag ...
e(V)  :- e(E), @"-", t(T), V is E-T.   Transforming ...
e(V)  :- t(T), V is T.                 e1(V,V3) :- @"+", t(T), e1(V,E2), E2 is V3+T.
                                       e1(V,V4) :- @"-", t(T), e1(V,E3), E3 is V4-T.
t(V)  :- t(T), @"*", f(F), V is T*F.   e(V)  :- t(T), e1(V,V2), V2 is T.
t(V)  :- t(T), @"/", f(F), V is T/F.   t1(V,V7) :- @"*", f(F), t1(V,T2), T2 is V7*F.
t(V)  :- f(F), V is F.                 t1(V,V8) :- @"/", f(F), t1(V,T3), T3 is V8/F.
                                       t(V)  :- f(F), t1(V,V6), V6 is F.
f(V)  :- num(N), V is N.               f(V)  :- num(N), V is N.
f(V)  :- @"(", e(E), @")", V is E.     f(V)  :- @"(", e(E), @")", V is E.
                                       e1(V,V).
                                       t1(V,V).
```

Figure 4.9   Input (left) and output (right) of the prototype

To sum up, the algorithm describes the transformation $AG \overset{A}{\mapsto} AG'$ of a arbitrarily attributed grammar $AG = (G, SD, AD, R)$ to an attributed grammar $AG' = (G', SD, AD', R')$ with $G \overset{G}{\mapsto} G'$, $AD \overset{A}{\mapsto} AD'$ according to (A.1) and $R \overset{A}{\mapsto} R'$ (A.2) to (A.5).

4.5 Practical Experiences

Prototypes.   The given approach has been implemented as proof-of-concept prototype for multi-pass attribute grammar, i.e., it demonstrates the algorithm for simple examples, but is not ready for practical applications. For the implementation TXL [CDMS02] was chosen. For the experiments, we used grammars as used by Laptob [LR01]. Grammars are represented as logic rules in Prolog. Predicates represent nonterminals, @ interprets strings as terminals, and variables are attributes addressed by position. In Figure 4.9 the input (left) and output (right) for the prototype is given. The prototype has been reimplemented in Prolog for a smoother integration with Laptob. [1]

A larger scenario.   We started to apply the approach to a 15 years evolutionary grown YACC specification[2] describing LPC, a language for interpreted scripts in a multi-user environment[3]. The grammar currently possesses 99 rules with 310 alternatives altogether, and it is likely to change in future. We have no influence on grammar and code as this is part of a kernel distribution for 100s of such environments. Since than five years, complex modernisations of the class library are being done. As a consequence, there are 1000s of changes in the area code. Tool support is desirable, where each necessary change is specified with semantic rules according to the known grammar. For several reasons, an LL(k) grammar based tool was chosen. Figure 5.1 shows an extract from the context-free grammar of the definition for the expression. Even without left recursion removal, real grown grammar rules are difficult to read. The grammar rules can be automatically extracted

---

[1]We refer to Appendix A.2 for a description of a more AG-like Prolog-notation and the Knuthian example.
[2]http://www.ldmud.de
[3]http://www.evermore.org

```
expr0 :                         (some of 34 alternatives)
    lvalue L_ASSIGN expr0 %prec L_ASSIGN
    | expr0 '?' expr0 ':' expr0 %prec '?'
    | expr0 L_LOR %prec L_LOR expr0
    | expr0 '|' expr0        | decl_cast expr0 %prec '~'    | cast expr0 %prec '~'
    | pre_inc_dec expr4 index_expr %prec '['
    | pre_inc_dec expr4 '[' expr0 ',' expr0 ']' %prec '['
    | L_NOT expr0 | '-' expr0 %prec '~'
    | expr4
    ...


expr4 :                         (some of 29 alternatives)
    | inline_func     | catch    | L_CLOSURE | L_SYMBOL | L_FLOAT
    | '(' note_start comma_expr ')'        | '(' '{' note_start expr_list ')' ')'
    | L_QUOTED_AGGREGATE note_start expr_list ')' ')'
    | '(' '[' ':' expr0 ']' ')'    | '(' '[' m_expr_list ']' ')'    | '(' '<' '>' ')'
    | '(' '<' identifier '>' note_start opt_struct_init ')'
    | expr4 L_ARROW struct_member_name    | '&' '(' expr4 L_ARROW struct_member_name ')'
    | expr4 index_range
    | '&' L_LOCAL                         | '&' '(' expr4 index_expr ')'
    | '&' '(' expr4 '[' expr0 ',' expr0 ']' ')'
    | '&' '(' expr4 index_range ')'
    | expr4 index_expr
    | expr4 '[' expr0 ',' expr0 ']' | L_LOCAL
    ...
```

Figure 4.10   Context-free extract from a yacc specification for expression definition

from the YACC specification and converted in the grammar notation used for the tool. The context-free part of the grammar is then reused to specify source-to-source transformations by giving appropriate semantic rules. The above approach can then be used to transform the transformation into a form suitable for the used tool, as is demonstrated in Figure 4.11. Several technical problems have still to be solved. For example, ϵ-productions violate the conditions to apply the algorithm for left recursion removal.

4.6 Related Work

There are several approaches to left recursion removal, all of them dealing with the context-free grammar only, without caring for attributes. The general algorithm for left recursion removal is given in many compiler books, as representative see Louden [Lou97]. He also demonstrates, how left recursion can be avoided using EBNF-notation, and an implementation using iteration is given. Rechenberg/Mössenböck [RM85] use a translation of the grammar to syntax graphs, from which they construct parsers. Left recursion is handled by transforming it into iteration, while preserving the accepted language.

We mentioned the use of top-down tools for their ease of use. Pepper [Pep99] unifies the paradigms for LR(k)- and LL(k)-parsing expressed by the formula LR(k) = 3NF + LL(k). The main aim is an easy comprehensible derivation method, easy to adapt, providing the power of LR parsing while providing efficiency known from LALR parsing. Grammars are enriched with null nonterminals, which do not change the language but may carry semantic actions or can act as assertions that guide reductions. Semantic rules are not

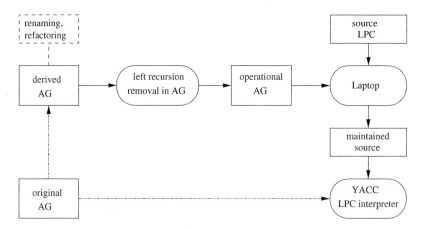

Figure 4.11 Reuse of the original grammar for small maintenance transformations

considered during the grammar transformation process. Schmeiser/Barnard [SB95] modify the standard table driven algorithm for bottom-up parsing to offer the programmer a top-down parse order while using a bottom-up parser. Besides states additionally rule lists are stored on the stack. When a rule is reduced, the rule lists are concatenated in suitable order.

We discussed that grammars are not only changed to implement compilers. The need of an engineering discipline for grammarware is emphasised in [KLV05a]. In [LV01b] the authors propose an approach to the construction of grammars for existing languages. The main characteristic of the approach is that the grammars are not constructed from scratch but they are rather recovered by extracting them from language references, compilers, and other artefacts. They provide a structured process to recover grammars including the automated transformation of raw extracted grammars and the derivation of parsers. Examples for tool support for grammar engineering are Grammar Deployment Kit (GDK) [KLV02] and *F*ramework for *S*DF *T*ransformation (FST) [LW01]. GDK provides support in the process to turn a grammar specification into a working parser. FST supports the adaptation of grammars based on the syntax definition formalism SDF, where, for example, EBNF patterns are removed (YACCification) or introduced (deYACCification). Transformations by Cordy et al. to enable agile parsing based on problem-specific grammars [DCMS02, DCMS03] are examples for grammar engineering as well as the transformations for deriving an abstract from a concrete syntax by Wile [Wil97].

Theoretical work on general grammar adaptations can be found in [Läm01]. A set of operators is defined together with properties. The operators can be used to describe grammar adaptations.

Lämmel et al. [Läm04b, LR99, Läm99b] also work on grammar evolution. For example, a general framework for meta-programming is developed in [Läm99b] together with an operator suite, where its operators model schemata of program transformation, synthesis and composition. Examples are fold and unfold operations defined on skeletons of declarative programs, i.e., attribute grammars, logic programs. Parameters are analysed and propagated through folded elements.

There is also a relation to refactoring [FBB+99, OJ90], which can be applied to grammars and transformation rules. Indeed, left recursion removal could be considered as a composite refactoring for grammars.

Related to this chapter is the next Chapter 5 on automatic migration of transformation rules after a grammar extension has been made (publication [LR03b]). There, we show how we make rewrite rules able to store layout information in the rewrite pattern. On the level for the rewriter that information is invisible. Hence, the approach helps to reduce complexity of rewrite patterns for users.

4.7 Concluding Remarks

Summary. The chapter contributes to the work on grammar adaptations and concentrates on semantics rules associated to grammar productions. The approach attempts to reuse existing semantic rules for the new grammar. Moreover, it offers the programmer of a program transformation the opportunity to specify semantic rules on a grammar closer to a grammar specification, while grammar and semantic rules can be adapted to meet technical demands, here left recursion removal. Hence, we provide the rewriter with a simpler grammar than necessary for the tool. The necessary transformation steps for the grammar are given, as well as a justification of the approach.

A disadvantage of the approach is the doubling of attribute numbers and the introduction of additional copy rules. Though the added complexity is hidden, the problem might be the time overhead it adds to the process of tool construction. Semantic rules using the original grammar have to be adapted each time a tool is built from rules and grammar. In the case of interpretative used environments, e.g., in a Prolog setting, this may become annoying for larger grammars.

Future work. We are going to make the approach real life usable, the current state is still a weak prototype. There is still the problem of ϵ-productions. The algorithm could benefit from improvement by the use of lazy evaluation strategies. The approach would then only be implemented with S-AG, all other variants are automatically supported. It is also possible to construct terms instead of applying operations, then interpret the term in the root attributes.

In future we will look for further grammar adaptations necessary during maintenance and investigate, if and how it is possible to derive changes for both, the software the grammar uses and for the semantic rules associated with the grammar. We will examine, how we can connect such combined grammar/ transformation rule adaptations to more complex operations.

Chapter 5

Towards Automatical Migration of Transformation Rules after Grammar Extension

The chapter addresses two problems in software maintenance. First, some maintenance tasks require modifications of a grammar. A change in a grammar can make abstract syntax and transformation rules outdated, which then themselves become subject to a maintenance process. Second, it is essential that after a repair programs look as much as possible as they looked before. Especially comments and principle readability by humans are indispensable for further maintenance. Term manipulation systems based on abstract syntax can be used for repair, but they often lack the facility of layout preservation.

We argue that necessary changes of both abstract syntax and transformation rules due to grammar extension can be made automatically. Thus, most of the original rules can be reused. The approach can be used to define and use simplified views on complex patterns to be analysed with transformation rules.

As a case study, we apply the described technique to extend rule-based program transformations with the facility of partial layout preservation. The migration relation is given. The programmer uses common rewriting techniques for program transformation without taking care of layout, which then is automatically included.

5.1 Introduction and Running Example

Software maintenance is concerned with repair and adaptation of software to new requirements. Repair includes the removal of errors, the change of data structures, refactoring [Opd92, FBB+99] to enable extensions to the program, or an optimisation, where, for example, a constant assignment is taken out of a loop. The latter one will be our running example, shown in Figure 5.1.

Modifications made during maintenance should be minimal, only the parts that need repair should be modified. Comments and existing layout should be preserved [Van01, Jon02]. Currently, changes are done in a mixture of manual and automatic procedures. A starting point for tool support is the grammar, from which parsers are generated. For our example, a grammar fragment is given in Figure 5.2.

Before optimisation	After optimisation
```if E(i,x) then while E2(n,x) do i := f(m,x); if E(n,m) then something; endif n := n - i; od -- some comment endif```	```if E(i,x) then i := f(m,x); while E2(n,x) do if E(n,m) then something; endif n := n - i; od -- some comment endif```

Figure 5.1 Loop optimisation

```
stmts : stmt stmts              . {stmts}
      |                           {empty} .

stmt  : "if" exp "then" stmts "endif"    {if}
      | "while" exp "do" stmts "od"   {while}
      | id ":=" exp ";"               {assign}
      | "something" ";"            {something} .

exp   : ...
      | id "(" args ")"               {funcall} .
```

Figure 5.2 A grammar fragment

Automatic changes require scanning and parsing of the source to yield an internal representation. Then a repair is done applying transformation rules to the internal representation. Finally, the resulting program is written out unparsing the transformed internal representation.

As many maintenance tasks can best be specified by rewrite rules [LdM01], we will concentrate on terms as internal representation. E.g., `assign(id(I),nat(N))` represents an assignment of a natural number to an identifier. See Figure 5.3 and 5.4 for Prolog rules, which describe the transformation of the program given in Figure 5.1. For simplicity, we only care of the first assignment in a while-body.

5.1.1 Two Problems with Maintenance Tools

Layout is missing in abstract syntax. Term manipulation systems based on abstract syntax often lack the facility of layout preservation. The problem is nontrivial and if layout information would be incorporated into abstract syntax trees the transformation rules would be soiled with unnecessary information (from the point of the rewriter), and needlessly unreadable. The use of a pretty printer after a transformation is not sufficient as much information gets lost.

```
loop_op( stmts( if(EXP, Ss), Ss2), stmts( if(EXP, NewSs), N2) ) :-
            loop_op(Ss, NewSs), loop_op(Ss2, N2).
loop_op( stmts( while(EXP, stmts( assign(ID, EXP2), Ss)), Ss2),
            stmts( assign(ID, EXP2),
        stmts( while(EXP, NewSs), N2) ) ) :-
            changes(ID, Ss, 0),
            loop_op(Ss, NewSs), loop_op(Ss2, N2).
loop_op( stmts( while(EXP, stmts( assign(ID, EXP2), Ss) ), Ss2),
            stmts( while(EXP, stmts( assign(ID, EXP2), NewSs)), N2)) :-
            loop_op(Ss, NewSs), loop_op(Ss2, N2).
loop_op( stmts( something, Ss), stmts( something, NewSs)) :-
            loop_op(Ss, NewSs).
loop_op( stmts( assign(ID, EXP)),stmts( assign(ID, EXP))).
loop_op( empty, empty).
```

Figure 5.3   Rules to extract the assignment of a loop invariant variable

```
changes(ID, empty, 0).
changes(ID, stmts( assign(ID, EXP), Ss), Cs) :-
            changes(ID, Ss, Cs1),
            Cs is Cs1 + 1.
changes(ID, stmts( while(EXP, Ss), Cs)) :-
            changes(ID, Ss, Cs).
changes(ID, stmts( if(EXP, Ss), Ss2), Cs) :-
            changes(ID, Ss, Cs1),
            changes(ID, Ss2, Cs2),
            Cs is Cs1 + Cs2.
```

Figure 5.4   Counting assignments of a variable

Maintenance tools have a maintenance problem, too.   Some maintenance tasks involve a change of the grammar. Consider, for example, the task to adapt software to a different version of the programming language. Grammar constructs might become obsolete, others are to be introduced, e.g., the tagged record in Ada95. An approved tool might be applied to different dialects of the same language (e.g., Cobol with 300 dialects [LV01a]), or, a grammar for island parsing [Moo02, Moo01] is to be extended to support a new type of island. As a result, a new parser has to be constructed and, more importantly, the internal representation changes. Transformation rules will usually not work on the new terms without change. Traversals may break and may have to be adapted, if they are still needed. For example, Ada95 was designed such that Ada83 became a sub-language. Old programs could be recompiled and reused. The reuse of approved transformation rules over those programs would now be desirable.

5.1.2 Aim and Result

```
stmt  : lay  "if" exp lay
                      "then" stmts lay  "endif" {if}
        |  ...

lay : white_space_or_comment+              {lay}
        |                                  {nolay}.
```

Figure 5.5 Extension by explicit layout

In the chapter we investigate how the change of the grammar induces changes of such rules. We show how rules can be migrated to work with a new internal representation automatically. This way, the old rules can be reused on programs according to the new grammar to some extent even if the program now contains constructs from the grammar extension. Especially, rules encoding an analysis can be reused to work on program parts, which are now embedded into the new grammar. For some rules this does not make sense, others might need to be extended. We concentrate on the general migration of rules from the syntactic point of view.

To demonstrate the usefulness, we apply automatic transformation rule migration to enable (partial) layout preservation without burdening the rewriter with more complicated rules. The grammar is extended by explicit layout nonterminals (see Figure 5.5). All existing rules can be reused without change from the rewriter's point of view. For an

```
loop_op( stmts(if( LAY_1,  EXP, LAY_3,  Ss ,LAY_5 ), Ss2),
         stmts(if( LAY_1,  EXP, LAY_3, NewSs ,LAY_5 ),N2)) :-
         loop_op(Ss, NewSs), loop_op(Ss2, N2).

changes(ID, stmts(if( LAY_1,  EXP, LAY_3,  Ss ,LAY_5 ),Ss2), Cs)  :-
         changes(ID, Ss, Cs1),
         changes(ID, Ss2, Cs2),
         Cs is Cs1 + Cs2.
```

Figure 5.6 Migrated rules for layout extension

example of automatically adapted rules, see Figure 5.6. The result will be discussed in more detail in Section 5.4.4.

5.1.3 Remainder of the Chapter

The rest of the chapter is structured as follows. In the next section, the need for layout in maintenance is discussed and motivated. Section 5.3 examines grammar extension and its effects on rules by the example of layout introduction. A generalised use of the approach is discussed. Section 5.4 describes the generation of internal presentation, the extension of the grammar, and discusses the induced migration of transformation rules. We give a relation which describes the migration including a heuristics to preserve layout to some extent. Section 5.5 points to some related work and evaluates the results. Finally, some concluding remarks are given in Section 5.6.

5.2 Layout in Software Maintenance

This section motivates the need for layout preservation for abstract syntax.

5.2.1 The Need for Layout Preservation

Manual maintenance is still indispensable. Not all changes can be performed automatically. Furthermore, it might be too costly to construct a tool for the removal of few errors. Manual adaptation of software requires readability of the sources. Readability of sources includes a certain layout of the program and comments. To support the understandability of programs is an important function of layout [Jon02]. Hence, blank lines, line breaks, and other instruments used by the programmer for structuring source code should be preserved as much as possible [Van01, Jon02].

Some repair can and needs to be done automatically for efficiency reasons. For example, we participated the class library renovation of a multi-user software. About 13900 files are based on the class library, which contains about 15000 methods. Changes in the library led to necessary adaptation of the source using it. One typical task was to migrate 4313 appearances of calls of a global function `environment(arg)` (`arg` is an optional expression) to a method call `(object)arg->environment()` in 1329 files. Simply loading each file into an editor alone would have taken 5:32 hours if we assume 15 seconds to browse for a file (containing a use of the global function) in the file hierarchy and open it. Manual adaptation was unacceptable in this case. The description of such a transformation was easy and the transformation of all appearances of the functions was done within minutes.

As mentioned above, tools transform source code into a suitable internal form. However, classic techniques in compiler construction skip whitespaces and comments as this information is not necessary for translation for most languages. It is then missing when the repaired program has to be written out. The matter is that layout information is usually not even contained in the grammar specification input for the parser generator. See Figure 5.7 for an output of our transformation tool without layout preservation support.

Pretty printers are tools to create a certain layout, and thus they improve readability. However, line breaks are not where programmers have inserted them (pretty printers usually insert line breaks at defined points in the program text), and lost comments mean lost

```
if E ( i , x ) then i := f ( m , x ) ; while E2 ( n , x ) do if E ( n
, m ) then something ; endif n := n - i; od endif
```

Figure 5.7 Result without layout preservation

information. Hence, transformations that will keep as much information on layout and comments are highly needed for software maintenance tasks. There are three locations where the layout has to be preserved in a transformation: around the program part to be changed, the part itself, and its substructures (e.g., a statement part while transforming the condition part of an if-statement).

5.2.2 Layout in Abstract Syntax

Program transformation systems can work on concrete or on abstract syntax. However, sometimes rewriting with concrete syntax is confusing if some syntactical entities can stand for both, the term to be rewritten, and for a variable containing it. For example, 'class' in a rule could be a variable at rewrite level, bound to a class definition, as well as beeing the keyword class as part of the concrete syntax term. A solution is quoting [Vis02], which again makes it difficult to read. Moreover, already existing rewriting systems and languages used for rewriting often use abstract syntax. Thus, it makes sense to support the layout preservation for abstract syntax, too.

Usually, abstract syntax does not contain layout information as the rewriter would be distracted by much information that is of no use in the rewrite process.

Our aim is to contribute to program transformation with layout in the field of rule-based program transformation on abstract syntax *without burdening* the programmer with complicated rules. Moreover, we want to *reuse existing specifications without changes*.

5.3 Introducing Layout Preservation to Existing Transformation Systems

The basic idea to allow (partial) layout preservation is to extend a grammar G to include layout (G_L). (This idea also appears in [Wag98, vdBSV98, SV00, Wes01].) By solving the problem of transformation rule migration the problem of layout preservation can be eased.

5.3.1 Grammar Extension and Transformation Rules

The first step is to extend the grammar by adding nonterminals (in our case lay). This can be done automatically. By grammar extension we mean the introduction of nonterminals to existing rules and possibly addition of new rules. For theoretical background on grammar adaptation, see [Läm01]. The adaptation A_g to include layout also controls the automatic migration M_r of user-given transformation rules R for abstract syntax without layout AS to one with layout included (AS_L). Given the automatic migration, most of the old transformation rules can be reused.

A change in the grammar leads to a change in the abstract syntax, leading to a change of syntax trees derived from programs. Moreover, as structure of patterns in rules directly corresponds to abstract syntax, we can now adapt them based on the same change of our grammar.

Figure 5.8 depicts possible relations. The construction C of an abstract syntax is based on a grammar. Hence, the migration M_{as} is usually not necessary. If the new grammar is not available, or if abstract syntax has to be modified for other purposes, abstract syntax can be adapted using A_{as}.

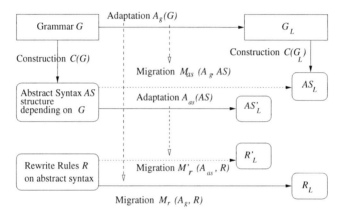

Figure 5.8   Adaptation of grammar, abstract syntax and rewrite rules

Transformation rules can now be migrated with either using (M_r) to work according to the changed grammar, or using (M'_r) to follow the modified abstract syntax. Note that AS_L and AS'_L as well as R_L and R'_L are not necessarily equal. If rules are migrated by M_r, AS has to be either migrated by M_{as} or constructed from G_L by C to ensure transformation rules are conform with new abstract syntax. The relations are summarised in Figure 5.9.

5.3.2 Generalised Use of the Approach

The relations can be used for more than just for layout preservation. Instead of introducing layout into the transformation process there can be other information that could be inserted into the grammar and/or into the abstract syntax, e.g., language constructs like the tagged record in Ada95 and additionally control statements for user-designed tools.

Furthermore, the existing grammar and/or abstract syntax itself can be considered as an already extended grammar to make especially the writing of analysing rules easier, as is described now. A programmer might be interested in some part of the grammar only,

$$G_L = A_g(G) \tag{5.1}$$
$$AS = C(G) \tag{5.2}$$
$$AS_L = C(G_L) \ \lor \ AS_L = M_{as}(A_g, AS) \tag{5.3}$$
$$AS'_L = A_{as}(AS) \tag{5.4}$$
$$R_L = M_r(A_g, R) \land (5.3) \tag{5.5}$$
$$R'_L = M'_r(A_{as}, R) \tag{5.6}$$

Figure 5.9 Relations between the grammar, the extended grammar, the abstract syntax and migrated abstract syntax, the rewrite rules, and the migrated rewrite rules

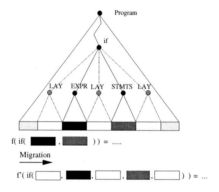

Figure 5.10 Interesting parts of a tree structure

or in a part of the term structure (cf. the dark boxes in Figure 5.10) representing abstract syntax or other information. The programmer only inquires certain values or properties. For example, counting appearances of assignments to a certain variable does not need the examination of expressions from while- and if-statements. Currently, he is forced to include the complete pattern for the structure into his rules. However, if the original structure is considered as the extended one, it is possible to describe the adaptation from an imaginary reduced one that presents the aspect interesting for the programmer. That means, the transformation rules are written as if there would be no uninteresting parts. Then, they are automatically adapted to the case with uninteresting parts. Thus, one is able to abstract from unnecessary details.

Now, the programmer defines rules over the restricted structure undistracted from task, thus, doing less errors and probably increasing productivity. The rules are then migrated

```
grammar    : rule+.
rule       : sort ":" alts "." .
alts       : alt alts-tail* .
alts-tail  : "|" alt annotation.
alt        : term* .
annotation : "{" basis "}".
term       : basis repetition?.
basis      : literal | sort .
repetition : "*" | "+" | "?".
```

Figure 5.11 Grammar of LLL-Grammars

to the original structure, so that no information gets lost during program transformation.

Adaptation A_{as} makes also sense, if different tools are used to extract/manipulate data based on the original structure. Several uninteresting parts of the grammar could be blended out, so the programmer only concentrates on those parts which are of interest for the special task. This could be applied to structured data exchange with, for example, XML documents between architect, builder, and employer.

5.4 Implementation

In the following subsections, we show how we construct an abstract syntax-like internal representation with a construction relation C to be used on any grammar. We then enrich the grammar with layout nonterminals using A_g and create the internal representation (AS_L) using C. Finally, we give the solution for an adaptation-controlled migration relation for transformation rules using the presented concept, and we thus prepare a grammar and transformation rules on its AS to support of (partial) layout preservation.

5.4.1 Notations and Used Tool

We use LLL (Lightweigt LL) as grammar description format, as BNF is too simple and EBNF too liberal for abstract syntax [KLV02]. Figure 5.11 shows the LLL definition taken from [KLV02] with slight changes. The head of a grammar rule (LHS) is separated by a ':' from the rule body (RHS), terminals are enclosed in double quotes, all other names are nonterminals. Moreover, we enrich the rules with annotations similar to [Vis97b]. They serve as address for a rule alternative and are used to construct the internal representation. Annotations are written in { }. For simplicity, we restricted ourselves to the BNF-expressiveness in the chapter.

The extension of the grammar is described with intuitive syntactic sugar. Of course, our approach is not restricted to this grammar type.

For our implementation we used Laptob [LR01], a Prolog-based tool supporting the definition of language processors. Grammar adaptations are done in a simple form of metaprogramming. Grammars are specified as logic grammars [RL88, SS97]. Hence, we can make use of the full power of Prolog. The production $'A : B C.'$ is written in Prolog as `a :- b, c.`, terminals are enclosed in quotes and prefixed with the operator `@`, e.g., `@"if"`. Attributes are given as parameters to predicates, e.g., `exp(EXP)`. Parsers are derived from logic grammars using metaprogramming. We introduce the convention that result parameters occur always at the last position. Thus, for a predicate $p(t_1, \ldots, t_n)$, we call $Is = \{t_1, \ldots, t_{n-1}\}$ input positions, and $O = \{t_n\}$ output position. Additionally, indices $_l$ and $_{r_i}$ denote, whether the predicate appears on the left or right hand sides of the Prolog rule. N indicates the number of predicates on the RHS.

The implementation idea is independent of Prolog and can be applied to any transformation tool. The difference will mainly concern the syntax of the rules. In Prolog, we use predicates to describe transformation. E.g., a predicate `f(A,B) :- p(A), B = A.` can be read as 'B is the (identical) result of transformation `f` applied to A, if `p(A)` holds'.

5.4.2 Generating an Internal Representation

Generating abstract syntax has been described, for example, in [Wil97, Jon02]. We will speak about generating internal representation (terms) only. A simple translation is given by the logic grammar version of `{if}`:

```
stmt :- @"if", exp, @"then", stmts, @"endif".
```

To enable the logic grammar to describe the construction of terms (representing syntax trees) we add an 'ast'-attribute to each nonterminal.

```
stmt( if(EXP_1,STMTS_2))  :-
    @"if", exp(EXP_1),
    @"then", stmts(STMTS_2), @"endif".
```

The name of the attribute is simply the name of the corresponding nonterminal in uppercase plus its ordinal number of occurrence as index. The node of a syntax tree corresponding to a grammar rule is named using the annotation of the rule (possibly plus an index, to distinguish different occurences of the same nonterminal). Furthermore, it is parameterised with attributes of the nonterminals on the RHS.

5.4.3 Extending the Base Grammar

```
add rule r to g where
  r = lay : whitespace_or_comment+ {lay}

insert lay with default = lay(" ")
  before $x in g
  where terminal($x)
```

Figure 5.12   Description of the transformation

Now, we describe the grammar adaptation A_g to include layout in some grammar G. Firstly, we have to introduce a new grammar rule for layout. Secondly, we insert layout nonterminals in front of each terminal of the grammar. For the inserted nonterminal, in our case lay, a default value can be given. See Figure 5.12 for the specification and Figure 5.13 for its result.

```
LLL grammar:

stmt : lay "if" exp lay "then" stmts lay "endif"        {if} .


Logic grammar:

stmt(if(LAY_1, EXP_2, LAY_3, STMTS_4, LAY_5)) :-
        lay(LAY_1), @"if", exp(EXP_2),
        lay(LAY_3), @"then", stmts( STMTS_4 ),
        lay(LAY_5), @"endif".
```

Figure 5.13   Resulting logic grammar rule

The grammar transformation can be tracked and attached to the internal representation of the new grammar or stored as an annotation to the new grammar. This information can later be used to adapt the transformation rules. We chose the following format to express the change:

```
trace += if([1:(lay,lay(" ")),
             3:(lay,lay(" ")),
             5:(lay,lay(" "))])
```

A trace for a rule is a collection of changes. It is named according to its annotation and contains a list of entries. The numbers represent the positions in the list of nonterminals of a rule, as these are the items which will be used in the transformation rules. To the position, the inserted nonterminal as well as the default value is associated.

If it is possible to give default behaviour for the new introduced nonterminals, transformation rules can be kept even without any change. The kind of default behaviour is dependent on the used grammar. Note that it is possible to provide different default values for different occurrences of the same nonterminal in a rule. In our example, it makes sense to insert a whitespace as default value (see Figure 5.14).

The solution to insert a whitespace for every empty layout nonterminal after the transformation (e.g., by a succeeding transformation) is not a good decision. It would change positions that have been subject to a change and do not possess explicit layout. For example, abstract syntax for a piece of code as a.b in an object-oriented language has empty layout, and a transformation afterwards cannot distinguish between new generated empty layout, and therefore inserts whitespace there.

If we now apply construction of internal representation to the modified grammar, the successful reduction of the grammar rule for {if} yields a term of the form

```
if(lay("  "), exp(..), .., stmts(...), lay("\n"))
```

5.4.4 Migration of Transformation Rules

Based on our internal trace of the grammar adaptation, the rules can now become automatically migrated to follow the new grammar structure by means of meta-programming on Prolog rules. As proposed in Section 5.4.1, the new term T to be constructed is assumed

```
loop_op(stmts(if( LAY_1, EXP, LAY_3, Ss ,LAY_5 ), Ss2),
               stmts(if( LAY_1, EXP, LAY_3, NewSs ,LAY_5 ), N2)) :-
       loop_op(Ss, NewSs), loop_op(Ss2, N2).

some_rule(stmts(while( LAY_1, EXP, LAY_3, Ss ,LAY_5 ), Ss2), Result) :-
       some_rule(Ss, NewSs),
       some_rule2(stmts(if( lay(" "), EXP ,lay(" "), NewSs ,lay(" ") ),Ss2),
                  Result).

some_rule4(stmts(while(..),..),
               stmts(if( lay(" "), EXP, lay(" "), NewSs ,lay(" ") ),N2)) :-
       ...
some_rule5(stmts( .., ..), ..) :-
       some_rule6(.., stmts(if( LAY_6, EXP, LAY_8, Ss ,LAY_10 ), Result)).
```

Figure 5.14   Some locations for term construction

to be the last argument in a Prolog predicate. If the result is given as a variable, which appears in Is_l, there is no loss of information. The problem emerges whenever new terms are constructed. See Figure 5.14 for some possible variants of term construction.

Case 1. This can be directly at O_l. Here, we distinguish: the term constructor is either a) the same as in at least one subterm $t_i \in Is_l$, then we get the information from there, or b) no subterm of any $t_i \in Is_l \cup \bigcup O_r$, then the term needs default values as it has to return something meaningful to the export, or c) a subterm of several $t_i \in \bigcup O_{r_j}, 0 \leq j \leq N$. Here, the programmer's intention is not clear, therefore we vote for a default value.

Case 2. The term might be constructed at some $Is_{r_i}, 1 \leq i \leq N$. Default values are necessary, as inside the predicate the nonterminals might be bound correctly with the output position, if, e.g., the term is just delegated like case 1a).

Case 3. The term might occur in one or more $O_{r_i}, 1 \leq i \leq N$, where it needs to have new variables matching against potential information delegated through the predicate.

If there is more than one t_i in 1.a), we offer the heuristics to take the first found occurrence while searching the Is_l. This will give wrong results in some cases, but mostly result in good layout preservation.

Though it will not make sense to keep all layout if an if-statement is replaced by a switch-statement, some further improvements are imaginable. For example, we can save the first appearance of the layout, as usually new syntactic entities replacing old ones, will use at least the same initial indentation. However, if a comment has been in the first place, it might become obsolete. One could also imagine that while performing traversals, information on the layout is collected, and from that conclude strategies to set layout into new constructed terms. There is a more detailed analyses in the next chapter.

5.4.5 The Migration Relation

```
% traverse rules
m( Head :- Body, T, _, NewH :- NewB) :-
  m(Head, migrate_h, (T,var,default), NewH),
  m(Body, migrate_b, (T,default,var), NewB).

% traverse body clauses
m( (A, B), M, P, (NewA, NewB)) :-
  m(A, M, P, NewA), m(B, M, P, NewB).

% migrate predicates
m(Pred, M, (T,CASE,CASE2),  NewPred) :-
  Pred    =.. [RewrName| AbsSynNs],
  RewrName \= (:-), RewrName \= (,),

  % separate input from output positions
  append(Ins, [Out], AbsSynNs),

  % create migration call for input positions
  % and traverse migration over input structure
  Mig    =.. [M, T, CASE, [] ],
  map(td(Mig), Ins, NewIns),

  % create migration depending on new inputs
  % and traverse over output positions
  Mig2    =.. [M, T,CASE2,NewIns],
  td(Mig2, Out, NewOut),

  % construct resulting predicate
  append(NewIns, [NewOut], NewAbsSynNs),
  NewPred =.. [RewrName| NewAbsSynNs].
```

Figure 5.15 Migration relation: top level

The relation is given as a Prolog metaprogram. As a sidemark, we remind the reader of the meaning of the Prolog univ-operator =.. and the predicate functor, necessary for understanding the given rules. The following holds:
$f(t_1, \ldots, t_n) = \ldots [f|t_1, \ldots, t_n]$, i.e., a term is decomposed into a list starting with the functor f and followed by the list of all argument terms t_i. The inverse way is also possible: a term can be constructed from a nonempty list, with the head of the list as functor, and its tail as arguments. | separates the head of a list from its tail. Thus, $functor(f(t_1, \ldots, t_n), f, n)$ is a valid predicate.

We roughly explain the migration relation. First of all we have to take care of the different abstraction levels, terms representing predicates of the original transformation rules, and terms that are arguments to the former. This is done by the top-level relation m in Figure 5.15 (some trivial cases are left out). The predicates arguments (i.e., terms of the internal representation, patterns given by the rewriter) are extracted (AbstSynNs) and a distinction is made between input and output positions, as described in Section 5.4.1. Two calls to migrations are constructed using, for example, the trace. map applies its first argument to its second, i.e., for all input positions of the predicate (terms on which the original rules are transforming) a top-down traversal (td) is initiated. The traversal applies Mig to all subterms. For more on second order programming in Prolog, see [LR01]. Note: Migration of the output position needs the newly generated input positions. If the term is constructed at the output position, and if it can be found at input positions, we can get the information, i.e., layout from them.

The migration migrate_b for the positions on the RHS initialises the weaver to weave default values or variables into the arguments of the current term depending on the actual case (see Figure 5.16).

```
% migration for body predicates          % find possible information
migrate_b(Trace,CASE,_I,AS,NewAS):-      % in input terms
   % get current trace for actual node   heuristics(AS,T,MInputs,AS_h):-
   AS =.. [Node| Atts],
   getTrace(Trace, Node, CT),               % create a pattern with
                                            % unbound variables
   % weave attributes using the trace      functor(AS, Node, Number),
   % and construct new term                length(T,Add),
   weave(CT, CASE,[], Atts,NewAtts,0),     N is Number + Add,
   NewAS =.. [Node | NewAtts].             functor(Pattern, Node, N),

% migrate input position of head          % look for a match and return
migrate_h(T, CASE, [], AS, NewAS) :-      % arguments of one of the
   migrate_b(T, CASE,[], AS, NewAS).      % patterns
                                          td(pm(Pattern), MInputs,
% output positions of the head              [],_,[PM|PossibleMatches]),
migrate_h(T, CASE, MI, AS, NewAS) :-      PM =.. [Node| AS_h].

   AS =.. [Node| Atts],                   heuristics(_,_,_,[]).
   getTrace(T, Node, CT),

   % what can we learn from the input
   % then weave head output positions
   heuristics(AS, CT, MI, AS_h),
   weave(CT, var, AS_h, Atts, NewAtts,0),
   NewAS =.. [Node | NewAtts].
```

Figure 5.16 Configuring the weaving and heuristics for layout preservation

If there are no migrated parameter input positions migrate_h is the same as migrate_b. Otherwise, we are migrating the arguments of the output position, and therefore need to find the corresponding term in the migrated input (MI). It initiates the weaving process using the trace for the current abstract syntax investigated, together with preserved knowledge calculated by the heuristics.

Our heuristics searches in the migrated input list of abstract syntax trees for a term, which has the same constructor. Its arity is that of the actual output term plus the number of nonterminals to be inserted. If such a term can be found as subpart in one of the trees, its arguments are returned. (Note that the constructor is of the same type, as for the same constructor the same trace has been used.)

The heart of the migration is the weaving predicate (see Figure 5.17). If the remaining

```
% weave hidden information into abstract syntax
weave([Pos:(NT, Def)|CT], Case, [], Atts, [NTind|NewAtts], Pos) :-
   % depending on the case use indexed nonterminal
   % or default for this position from the trace
   ( Case = default
        -> NTind = Def ;
             index(NT, Pos, NTind)
   ), N is Pos + 1,

   % weave for the rest
   weave(CT, Case, [], Atts, NewAtts, N).

% trace contains no information for this Pos
weave([P1:(NT,Def)|CT], Case, [], [A|Atts], [A|NewAtts], P) :-
   P1 \= P, N is P + 1,
   weave([P1:(NT,Def)|CT], Case, [], Atts, NewAtts, N).

% if heuristic information exists (H) take that
weave([P:Inf|CT], Case, [H|Hs], Atts, [H|NewAtts], P) :-
   N is P + 1,
   weave(CT, Case, Hs, Atts, NewAtts, N).

% but not, if it is the wrong position
weave([P1:Inf|CT], Case, [H|Hs], [A|Atts], [A|NewAtts], P) :-
   P1 \= P, N is P + 1,
   weave([P1:Inf|CT], Case, Hs, Atts, NewAtts, N).

weave([], Case, _, NewAtts, NewAtts, _ ).
```

Figure 5.17 Weaving nonterminals into terms

trace (first position) is empty, the remaining attributes can be adopted unchanged. If there is no list of arguments (third argument) that are from the corresponding migrated input term, and if it is the correct position, then we adopt the default value or generate a new variable depending on the case. The next case just copies the attribute. The next two rules cope the cases that attributes of a migrated term are to be used instead of the information in the trace.

5.5 Discussion and Related Work

Format evolution. The approach is another co-transformation, where the migration of an artefact (the abstract syntax, and the transformation rules) is induced by the adaptation of an artefact on another layer (the grammar). It is related to Chapter 3, where a change of the underlying document structure is described. Based on the description both is controled, the adaptation of the defining structure, i.e., DTD, and the migration of XML documents with the old structure to documents following the new structure.

Transformation of rewrite rules. With our approach, we can reduce complexity of several rewrite rules. Automatically applied fusion transformations [SdM01] is related to this: Many quite complex program transformations can be expressed by rewrite rules that are easy to understand.

Grammar extension. Much work has been done on the field of grammar transformation. Especially related to the chapter, however, is [Läm01], which provides a theoretical foundation for grammar adaptation. [KLV02] presents a tool box that is tailored to grammar adaptations.

Dean et al. [DCMS03] introduce (grammar) overrides in TXL to support their *agile parsing* philosophy to program a grammar to support the task at hand by grammar overrides.

Layout preservation. A recent approach in pretty printing [Jon02] is able to preserve old layout of the source to be pretty printed and adapted to customer specific format guidelines. It is a precondition for layout preserving pretty printing after a transformation that much information on original layout has to be preserved by the preceding transformation.

Rewriting with layout [BV00] using ASF+SDF [DHK96] in the Meta-Environment [Kli93] provides an approach which can be combined with [Jon02]. Full parse trees are used during rewriting over *concrete syntax*. This is supported by powerful SGLR-parsing [BSVV02, Vis97a]. Thus, the addition of layout support is hidden because the rewriter will not realise that a whitespace in his rule stands for any layout. Moreover, the introduction of (default) whitespace in newly constructed terms is done intuitively by the user, who simply writes the desired code in concrete syntax taking care of the layout. Variable productions match and are instantiated to any subtree of the same sort. Any two layout nodes always match. Layout in the left hand side of the production is left unchanged. Bound variables keep their contained layout. All rewritten terms will lose their original layout.

Our automatic migrated adaptations achieve similar results for abstract terms. Bound variables keep layout. If the term constructor matches one of the inputs, it will take layout of that. It might be wrong, but on the other hand it preserves more layout in average than what is described by [BV00]. This is due to the fact that the rewriter in the above mentioned approach inserts layout by concrete syntax when rewriting terms, while our automated migration can try to find and insert variables used on the input positions. Layout in an untouched subpart of a rewritten term is kept. Moreover, our approach is more general in two ways: it offers a way for several transformation tools without changing them and, besides layout preservation, other applications are possible, e.g., working on abstractions of the grammar or extending a grammar in general.

Our approach to layout preservation is similar to [Wag98, vdBSV98, SV00]. This has also been implemented by [Wes01] for the system CobolX. They generate signatures containing a layout sort for strategies in Stratego [Vis01], but they had to rewrite a lot of Stratego library strategies manually, and changed a lot of XT utilities [JVV01]. Their approach is restricted to layout support. They derive signatures from grammars, plus overlays, instead of including the layout into grammar. Old (1) and new (2) rewrite rule differ, and are similar only through syntactic sugar:

```
rules D: A(v,B(e)) -> A(v,e)       (1)
rules D::A(?v,?B(e)) --> A(!v,!e)  (2)
```

They do not support other forms of transformations.

TXL [CDMS02] allows to specify commenting conventions of a language and to specify comments as part of a grammar. Rules can then make use of the information provided in the internal representation.

Our migration can be done by a preprocessor and therefore can simply be integrated with existing tools. The rewrite tool does not need to be changed to work with our approach. Rewrite rules from the point of the rewriter do not change.

A disadvantage of our approach is the size of the internal representation, as it carries all characters of the source. To avoid this, [BV00] use ATerms [vdBdJKO00], which allow maximum sharing, and thus they provide some space efficiency. Moreover, our migration relation is not very efficient and offers room for optimisation.

There is still room to save more layout, e.g., if a data flow analysis is made on the RHS. The difficulties to determine, which comment is attached to which piece of code is described in [Van01]. We cannot solve that problem.

5.6 Concluding Remarks

Summary. In the chapter we have examined changes for abstract syntax and transformation rules caused by a grammar extension. We have shown a relation which migrates abstract syntax and transformation rules accordingly. Migration means that rules can match on a more complex structure. This reduces the amount of work to adapt rules to new grammars. We argued that if it is possible to give default behaviour for newly introduced nonterminals, transformation rules do not need any change by the rewriter to work. The idea and implementation are simple and straightforward. Thus, they are easy to apply to other transformation systems.

We applied the approach to introduce partial layout preservation into rewriting based on abstract syntax. The adaptation is done by metaprogramming on rewrite rules, and controlled by the description of the underlying grammar extension. We showed how the internal representation and all transformation rules can be adapted automatically to work with layout. Transformation rules for the programmer *do not change*. He continues creating rules without layout. They can then be migrated to work with a layout-enriched grammar by a preprocessor. The remaining problem is at those points, where new abstract syntax terms are introduced (which do not appear anywhere on the input of the transformation), as there is no information on layout. Moreover, for some rewritten terms it can not be said what the intention of the programmer is, and thus a decision can not be made. There, layout will simply be whitespace.

Our approach is general: it offers a way for layout preservation for several transformation tools, without changing them, and, besides layout preservation, other applications are possible, e.g., grammar abstractions.

Future work. Future work will include the search for more grammar extensions, where this approach is applicable. It is necessary to clearly identify its limits. During the work on the topic several questions arose:

How many parts of the grammar could be abstracted from for the rewriter without losing the help of automatic rule migration, thus supporting avoidance of boring aspects for the programmer? Can some other grammar adaptations be found, where adaptation of rewrite rules also make sense, i.e., not only extensions? How much can we combine migrations? What about default values? Can they be automatically determined? We can describe a change and as a consequence automatically adapt all places where the change of the grammar has an influence. We would like to apply this approach to library migration.

Chapter 6

Automatic Layout Preservation in Declarative First Order Rewriting

Layout preservation is essential in software maintenance. Declarative rules in source to source transformations describe transformations on an abstract syntax tree. They can support layout preservation during the transformation, if the abstract syntax tree additionally provides layout information. This requires that argument positions of the rules are added to take care of the layout information. However, to avoid unreadability of transformation rules, positions concerning layout information should be hidden. The chapter examines cases for automatic introduction of layout positions for a simple traversal scheme.

6.1 Introduction

The need for layout preservation in software maintenance has been discussed in the literature, for example, [Van01, Jon02] or Chapter 5 ([LR03b]). Shortly, it is essential that maintained programs look similar to their original. Programmers want to recognise their programs. Moreover, comments contain valuable information or even control statements for tools. In the context of source to source transformation the part of a program text that determines the arrangement of the program together with the comments is often referred to as layout.

A typical maintenance using source to source transformations is done in three phases. The program is transformed in some internal representation. Then suitable maintenance operations are applied to the internal representation. Finally, the internal representation is written out using some pretty printer. The pretty printer generates keywords and some layout. The layout, however, is not the original one, and comments are missing.

Common transformation tools are either constructed based on a grammar, e.g., the YACC-approach, or they take a grammar description, which is then used to generate a parser/ unparser for the special transformation task [Kli93, Vis01, LR01] while constructing the internal representation.

Language specifications define locations of layout often informally. In compilers comments and whitespace as well as the representation of keywords and other symbols are skipped usually. The 'important' information is attached in abstract syntax trees. This is not sufficient in software maintenance.

6.1.1 Common Approach to treat Layout

One solution usually applied is to introduce a nonterminal `layout` into the grammar representing sequences of whitespace and comments (cf. [Wag98, vdBSV98, SV00, Wes01]). The nonterminal is then inserted in front of each terminal. For practical reasons, a catch-all nonterminal is introduced at the end of the program to gather the remainder of the program text. Now, using a tool derived from the grammar, an abstract syntax tree can be constructed carrying the program information as well as the layout preceding the terminals.

We are interested in the use of declarative first order rewriting to implement transformations because it is well-suited for program transformation [LdM01]. Abstract syntax trees (AST) in declarative first order rewriting are represented as ground terms. Rewrite rules provide several argument positions, which are terms to match against components of the abstract syntax tree. We will use the term representation of an **if**-statement defined by the grammar rule

```
<stmt>  ::=  if <exp> then <stmts> fi.
```

as example for terms that are to be extended with layout in the rewrite rule. A term representation is `if(E,S)` where `E` and `S` would be terms representing expressions and statements. We will adopt the convention to denote variables with a starting capital letter.

The extension of the grammar rule by layout nonterminals results in the following grammar rule:

```
<stmt>  ::=  <layout> if <exp> <layout> then <stmts> <layout>fi.
```

The term representation changes to `if(L1,E,L2,S,L3)` with `Li` being variables matching the layout structure, for example, `lay(' ')`. It is now possible to construct transformations that take care of the layout.

6.1.2 Problem Description

However, layout information is a mainly uninteresting concern from the programmer's point of view of the transformation and distracts from the main task. Writing transformation rules with many argument positions and complex terms to match against the AST is error-prone. Therefore, our aim is to separate both concerns, the main transformation as well as transformation of the layout portion according the idea of AOP [KLM+97a]. Moreover, we are interested in how the layout information can be treated automatically, that is, in where and how to weave necessary layout-representing terms into the rewrite rules.

Imperative vs. declarative description. In transformations described using imperative languages components of an AST node are modified destructively, usually using pointers. To implement a traversal it is sufficient to recursively traverse a node's components or to apply a transformation. A modification of a subcomponent will affect the original syntax tree *directly*. The modifications are done in place. Hence, in a tree enriched with layout information the layout of a node in the abstract syntax tree will be preserved in traversals even when subcomponents are changed. In declarative rewriting, transformation rules describe relations between terms. Rules are applied if their parameter positions match structurally with arguments they are applied to. The matching is described using terms, which can contain variables (the declarative way of pointers). However, the result of a successful applied rule is a *newly*-created term even if it has the same functor as well as the same variables like the pattern. This is one reason why automatic introduction of layout preservation capability into transformation rules is more difficult in declarative rewriting than in transformation based on imperative languages.

Extending terms.   After the extension of the internal structure with layout information each argument of the rule now has to treat layout information. This means for existing rules that the terms of every argument position of a rule have to be adapted accordingly. Variables in terms can match immediately to layout containing structures. Nodes of the AST corresponding to grammar rules that do not contain terminals do not contain layout information. The other nodes of the AST correspond to grammar rules that contain terminals and require an adaptation of rules applied to these nodes. Terms in the arguments of these rules need new positions to match against layout information, e.g., `if(E,S)` vs. `if(L1,E,L2,S,L3)`. Each position has to be filled by a default value or by a variable, either fresh or bound somewhere in the same rule.

To achieve layout preservation the problem is to decide when and which of the variants has to be used, i.e., how layout is delegated from input to the output to achieve a transformation with the least possible loss of information. The main problem appears in rules at those positions, where new terms are constructed. While other work use a more pragmatic approach, we attempt to examine it from a more formal perspective.

In the remainder, we will give simplifying assumptions in Section 6.2 and notions in Section 6.3, which will be used in Section 6.4. Then, that section examines cases which can appear, and what the automatic answer could be. Related work is given in Section 6.5. Finally, a summary and a discussion of further work in Section 6.6 concludes the chapter.

6.2 Simplifying Assumptions

We use Prolog to describe transformations. Hence, our transformation rules are predicates. We make several simplifications to concentrate on few cases:

Functional use   Transformation rules are written in a directed style where certain input values are used to compute output values. For this we introduce input and output positions where input positions are bound with intermediate results and output positions contain results. Usually, program transformations have a functional intention. This is a minor restriction and helps to evaluate the intention of the rewriter.

Ordered predicates   Predicates on right hand sides (RHS) of transformation rules are ordered according data dependencies, i.e., a literal l_1 with an input position that refers to some output position of a literal l_0 is ordered behind l_0 (assuming the procedural interpretation of logic programs). Cases where this is not possible are left out. This also makes it easier to adapt the case discrimination for other instances of the first order rewriting.

Data flow information is valuable help in transformation. Note, however, that we transform transformation rules. The data flow of the programs that are transformed by original transformation rules is not available. Hence, it cannot help to reason about layout in source programs.

Defined layout positions We have to pay attention to two levels of intention. Firstly, a programmer, whose program is being transformed, can write comments concerning the same syntactical construct at different locations. The suggested grammar extension formalises the locations where layout can be used in a program text. We will assume that layout is used according the given grammar extension, i.e., comments are written before the syntactical entity, so that we can concentrate on rewrite rules.

Secondly, to automatically adapt existing transformation rules to preserve layout information we have to guess the intention of the rewriter, i.e., what might be the aim of the transformation: Does an argument in a rewrite rule match against original code containing layout to be preserved or is it just an additional argument to control the transformation (i.e., layout information of it is uninteresting)?

Traversals Layout bound to a term is probably of interest if a term is constructed using the same functor again.

Recursive case discrimination Each case will examine one position in a rewrite rule depending on its role, e.g., input position on RHS. For composed terms, apply the case discrimination first for the outer term level, then for its subterms.

6.3 Notions

In this section we introduce some notions necessary for the analysis. Transformation rules are represented as logic rules of the form

$$f_l(t_1, \ldots, t_{n_0}) : -f_{r_1}(t_1, \ldots, t_{n_1}), \ldots, f_{r_k}(t_1, \ldots, t_{n_k}). \qquad f_l(t_1, \ldots, t_n).$$

For simplicity, we consider $n_i > 1$ only. Other cases can be simulated by adding a neutral parameter, e.g., *true* in the logic paradigm.

Variables are denoted using capital letters. All other terms will be denoted using s, t, u. $var(t)$ expresses that t is a variable. Functors will be denoted by f. $F(t)$ will denote the functor of t. $F(p)$, where p is a predicate, denotes the predicate symbol. $A_t(t)$ will denote the arity of $F(t)$, that is, the number of terms t is constructed of. E.g., for $t = f(a, b(c), d), A_t(t) = 3$. Similarly, $A_p(p)$ denotes the arity of predicate symbol $F(p)$. We leave out the index, when it is clear from the context, which arity we mean. For simplicity, we require $F(s) = F(t) \rightarrow A(s) = A(t)$, i.e., overloading of functors is not allowed.

We will use $\pi_i(X)$ to denote the ith projection of X, where X can be a predicate or a term, e.g., $\pi_1(f(a, b, c)) = a$. Sequences of indices i of π_i behind terms will be used to address subterms, e.g., $t[1, 2, 3]$ stands for $\pi_3(\pi_2(\pi_1(t)))$. Such a sequence is also called a path. We apply lexicographic ordering between paths.

The set ST of terms and subterms of t is defined as $ST(t) = \{t\} \cup \bigcup_{1 \leq i \leq A(t)} ST(\pi_i(t))$. The set ST will also be defined for terms and subterms of p: $ST(p) = \bigcup_{1 \leq i \leq A(p)} ST(\pi_i(p))$. We will be interested in cases, where functors of terms correspond. Therefore, we write $s \doteq t$, if $F(s) = F(t)$. $s \subseteq t :<=> \exists u : u \in ST(t) \wedge s \doteq u$ describes that there is a subterm of t or the term itself, which has the same functor as s.

For a predicate $p = ps(t_1, \ldots, t_{A(p)})$ we will call $I_{side} = \bigcup_{1 \leq i \leq A(p)-1} ST(\pi_i(p))$ input positions, $O_{side} = ST(t_{A(p)})$ output position, $side = l$ for LHS predicates and $side = r_i$ for RHS predicates with i denoting the position of the predicate.

We introduce following notions, which can be used to describe the quality of layout preservation capabilities of a predicate: Pattern position will denote a term in a predicate addressable using a path with subterms not being of interest. A pattern position is *strongly layout preserving*, if no layout information gets lost. A pattern position is *conditional strongly layout preserving*, if it is *strongly layout preserving* wrt. the bound structure, but we have no indication if the contained layout is reliable. A pattern position is *weakly layout preserving*, if layout information is copied from elsewhere, but it is unprovable, whether it is the correct one.

A predicate is *used* if it is used to define an other predicate that is then called *defined*. A predicate is *used strongly layout preserving*, if all pattern positions $t \in I \cup O$ are *strongly layout preserving*. A predicate is used *conditional strongly layout preserving*, if all pattern positions $t \in I \cup O$ are *strongly layout preserving* or *conditional strongly layout preserving*. A predicate is used *weakly layout preserving*, if all pattern positions $t \in I \cup O$ are *strongly layout preserving* or *conditional strongly layout preserving*, or *weakly layout preserving*. Other predicates are called *not layout preserving*ly used.

A predicate is *defined strongly layout preserving*, if it is *strongly layout preserving* and all used predicated $t \cup O_l$ depends on are *strongly layout preserving*. A predicate is defined *conditional strongly layout preserving*, if all pattern positions $t \in I_l$ are defined *strongly layout preserving*, all $t \in O_l$ are at least defined *conditional strongly layout preserving*, and all predicates used to compute $t \in O_l$ are *conditional strongly layout preserving*. A predicate is defined *weakly layout preserving*, if all $t_i \in I_l$ are *conditional strongly layout preserving*, $t_i \in O_l$ are defined *conditional strongly layout preserving*, and used predicates to compute $t_i \in O_l$ are *weakly layout preserving*, *conditional strongly layout preserving*, or *strongly layout preserving*. Other predicates we denote as *not layout preserving* defined.

6.4 Case Discrimination over Argument Positions

To modify transformation rules with layout, the case discrimination examines each argument position in a rewrite rule. The form of the terms as well as its influence on layout preserving transformation are investigated. We will consider only terms which will be matched against components of a AST derived from layout extended grammar rules. For each case, we give the property *strongly layout preserving*, *conditional strongly layout*

preserving, **weakly layout preserving** or **not layout preserving** for pattern positions. The case discrimination is to be applied recursively to all subterms of the term per position.

6.4.1 Input Position on LHS

$(t \in I_l)$

1. $var(t)$

   No change of the term is necessary. t matches full available information. If the term structure is extended by layout information, a variable will match immediately against this structure. The pattern position is ***strongly layout preserving***.

   Example:
   before layout introduction:
   ```
   f( V , Result) :- ...
   g(if( B ,S), ..., Res) :- ...
   ```
   after layout introduction:
   ```
   f( V , Result) :- ...
   g(if(L1, B ,L2,S,L3), ..., Res) :- ...
   ```
   If v and b were bound to a term without layout representing structure before layout introduction, they will also be bound to terms with layout presenting structure.

   Possible problem: The use of the same variable for several positions
   `f(V,V,Result) :- ...` could be written if the rewriter wants to check, if two pieces of code are syntactical similar. Usually, the rewriter would consider the code to be equal also, if its layout is different, but common pattern match would now fail. Therefore, one needs layout tolerant matching at some positions.

2. $\neg var(t)$

   Fresh variables are necessary: To match against a structure enriched with layout corresponding positions for layout in the term have to be added. Fresh variables are necessary for each of these positions, because they will be bound to possible different layout. The pattern position is ***strongly layout preserving***.

   Example:
   before layout introduction:
   ```
   f( if(B,S) , Result) :- ...
   ```
   after layout introduction:
   ```
   f( if( L1, B, L2, S ,L3 ) , Result) :- ...
   ```

6.4.2 Input Position on RHS

($s \in I_{r_i}$)

1. $var(s), s \in I_{r_i} \wedge \not\exists t, u \in I_l \cup \bigcup_{1 \le j < i} O_{r_j} : s \doteq u, u \subseteq t$
   (s is an unbound variable)
   According to section 6.2, it is an error.

2. $var(s), s \in I_{r_i} \wedge \exists t, u \in I_l \cup \bigcup_{1 \le j < i} O_{r_j} : s \doteq u, u \subseteq t$
   (s is bound at input position on LHS or some output position on RHS)
   s is as much layout preserving as u. s is bound to a term possibly enriched with
   layout information. The layout of this term is preserved while the term is bound to
   the input of p_i. The pattern position is ***strongly layout preserving***.

   Example:
   before layout introduction:
   ```
   f(IF, Result) :- g( IF , ...), ...
   g(t(V, t2(...), ...), ..., Result) :- g( V , ...), ...
   ```
   after layout introduction:
   ```
   f(IF, Result) :- g( IF , ..), ...
   g(t(V, t2(...), ...), ..., Result) :- g( V , ...), ...
   ```

3. $\neg var(s)$

   a) $\not\exists t, u \in I_l \cup \bigcup_{1 \le j < i} O_{r_j} : s \doteq u, u \subseteq t$
      subterm (s is not term or subterm at some input position on LHS or at output
      position of a predicate on RHS)
      Layout positions in the term have to be default values, e.g., a whitespace. This
      is necessary because the layout position can be used by the predicate to create
      output term, and non-defined or wrong (e.g., empty) layout would be used to
      generate an invalid source (e.g., publicintcreate-problem in Java). The pattern
      position is ***not layout preserving***.

      Example:
      before layout introduction:
      ```
      f(..., NT) :- ..., g( if(B,S) , ..., NT)
      ```
      after layout introduction:
      ```
      f(..., NT) :- ...,
              g( if( lay(' '), B, lay(' '), S , lay(' ')) , ...,NT)
      ```

   b) $\exists t, u \in I_l : s \doteq u, u \subseteq t \wedge \not\exists t', u' \in \bigcup_{1 \le m < i} O_{r_m} : s \doteq u', u' \subseteq t'$
      (s is a similar term or of in the input position on LHS, but not at some output
      position of a predicate p_m on RHS)

      i. $\exists! u$
         s can reuse the layout of u. Copy terms (i.e., variables) from correspond-
         ing layout positions, as the probability is high it describes a traversal.

However, it might be that a new term with different components is being constructed. Hence, this pattern position is ***conditional strongly layout preserving***.

Example:

before layout introduction:

```
f(..., if(B,S), ...)   :- g( if(B,S) ,..)
```

after layout introduction:

```
f(..., if(L1,B,L2,S,L3),...)   :-
            g( if( L1, B, L2, S ,L3 ) ,...)
```

ii. Otherwise

It is not clear from which term the layout should be copied. Use a heuristics to choose one. Suggestion: From the terms in question choose that with the smallest path according lexicographic order, and reuse variables generated for layout from the pattern denoted. This pattern position is only ***weakly layout preserving***.

Example:

before layout introduction:

```
f(..., if(B1,if(B2,S)), ...)   :- g( if(B2,S) ,...)
```

after layout introduction:

```
f(..,if(L1,B1,L2, if(L4,B2,L5,S,L6),L3),...)   :-
            g( if( L1, B2, L2, S ,L3 ) ,...)
```

The example demonstrates the failing of the heuristics. The quality of the heuristics can be improved by analysis of subterm.

c) $\nexists t', u' \in I_l : s \doteq u' \subseteq t' \land \exists t, u \in \bigcup_{1 \leq j < i} O_{r_j} : s \doteq u, u \subseteq t$

(s is also term or subterm of in the output position of a predicate p on RHS, but not at input position on LHS.)

i. $\exists! u$

s can reuse the layout of u copy terms (i.e., variables) from corresponding layout positions as it is very probably it is describing a traversal. However, it might be that a new term with different components is being constructed. Hence, this pattern position is ***conditional strongly layout preserving***.

Example:

before layout introduction:

```
f(...,...)   :- g(..., if(B,S)), ..., h( if(B,S) , ...)
```

after layout introduction:

```
f(...,...)   :-
            g(..., if(L1,B,L2,S,L3)), ...,
            h( if( L1, B, L2, S ,L3 ) ), ...)
```

ii. Otherwise

It is not clear from which term the layout should be copied. Use a heuristic to choose one. Suggestion: From the terms in question choose that with the smallest path according lexicographic order, and reuse its variables generated for layout. This pattern position is only ***weakly layout preserving***.

Layout might be preserved if the predicate with u preserves layout. If not, it will return default values. These are the same default values as would have been introduced here if no reuse of layout information was possible. This might miss the intention of the programmer, as the reused term on the output might depend on the actual input to be determined.

d) $\exists t', u' \in I_l : s \doteq u', u' \subseteq t' \wedge \exists t, u \in \bigcup_{1 \le j < i} O_{r_j} : s \doteq u, u \subseteq t$

(s is term or subterm of at least one term at the input position on LHS, *and* in at least one at output positions.)

No definite statement can be made. Suggestion: From the terms in question choose that with the smallest path according lexicographic order, and reuse its variables generated for layout. This will use at least original layout information from the LHS, but might be obsolete, as new computed layout could be available in the output positions on RHS. The pattern position is ***weakly layout preserving***.

6.4.3 Output Position on RHS

$(s \in O_{r_i})$

1. $var(s)$

   Layout from the new computed result is bound. The extent of preservation is determined by the body of the predicate the output position is from. The pattern position is ***strongly layout preserving***.

   Example:
   ```
   f(T,..., NT)  :- g(T...,...,|NT|).
   g(T,..., NT)  :- h(T...,...,|V|), ..., i(V, ..., |NT|).
   f(T, A, R )  :- g(T,|R|).
   f(T, A, R )  :- g(T,|R0|),h(R0,R).
   ```

2. $\neg var(s)$

   Using other terms than simply variables at output positions on RHS makes sense only to constraint the result to be of a certain form, e.g., that an `if`-statement is to be constructed, and/or to bind subparts of the returned structure with variables to be used in the following transformation. Fresh variables are necessary to bind preserved layout from the inside of the predicate, otherwise a desired match could fail because of different layout information. Or, layout tolerant matching is necessary.

The pattern position is ***conditional strongly layout preserving***.

Example:
Before layout introduction:
```
...:- f(..., if(B,S) ), ...
```
After layout introduction:
```
...:- f(..., if( L1, B, L2, S ,L3 ) ), ...
```

6.4.4 Output Position on LHS

$(s \in O_l)$

1. $var(s)$

   a) $\exists t, u \in I_l : s \doteq u, u \subseteq t$

   (s is term or subterm on an input position on LHS)

   s is bound to a layout containing term. The pattern position is ***strongly layout preserving***.

   Example:
   ```
   f(T, T ) :- ...
   g(T,_, T ) :- ...
   h(T1,T2, T2 ) :- ...
   ```

   b) $\not\exists t', u' \in I_l : s \doteq u', u' \subseteq t' \wedge \exists t, u \in O_{r_i} : s \doteq u, u \subseteq t$

   (s is term or subterm in an output position on RHS)

   The bound layout is preserved depending on the layout preservation of the predicate s is bound. The pattern position is ***conditional strongly layout preserving***.

   Example:
   ```
   f(..., T ) :- ..., g(..., T),...
   ```

2. $\neg var(s)$

   (new term constructed at output position of LHS)

   a) $s \notin I_l \cup \bigcup_j O_{r_j}$

   (no similar term on input positions of LHS or output positions on RHS)

   There is no available layout information. Default values are necessary, for example, a space $lay(' ')$. The pattern position is ***not layout preserving***.

   Example:
   before layout introduction:
   ```
   f(..., NT) :- ..., g( if(B,S) , ..., NT)
   ```
   after layout introduction:

```
f(..., NT) :- ...,
     g( if( lay(' '), B, lay(' '), S ,lay(' ') ) ,..., NT)
```

b) $\exists t, u \in I_l : s \doteq u, u \subseteq t \wedge \not\exists t', u' \in O_{r_i} : s \doteq u', u' \subseteq t'$

(only appears on LHS)

   i. $\exists! u \in I_l$

   The layout information of the term in I_l can be taken. If the term with the same functor is bound to the same program, the layout is preserved. The pattern position is ***conditional strongly layout preserving***.

   ii. several $u \in I_l$

   The intention of the rewriter is not clear. Hence, one could decide between default values and layout from one of the terms in I_l. For the latter, it might be a good solution to take the layout from the term with the shortest path from the set of lexicographic ordered paths of all $t \in I_l$. The pattern position is ***weakly layout preserving***.

c) $\not\exists t, u \in I_l : s \doteq u, u \subseteq t \wedge \exists t', u' \in O_{r_i} : s \doteq u', u' \subseteq t'$

(only appears on RHS)

This should not be the case often, as terms at output positions on RHS deconstruct terms, restrict possible solutions. Layout information in the terms of O_r can be originally some of subterms of I_l, which are delegated/ changed/ traversed in inside the predicate. Hence, the copy of layout matching variables may be desired.

Example:

```
f( ..., if(B,S) ) :- ..., g(..., if(B,S)), ...
```

   i. $\exists! u' \in O_{r_i}$

   If u' contains the layout of interest, the layout can be preserved by this position. The pattern position is ***conditional strongly layout preserving***.

   ii. Otherwise,

   the intention of the rewriter is not clear. We can choose an heuristics to determine which pattern we copy the layout from. Therefore, the pattern position is ***weakly layout preserving***.

d) $\exists t, u \in I_l \wedge \exists t', u' \in O_r : s \doteq u, u \subseteq t \wedge s \doteq u', u' \subseteq t'$

(appears on both sides)

Again the intention of the rewriter is not clear. The probability that layout of term in I_l is original is higher than that of those in O_r. The latter, however, could contain original layout of a substructure of the input term, identified in some of the predicates on RHS. The predicate is ***weakly layout preserving***.

6.4.5 Remarks

The case discrimination ignores types. Hence, it might be necessary to change the type of variables that will be bound to a term enriched with layout information.

Note that even some pattern positions could be identified as *conditional strongly lay-out preserving* assumed that appearance of equal functors in argument positions means a traversal is specified, where the layout should be reused. The case discrimination tried to find subterms that could be traversed according to the same functor. This might miss the intention of the rewriter completely. See, for example, the replacement of a `switch` with only one `case`, which is rewritten as `if`-statement:

```
f(switch(Cond, stmts(case(Cond2, stmts(if(A, B), S)), empty)),
        if(eq(Cond,Cond2), stmts(if(A, B), S)) )
```

Here, it is not desired to reuse layout attached to the `if` inside of the `case` for the newly introduced `if`, but rather that of `switch`. Moreover, here we can see a second problem. With the strategy given in the case discrimination, original layout would be used twice in the result. A solution is perhaps to use counters, which ensure to use every layout term once only, and to apply strategies along the line: inner terms in results should reuse layout of inner terms in input positions, or default values.

6.5 Related Work

Other approaches support the presented cases partially only. They leave out different variables, and just allow tolerant matching, i.e., they already have lost information while binding the input information. Only layout of terms wholly bound to a variable will be preserved, see, for example, rewriting with layout [BV00] using ASF+SDF [DHK96] in the MetaEnvironment [Kli93]. Full parse trees are used during rewriting over *concrete syntax*. Thus, the addition of layout support is hidden, because the rewriter will not realise that a whitespace in his rule stands for any layout. Moreover, the introduction of (default) whitespace in newly constructed terms is done intuitively by the user who simply writes the desired code in concrete syntax taking care of the layout unconsiously. Variable productions match and are instantiated to any subtree of the same sort. Layout in the left hand side of the production is left unchanged. Bound variables keep their contained layout. All rewritten terms will loose their original layout. Any two layout nodes always match. They loose more layout than necessary in their approach. This is due to the fact that the rewriter in the above mentioned approach inserts layout implicitly by concrete syntax when rewriting terms. Consequently, default values are used too often. The given case discrimination indicates, how to restrict layout-tolerant matching, and how to find variables and layout to be reused in patterns. The problem of finding the right pattern for a traversal is solved by using traversal functions. The traversal is automatically generated, and thus it can preserve the layout. The pattern position for traversals is fixed.

The approach to layout preservation using a grammar extension is described in [Wag98]. This has also been implemented by [Wes01] for the system CobolX where signatures are generated containing a layout sort for strategies in Stratego [Vis01]. They derive signatures from grammars, plus overlays, instead of including the layout into grammar. Old (1) and new (2) rewrite rules differ, and are similar only through syntactic sugar:

```
rules D: A(v,B(e)) -> A(v,e)           (1)
rules D::A(?v,?B(e)) --> A(!v,!e)       (2)
```

Another approach is [KL03]. Parse trees are enriched with annotations, which among others can provide layout information as well as history information of the transformation so far. Additionally, access methods for annotations are provided. This is also related with origin tracking [DKT96], a method to keep track of the change during a transformation. In Chapter 5 (Publication [LR03b]) we suggested to derive automatic migration of transformation rules after a grammar extension. We demonstrated the algorithm for the introduction of layout preservation. An approach in pretty printing [Jon02, Jon03] is able to preserve old layout of the source to be pretty printed and adapted to customer specific format guidelines. Precondition for layout preserving pretty printing after a transformation is that much information on original layout is preserved by the preceding transformation already. In [Van01], several problems concerning layout preservation are discussed.

6.6 Concluding Remarks

Summary. In the chapter we investigated, what cases are interesting to automatically adapt transformation rules to preserve layout in program transformation. We focussed on traversals, i.e., we assumed that equal functors of terms on input positions and output positions mean the specification of a traversal. While other pragmatic approaches exist, this is the first attempt to analyse the possible situations more formally and to give a receipt how to modify transformation rules to support layout preservation. Pragmatic approaches can be improved using our case discrimination. We showed that, though we used a simple strategy with many restrictions, automatic introduction of layout preserving is difficult in rewriting. It is non-trivial already for traversal schemes.

We defined notions of strongly, conditional strongly and weakly layout preserving definitions and uses of predicates. These notions can be used to describe the role of a predicate in a layout preserving transformation, but they are still insufficient as a metrics.

Future work. However, there is much room for further investigation. Some cases of the discrimination appear more often than others. It is an interesting question, if a statistical analysis of rewriting behaviour can help in the adaptation of the transformation rules.

Default values are appropriate, if a determined state is desired, i.e., it is better to have values to be replaced by the use of pretty printing than to have possible wrong layout for this term. It would be interesting to examine, if there are better default values than simple whitespace, and which. Are there classes of default values depending on the syntactical category they are attached to? It might be desired that the transformation tool generates a mark indicating that a comment is not trustworthy. A programmer should always be informed about what is done with/to his program.

It is interesting to note that tolerant matching is necessary. This is the case always, where a variable is bound to a layout containing term structure. We could imagine to improve transformation rules in a way that a user gets means to describe, which part of a rule can match tolerant. What is a good way to describe it? Note that general tolerant matching for one pattern kind is insufficient, as can be seen with the approach [BV00].

The degree of layout preservation seems to depend on the complexity of rewrite rules. The smaller the transformation steps the higher the probability to increase layout preservation. Similarly, the higher the degree on automatically generated rules (e.g., traversal schemes can be generated) the higher the degree of layout preservation. These suppositions have been substantiated in a study research project [Wal07]. To measure the degree of layout preservation, a metrics is needed as well as to adapt the given notions to describe and make use of it.

Layout should belong to the formal language definition as it is part of the program. It is simply on a different level. It can be considered as an aspect of the program text. One could imagine different kinds of layouts. This leads to two further research directions. Firstly, there are different aspects in the program from the point of view of dynamic behaviour as well as different layout aspects. This leads to classes of aspects. Secondly, documentation of what a function computes, why it does this way, theoretical background for the algorithm, how the function is to be used, or a general description all form different aspects of the same problem similarly to the idea of literate programming. The program text itself can be understood simply as a description of the problem suitable for compilation. This suggests the use of XML to integrate all together. We call this multi-layered documents. Programming environments can provide the programmer with a view desired.

A problem with layout around a language construct is the assignment to where it belongs. For example, a line comment can stand after the function header or before the list of variable declaration. When declarations are moved, it is difficult to determine, whether or not the comment has to be moved, too. We propose to introduce at least guidelines for comment locations, and to adapt the creation of abstract syntax to it. We chose the guide line to take all layout before a terminal to be assigned to the grammar rule containing this terminal, hence to program parts derived from the rule. One could extend this to include layout after a terminal till the next line break, or to include lines of layout as long until there is a first empty line, for example, showing that a new kind of comment is starting. To formally associate layout to one syntactical component, the location of layout has to be defined in the grammar. Though the common approach is to adapt `A -> if B then S` to `A -> L1 if L2 B then L3 S`, we came to the conclusion that `A -> L1 if B' then S'`, `B' -> L2 B` and `S' -> L3 B` describes better the intended location. However, this results in an even more difficult adaptation of the transformation rules along the lines of Chapters 4 and 5.

A research issue is also, what means we can offer to the rewriter to aid in layout preservation without bothering him too much with the secondary aspect. An example is the order of the arguments in a predicate to say which will be preferred for layout preservation.

It is necessary to research for functionality to control the use of layout unobtrusive in a rewrite rule. An approach can be to use the given case discrimination as default approach, and give the rewriter a means to overwrite where appropriate. A resulting question is, how can we avoid to force the rewriter to use two different representations of patterns (one with, one without layout patterns). Also, we think it is possible to describe the layout introduction for chosen rules in a separate modul. This would allow for experiments with different layout preservation behaviour without risking the introduction of errors in already written rules. Can a layout strategy perhaps be described abstractly (without mixed patterns)? Maybe there are some typical reuse patterns, which could be named and activated by name.

The next steps are to experiment with different object languages (transformation on programs of different languages) and compare the similarity of layout preserved results.

An important question is, how to preserve layout in patterns, which have different functors, i.e., in rules other than traversal schemes. Can one derive such information somehow? How can the rewriter give additional information without being bothered too much with this aspect. Furthermore, we are interested in how we can measure the quality of layout preservation, and investigate ideas to increase reasoning for layout.

Chapter 7

Aspect-Oriented Prolog in a Language Processing Context

Language processors can be derived from logic grammars. This chapter demonstrates that several concerns in the processor such as parsing, several kinds of analysis, or transformations, can be specified as aspects of the logic grammar. For that purpose, we bring the concepts of aspect-oriented programming to Prolog in a systematic way, based on established Prolog technology. We illustrate that typical Prolog programming techniques can be described as generic aspects and provided in a library to support reusable concerns. A DSL is developed to improve readability of the aspect-oriented specifications.

7.1 Introduction

Separation of concerns in language descriptions is desirable just as well as in any other software artefact to improve understanding and maintenance. As language descriptions are the base for derived language processors those immediately profit from modularity. Besides maintenance, also experiments with different variants of a language and a corresponding implementation are facilitated.

For that purpose, we combine aspect-oriented programming (AOP) with Prolog to enable descriptions of different concerns in a logic grammar in a modular way, allowing a better construction of language processors from a software engineering point of view.

7.1.1 Motivation: Modularisation for Logic Grammars

Prolog and language processing. Prolog is generally suited for prototyping. It is also very suitable for language processing and related problems [Rie91, Paa91, LR01, CH87, War80, BP89, SK94]. Due to its facilities for symbolic term manipulation, Prolog is particularly suited for the phases of language processing which can be performed at the level of abstract representations. It is well established that logic programs are well-suited to describe analysis, evaluation and transformation of abstract representations. Additionally, Prolog programs are structured grammar-like. This simplifies representations of grammars including attribute grammars. Thus, language processing can be mapped easily to Prolog.

Logic grammars. It is very easy to derive interpreters from logic grammars [LR01]. A logic grammar (as described in [LR01]) is a Prolog program where predicates represent nonterminals and terminals are represented by strings or are constructs especially marked by operators. When these operators are interpreted as predicates consuming lexemes, Prolog's evaluation mechanism immediately provides a recursive descent parser with backtracking already included. Logic grammars are interesting because transformations on grammars are conventional meta-programs on Prolog programs, which is natural in Prolog. In contrast to definite clause grammars [PW80] their external and internal representation do not differ. This simplifies treatment of grammars in several transformation steps. Logic grammars can easily be extended with semantics by adding variables and other predicates which, when deriving a prototype interpreter, perform several kinds of analysis or other tasks in a language processor. This resembles defining a language using attribute grammars. A logic grammar can then be considered as a special kind of attribute grammar. The strong relationship between Prolog and attribute grammars has been discussed in [DM93, RL88, DM85].

Crosscutting in language processing. Usually, there are different concerns in a logic grammar, e.g., construction of abstract syntax trees, type checking, analysis, several transformations, code generation, scanner integration, and pretty printing. Their descriptions are scattered along the grammar and tangled with each other. This obfuscates the context-free part of the grammar. Unfortunately, separate examination and change of each concern is not possible. Relying on just common modularisation concepts (clauses, predicates, and modules) it is impossible to implement these concerns separately. Instead, meta-programming or a computation in several phases is necessary. The inherent relation between concerns, independent from their implementation, is called *crosscutting*. Moreover, we would like to add the concerns in a stepwise enhancement manner. Therefore, it should be possible to switch concerns on or off easily or to replace them with alternative versions for experiments. Manipulating those concerns manually is error-prone. Additionally, maintainability is decreased as changes in modular units and in added concerns can influence each other and might have to be implemented manually, which again is error-prone. Furthermore, the implementation of crosscutting concerns is hardly reusable.

Aspect-oriented programming. Aspect-oriented programming (AOP) [KLM+97b, AFCE04] addresses modularisation of crosscutting concerns providing *aspects* as a new concept. Aspects are modules containing crosscutting expressions (pointcut descriptions, advice) encapsulating the described concern in one place. Aspects can be added to and removed from the program and are reusable components that can be composed with other components. The places where modules can be affected at runtime, are called *join points*. The kind of place determines the *kind of join point*. Corresponding points in the program text are called *join point shadows*. A *join point model* defines all possible join points, from which subsets – so called *pointcuts* – can be chosen to associate *advice*, i.e., additional program code. Pointcuts are specified using a *pointcut description* (a predicate, which quantifies join points). The same advice can be associated with more than one join point.

Also, more than one advice can be added at the same join point. A further central concept of AOP is the *weaver*, which transforms the descriptions with their associated advice and the original program into a woven program implementing the crosscutting. The moment of weaving – at compile time, run-time or a mixed form – influences the instance of AOP due to the available information.

AOP for logic grammars. The concerns given above can be seen as aspects of language descriptions respectively language processing. Further aspects in language descriptions are discussed elsewhere, e.g., layout preservation [LR03b] and debugging [WGRM05]. We apply the concepts of AOP to separate these concerns. As logic grammars are Prolog programs, this means providing AOP in Prolog itself. AOP lifts typical meta-programming tasks to language description level. Advantages that come with this approach are a modular description of different aspects in a grammar (hence, also in the derived language processor) and beyond it a formalisation of typical programming techniques by generic aspects allowing to describe reusable aspects such as parser construction. This formalisation furthermore leads to a disciplined procedure for stepwise enhancement in comparison to earlier approaches.

7.1.2 Overview on Key Concepts in the Chapter

In the chapter we demonstrate how scanner integration, abstract syntax tree construction, several kinds of analysis, and transformation in a language processor can be described as aspects of a logic grammar (see more details in Section 7.2). We provide a three level framework:

1. At the first level, the basic concepts of AOP are defined for Prolog in Prolog using Prolog syntax and semantics (Laola - Logic aspect-oriented language), and therefore we make use of established Prolog technology such as logic variables, the port model, and hooks to modify programs at load-time. Base is the control flow as described by an extended port model (see Figure 7.1 and Section 7.4.1 for an explanation). Goals and clauses are *Join point shadows*. They are represented as boxes in the port model. The ports in the port model are *Join points* with the kind of a port determining the *kind of join point*. This allows to place advice at desired points of execution, e.g., at failure or matching. There are three kinds of advice. *Port advice* is Prolog code to be attached at any port of the port model. *Around advice* is Prolog code which replaces or surrounds a box from the port model. *Term advice* describes a transformation on terms representing goals or clauses. *Pointcuts* are sets of join points. *Pointcut descriptions* are predicates quantifying join points. Patterns are used to denote sets of join points implicitly by addressing goals and clauses (i.e., the join point shadows of ports). Furthermore, pointcut descriptions can restrict the set of join points by additionally given properties of goals and clauses. The kind of join point is chosen by the advice. *Aspects* in this approach are grouping mechanisms for pointcuts and advice.

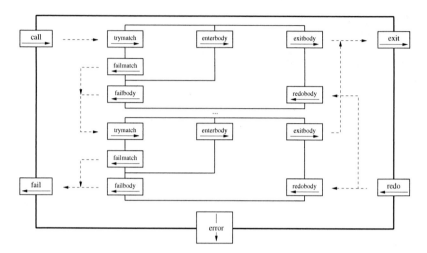

Figure 7.1   Extended port model of the IF/Prolog-Tracer. The outer goal box contains two clause boxes. Possible control flows are visualised by arrows.

A very important concept is the use of *pointcut contexts* of goals and clauses to exchange information between aspects and program code using logic variables. The use of logic variables supports communication between aspects and core concerns. A *weaver*, also provided as a logic program, weaves Prolog advice code at compile-time. It can also be easily integrated at load-time by common mechanisms such as `term_expansion`. A typical weaving transformation, such as weaving advice to the end of a clause (`exitbody` port), looks as follows (more details in Section 7.4.6):

$$p(X_1, \ldots, X_n) \leftarrow Body. \quad \overset{\text{exitbody}}{\leadsto} \quad p(X_1, \ldots, X_n) \leftarrow Body, Advice.$$

The above means the clause is extended with the advice at the end of the body. Other possible places are all ports in Figure 7.1, allowing a very fine-grained control over execution of Prolog programs. Section 7.4 discusses this level in detail.

2. The second level is formed by a library of generic aspects including, for example, `token/1`, `parser/1` or `traverse/1`. Generic aspects may contain generic pointcuts and are used to abstract typical Prolog programming techniques like `calculate`, `accumulate`, and `build`, making them independent of a particular skeleton. Generic aspects form the basis for construction of language processors, e.g., `build` to construct abstract syntax trees. The description of generic aspects is illustrated by the example of the `calculate`-technique in Section 7.5.

3. For easier use and understanding, the DSL Swell is provided being syntactic sugar for Laola for describing aspects. Section 7.6 discusses its systematic development and gives an informal mapping to Laola by example.

7.1.3 Remainder of the Chapter

Section 7.2 demonstrates how an example language processor can be achieved using aspects of a logic grammar. Next, we introduce a very simple running example in Section 7.3, which forms the basis for a detailed description of AOP in Prolog in Section 7.4. Section 7.5 exemplifies the specification of generic aspects for the aspect library. In Section 7.6, a DSL is described, before the chapter ends with related work and some concluding remarks in Section 7.7 and 7.8.

7.2 Aspects in Grammars for Language Processors - a Motivating Example

This section illustrates the use of AOP to describe concerns in a simple language processor example (taken from [LR01]) to eliminate dead `let`-assignments in programs of a simple expression language (cf. Figure 7.2) in a modular way. First, we start with the logic grammar, from which the language processor is derived manually. Subsequently, we describe the processor (and the dead `let` removal) again, this time modularly using aspects based on generic aspects from an aspect library while giving examples for the AOP concepts in our approach.

7.2.1 Grammar Example and a Derived Parser

```
Task:   let a = 1 in let b = 2 in  a + 3    ⟹    let a = 1 in a + 3
```

```
exp :- sexp.                         sexp :- nat.          uop :- "-".
exp :- sexp, bop, exp.               sexp :- id.           bop :- "+".
exp :- "let", id, "=", exp, "in", exp.  sexp :- uop, exp.  bop :- "-".
```

Figure 7.2 A logic grammar is the starting point for derived language processors.

Figure 7.2 shows a logic grammar for a simple `let`-expression language as a starting point. `id` and `nat` are lexeme classes for identifiers and naturals, respectively. Strings mark keywords. Due to the evaluation order in Prolog we achieve a recursive descent parser (with potential infinite look-ahead) immediately when lexeme classes and keywords are replaced by a predicate `get_token/1` responsible for tokenising the input. The predicate is provided by different scanners in our system called Laptob [LR01]. The result of adding `get_token/1` around keywords and lexemes is given in Figure 7.3. From an

AOP perspective, lexeme classes and keywords represent join point shadows of interesting join points.

```
exp :- sexp.
exp :- sexp, bop, exp.
exp :- get_token(kw("let")), get_token(id(Id)),
                  get_token(kw("=")), exp, get_token(kw("in")), exp.
...
```

Figure 7.3   Result: Keywords and lexeme classes need to be scanned.

The next step is to add the construction of abstract syntax trees (AST). Therefore, we add a parameter to each nonterminal (predicate). The first parameter of the nonterminals represents the corresponding AST; particularly the nonterminals on the left-hand side of a rule define the construction of an AST. At the same time we collect variables not used in let-expressions in a second parameter of the nonterminals. They can be used in a later traversal to eliminate dead let expressions. See Figure 7.4 for the resulting parser. Adding further tasks, e.g., type-checking and code generation, becomes increasingly tedious and error-prone.

```
exp(SExp, FreeSExp) :- sexp(SExp, FreeSExp).
exp(bop(Bop, Exp1, Exp2), Free) :-
  sexp(Exp1, Free1), bop(Bop), exp(Exp2, Free2),
                  union(Free1, Free2, Free).
exp(let(id(Id), Exp1, Exp2), Free) :-
  get_token(kw("let")), get_token(id(Id)), get_token(kw("=")),
  exp(Exp1, Free1), get_token(kw("in")),  exp(Exp2, Free2),
                  ( select(Id, Free2, Free3) ;  Free2=Free3   ),
                  union(Free1, Free3, Free).

sexp(nat(A), [])    :- get_token(nat(A)).
sexp(id(Id), [Id]) :- get_token(id(Id)).
sexp(uop(Uop, Exp), FreeExp) :- uop(Uop), exp(Exp, FreeExp).

uop(minus) :- get_token(kw("-")).
bop(plus)  :- get_token(kw("+")).    bop(minus) :- get_token(kw("-")).
```

Figure 7.4   Result: Parsing, AST construction, and determination of free variables.

7.2.2 Scanner Integration is a Concern

Viewing Figure 7.3 from an AOP perspective, it can be seen that the predicate get_-token/1 is tangled within the grammar. It corresponds to around advice (see Section 7.4.4), which is placed to all interesting join points. We add the scanner concern by instantiating two generic aspects from the aspect library.

1. `token/1` marks points in the grammar where lexemes are to be consumed, i.e., keywords and lexeme classes, and

2. `parser/1` employs `token/1` and binds the scanner via around advice to these places using the predicate `get_token/1` with the expected token.

To apply the generic `parser` aspect, information is needed about concrete lexeme classes. The desired join points form a set - the corresponding pointcut. The `parser` expects the definition of the pointcut `lexeme`. We define it by aspect `let` to describe appearances of lexeme classes, i.e., every appearance of goals `nat` and `id` belong to this set (Figure 7.5). Note that keywords do not need to be included as their form is known (a string in the gram-

---
Aspect `let`
  Define Pointcut `lexeme` :
      `goal(nat), goal(id)`

Figure 7.5 The pointcut `lexeme` describes positions to scan lexeme classes.

mar) and they are already addressed by the pointcut of aspect `token/1`. Instantiating the generic `parser` aspect by aspect `let` is done at weave-time using a weaver specification (Figure 7.6).

Weave   `% Instantiate`
  `parser(let)`   `% generic aspect 'parser'`
  into   `% with aspect 'let'`
  `'grammar/let.pl'`   `% in program of file 'let.pl'`
  yielding   `% and store the result`
  `'programs/letparser.pl'`   `% in file 'letparser.pl'`

Figure 7.6 Weaving scanner integration into the grammar using a specialised parser aspect.

7.2.3 AST Construction while Parsing is a Concern

Similarly, we consider the first argument of predicates for construction of an AST in Figure 7.4 as an aspect for the logic grammar from Figure 7.2. The logic grammar provides two kinds of rules: recursive rules, where a part of the AST is constructed from substructures, and initial rules where leaves of the AST are created. An aspect for AST construction has to add term construction to all clauses contributing to an AST.

The specification of the aspect `ast` as given in Figure 7.7 is based on the generic aspect `build/3` from the aspect library, which implements the build-technique from [SK93] while abstracting from the concrete skeleton. The build-technique is a design pattern in Prolog for building term structures along the control-flow. New parameter positions are added to predicates for collecting substructures, and a new goal is inserted to combine them. The parameters of the generic `build/3` aspect need to be instantiated. We choose a the aspect name `ast`, the name of the aspect which addresses the lexeme classes (`let`), and a list of nonterminals involved in the construction (`exp`, `sexp`, etc., line 2). Furthermore, the aspect contains generic pointcut descriptions to classify two kinds of clauses:

- in build-clauses a structure is constructed from substructures (here, we will construct an AST), and

- in init-clauses leaves are created (terminals in our example).

These generic pointcuts need also to be instantiated to describe where individual advice are to be placed for construction. The first argument points to nonterminals defined by the clause, whereas the other arguments point to substructures, nonterminals not contributing to the construction, lexemes, or keywords of the clause body in order of appearance in the clause body. Finally, the last argument denotes the structure to be constructed.

```
1   Aspect      ast
2     requires  build(ast, let, [exp, sexp, uop, bop])
3     TermAdvice
4         Pointcut: build_clause(exp, "let", Id, "=", Exp1, "in", Exp2, Exp)
5         Advice  : unify (Exp, let(Id, Exp1, Exp2))
6
7         Pointcut: build_clause(exp, Exp1, Bop, Exp2, Exp)
8         Advice  : unify(Exp, bop(Bop, Exp1, Exp2))
9         ...
10        Pointcut: init_clause(bop, "+", Bop)
11        Advice  : unify(Bop, plus)
```

Figure 7.7   Description of AST construction for `let`-Expressions using the generic aspect `build` from the library (`build/3` implements the build-technique using AOP).

The generic pointcuts are instantiated for build- and init-clauses (lines 4,7,10). Here, the kind of advice is term advice, which performs a term manipulation on goals and clauses addressed by pointcuts, i.e., AST construction. For example, a clause for `exp` is addressed, where a structure is created using `Exp` (4). The associated advice creates the term `let(Id, Exp1, Exp2)` and unifies it with `Exp` (5).

7.2.4 Program Analysis is a Concern

An analysis of unused variables can be described by aspect `free` (Figure 7.8). Again, we utilise the generic aspect `build/3` to construct the set of variables not used in `let`-expressions.

For this purpose, we want to add new code at the end of recursive clauses in the logic grammar. Hence, the generic pointcut `build_clause` is instantiated to address building

```
 1  Aspect free
 2    requires  build(free, let, [exp, sexp])
 3    PortAdvice
 4      Pointcut:
 5        build_clause(exp, "let", id(Id), "=", Free1, "in", Free2, Free)
 6      Advice at exitbody :
 7        ( select(Id, Free2, Free3); Free2=Free3),
 8        union(Free1, Free3, Free)
 9
10      Pointcut: build_clause(exp, Free1, bop, Free2, Free)
11      Advice at exitbody : union(Free1, Free2, Free)
12
13    TermAdvice
14      Pointcut: build_clause(exp, FreeSExp, Free)
15      Advice : unify(Free, FreeSExp)
16      . . .
```

Figure 7.8 Generic build and its pointcuts are instantiated to describe the construction of program analysis for unused variables.

clauses of interest, e.g., the rule for `let`. We provide port advice for adding new Prolog code to ports (i.e., the join points). To evaluate code at the desired point in the execution, positioning of code is based on the port model (cf. Section 7.4.1). This allows port advice to be at `call`, `exit`, `fail`, or, as in our example, at the `exitbody` port, i.e., code to be evaluated before exiting the clause. In Figure 7.8, we add code to collect unused variables at the end of the recursive clause for `exp` (lines 6-8, 11, 15). A term advice can be used (13-15) to describe a simple copy of values by unifying the variable names (cf. second arguments in Figure 7.4, first rule). Note that in our approach the kind of join point to be used is specified by the advice specification.

7.2.5 Program Transformation Based on a Generic Aspect traverse/1

A program transformation can also be described as an aspect. The aspect library provides a generic aspect `traverse/1`, which removes predicates representing keywords and lexeme classes. When the aspect for AST construction is added, it describes a complete traversal of the AST. The aspect will be instantiated by the program transformation aspect.

The aspect `edl` in Figure 7.9 describes a transformation, which eliminates those `let`-assignments of variables not used in an expression (e.g., `'let b = 2 in'`). It is based on the aspect `free` and instantiates the generic `build` aspect to construct the AST along the logic grammar from Figure 7.2. A new pointcut `eliminate` is defined (3), which addresses building clauses defining `let`-expressions. It is used to place port advice at the end of a clause body addressed by the pointcut removing an unnecessary `let`-assignment.

Properties of goals and clauses, here the pointcut context, are used to restrict the set of identified join points. Simplified, a context is a list of pointcuts (for more detail, see Sec-

```
1   Aspect edl
2     requires  free, build(edl, let, [exp, sexp, uop, bop])
3     Define Pointcut eliminate(FreeVars, Id, Exp1, Exp2, Exp) :
4       Any
5       where
6         parallel context contains
7                   build_clause(exp, "let", Id, "=", Exp1, "in", Exp2, Exp)
8               of aspect edl
9         first left context contains
10                  struct(exp, FreeVars) of aspect free
11    PortAdvice
12    Pointcut: eliminate(FreeVars, Id, Exp1, Exp2, Exp)
13    Advice at exitbody
14        member(Id, FreeVars) -> Exp = let(Id, Exp1, Exp2) ; Exp = Exp2
15        ...
```

Figure 7.9 Aspect edl: Describing removal of dead lets based on a generic aspect traverse/1 similar to parser/1.

tion 7.4). The role of the context is two-fold: It can be used to restrict the set of join points belonging to the pointcut. But more importantly, it establishes communication between pointcuts, and thus between advice. In Figure 7.9 the first property (6-8) means: 'the join point shadow has pointcut `build_clause` of aspect `edl` in its parallel context'. The parallel context contains pointcuts addressing the same goal or clause. The pointcut `build_clause` is described as part of the generic aspect `build` instantiated by aspect `edl`. Pointcut `struct/2` is defined by another instance of aspect `build` used by aspect `free` (10) and refers to the structure built by this aspect, i.e., the set of unused variables in the last sub-expression. The pointcut `eliminate` combines information of both pointcuts, which is then used by the port advice (12) to decide whether the `let`-expression is necessary.

7.2.6 A Note on Description Size

Our description of aspects in the previous example may seem too large compared to the result. However, the reader should note:

- When extending the grammar to a larger more realistic one, the aspect descriptions may grow slower. Only relevant clauses need to be treated with advice. Some pointcuts are reused. This depends on the specific concern. For example, it is in the nature of AST construction that it nearly doubles the grammar.

- An important advantage, however, is the modular description. This allows development of the grammar / language processor by stepwise enhancement, which is an accepted engineering method. Also, it includes separate maintenance and avoids bugs by manual editing in unreadable code, when more concerns are added. Moreover, aspects can be switched on/off without modifying the code. This allows to use the debugging aspect when needed only or to experiment with several implementations of the concerns. Different choices for aspects support experimenting with different variants of a language processor.

- Additionally, places of interest are defined using a property-based approach as opposed to the use of unique selectors (e.g., marked by programmer given tags). Thus, the aspect can take future Prolog code into account or modules of other programmers. Goals and clauses are addressed, as long as they possess the required properties. For example, the extension of the grammar by new rules would not require a change in the scanner integration (if no new lexeme classes are added). This is even more interesting for other Prolog programs, as pointcuts are defined property-based and will catch join points the programmer does not know yet.

7.3 A Simple Running Example

In the previous section, we have discussed how parts of a language processor can be described modularly as aspects in the grammar. In this section, we introduce the very simple example $list \rightarrow list|\epsilon$, which will be used in Section 7.4 to explain the representation of aspect-oriented concepts in Prolog in detail.

7.3.1 Computations on Lists

Many computations along the grammar are similar and can be introduced in a systematic manner by applying *techniques* [SK93], which can be considered as design patterns in Prolog. For example, the generic `build`-aspect implemented in the library is the most used technique in the language processor context for building structures.

A simple example of a technique is the `calculate`-technique to add values and their computation along a skeleton, i.e., the initial situation before the next enhancement is applied. (Note, instead of values an AST could be constructed.) Figure 7.10 (b)-(d) depict Prolog programs, which are results of extending Figure 7.10 (a), renaming and merging them. They work similarly as different phases/ aspects in a language processor. Figure 7.10 (b) is the result of extending the basic structure by the summation of elements (changes are underlined). Figure 7.10 (c) shows that another result can be achieved based on the same skeleton. Figure 7.10 (d) gives an example how different "phases" are woven together (this corresponds to the loop optimisation problem used in [KLM+97b] to introduce AOP concepts).

7.3.2 Aspect-Oriented Description of sumlist

Using aspects we will describe how to add code to achieve the step from Figure 7.10 (a) to (b). As we will discuss at the technical level in Section 7.4, we give the basic Prolog representation of the aspect (Figure 7.11).

The pointcut `sum` (2-3) addresses all goals and clauses in the skeleton which ought to be affected by the summation aspect. Every such appearance is renamed to `sumlist`

```
 1   (a)                              (b)
 2   list([]).                        sumlist([] , Sum) :- Sum is 0.
 3   list([H|T])                      sumlist([H|T], Sum)
 4       :- list(T).                      :- sumlist(T , TSum)
 5                                         , Sum is TSum + H.
 6   (c)                              (d)
 7   listlen([], Len)                 sumlistlen([] , Sum , Len)
 8       :- Len is 0.                     :- Sum is 0, Len is 0.
 9   listlen([H|T], Len)              sumlistlen([H|T], Sum, Len)
10       :- listlen(T, TLen)              :- sumlistlen(T , TSum , TLen),
11         , Len is TLen + 1.             Sum is TSum + H
12                                         , Len is TLen + 1.
```

Figure 7.10   Computations on a list skeleton

```
 1   %        Pattern,           Context, Aspect, PC name
 2   pointcut(clause(list(L), Body),   C, sumlist, sum(Sum)).
 3   pointcut(goal(list(L)),           C, sumlist, sum(Sum)).
 4
 5   %          Aspect    Pointcut       Advice (term transformation)
 6   term_advice(sumlist, sum(Sum),     rename(sumlist)).
 7   term_advice(sumlist, sum(Sum),     extra_args([Sum], last)).
 8
 9   %   -    -    -    -    -    -    -    -    -    -
10   pointcut(clause(list([]), _),   C, sumlist, init_clause(Sum))
11    :-      context(C, parallel,     sumlist, sum(Sum)).
12
13   %          Aspect    Pointcut       Port        Code
14   port_advice(sumlist, init_clause(Sum), exitbody) :- Sum is 0.
15
16   %   -    -    -    -    -    -    -    -    -    -
17   pointcut(clause(list([H|_]), _), C, sumlist, rec_clause(H, TSum, Sum))
18    :-      context(C, parallel,       sumlist, sum(Sum)),
19            context(C, left(first),    sumlist, sum(TSum)).
20
21   port_advice(sumlist, rec_clause(H, TSum, Sum), exitbody)
22    :-      Sum is TSum+H.
```

Figure 7.11   Pointcut and advice of aspect `sumlist` to sum up the elements of a list

(6) and gets an extra argument using term advice (7). Next, code for initialisation of the computation is added (using port advice) at the end of the body (port exitbody) of the initialisation clause (14) for the list traversal, which is addressed by pointcut `init_-clause` (10). Finally, the code for summation is added at the end of recursive list clauses, again using port advice (21). The necessary values are provided via logic variables being arguments of the pointcut `rec_clause`. The pointcut examines the pointcut context of the current clause to refer to the pointcut `sum` addressing the same clause (18), and to the pointcut addressing a preceding goal in the computation for intermediate results (19). Values are passed using logic variables, which are arguments of pointcuts. Note that matching of the structure of the arguments is done at weave time. Thus, `init_clause` (10) addresses only the first clause (2) in Figure 7.10.

7.4 Representing Concepts of AOP in Prolog - Level 1

In this section we discuss how in our approach the concepts of aspect-oriented programming are represented in Prolog and show how they can be specified by the user. The notation is code-named Laola (Logic aspect-oriented language). The basis for Laola is the operational semantics of Prolog (i.e., the procedural interpretation of Horn clauses), and the port model from Figure 7.1, which will be explained in the following section.

7.4.1 Control Flow in Prolog and Join points

Intuitively, the aim is to attach additional program code at desired places in the program to affect the execution in some way. This requires an understanding of the control flow. To describe and understand that of Prolog port models are used. The ports are the join points in our approach. The kind of kind of port advice is placed to is determined by the advice description.

We use the fine-grained port model borrowed from IF/Prolog [Sie99] given in Figure 7.1. It is an extension of that presented by Byrd [Byr80], which has been used as basis for the implementation of Prolog tracers. The main difference between our approach and the Byrd model is the distinction of two kinds of boxes for goals and for clauses extended by an *error* port (which is passed when an exception is raised). Ports to enter and leave a box representing a goal correspond to those in the Byrd model. Note that we need the ports of clauses, too, e.g., to add advice to a single clause of a predicate.

For completeness, we summarise the control flow. If such a goal box is entered by the *call* port, a corresponding clause box is created inside of the goal box for each clause of the treated predicate. When evaluating the actual goal, those clause boxes can be entered/left through different ports. To unify the actual goal with the clause head the first clause box is entered via the *trymatch* port. If the head and actual goal are not unifiable, it is left through the *failmatch* port and the next clause box is evaluated. Otherwise, the clause body is entered through the *enterbody* port.

In the clause body, goal boxes of subgoals are evaluated successively to satisfy the actual goal. The goal boxes created inside of the clause body are predetermined by the clause used and the unification of the actual goal with the clause head. If the subgoals were successful, the clause box is left through the *exitbody* port and the surrounding goal box is left through the *exit* port. Otherwise, the clause box is left via the *failbody* port, and the next clause is evaluated for the actual goal.

If the last clause box within a goal box is left through the *failmatch* or *failbody* port, the actual goal fails, and the surrounding goal box is left through the *fail* port. If the goal box is entered through the *redo* port, the clause box most recently left through an *exitbody* port is re-entered through the *redobody* port. Inside the clause box the last subgoal is entered again by the *redo* port implementing the backtracking.

7.4.2 Pointcuts and Pointcut Descriptions

Pointcuts are sets of join points (i.e., sets of ports). In our setting, a pointcut can be denoted by a possibly parameterised name and is associated with an aspect. Join points are quantified implicitly by denoting goals and clauses in the program text, and thus specifying the corresponding ports. The set can be restrained by additional properties of these goals and clauses. The kind of join point (kind of port) the advice is placed to is determined by the advice. We will say a goal or a clause is addressed by a pointcut when we mean a goal or a clause which has at least one of its ports in the pointcut.

As natural for Prolog, pointcuts are specified using a predicate. Thus, the pointcut description is a set of clauses of the form $\text{pointcut}(P, C, A, N) \leftarrow G_1, \ldots, G_n$, where P is a pattern for goals and clauses, C is a term representation of the context of the addressed goals and clauses, A is a term denoting the aspect the pointcut belongs to, N is a term denoting the name of the pointcut, and G_i are goals describing additional properties of the goals and clauses.

Patterns are needed for both, goals and clauses. This allows to address, e.g., a special single appearance of a goal or to choose one alternative clause to add advice at a corresponding port. Note that only static information is available before run-time. Each appearing atomic goal $p(X_1, \ldots, X_n)$ can be denoted by $\text{goal}(p(X_1, \ldots, X_n))$. Each clause $p(X_1, \ldots, X_n) \leftarrow G_1, \ldots, G_m$ can be denoted by $\text{clause}(p(X_1, \ldots, X_n), (G_1, \ldots, G_m))$. Using variables several program points can be described at once. For example, `goal(list(X))` includes every occurrence of a goal `list/1`. The pattern `clause(list([H |_]), _)` denotes all clauses of predicate `list/1`, where the clause head separates a list in head H and some tail (Figure 7.10 (a) line (3)). Facts can be treated as clauses with body `true`. Composite goals, goals as arguments of meta-predicates, queries, and whole modules have not been included for simplicity. However, they could be treated similarly or simulated using aspects.

Properties are used to restrain the set of join points. The property-based selection is more general and more insusceptible to adding new modules in contrast to unique selectors. A special property pertains to the pointcut context. The context of a given goal or clause consists of special pointcuts containing join points corresponding to goals and clauses from the neighbourhood of the given goal or clause. This is discussed in the next section.

A possible parameter for the pointcut name can refer to data from the goal or clause, to data from the context of the goal or clause, and/or to temporary variables used for intermediate results to support communication between join points with program code to be introduced by the weaver.

The pointcut descriptions in Figure 7.11 specify places of interest in Figure 7.10 (a): `sum` contains join points marking goals and clauses of `list/1` to be renamed and get a parameter added to, `init_clause` those to add an initialisation, and `rec_clause` those to add a summation. Also, the pointcut names have arguments to provide data to be used in advice, e.g., `rec_clause` summarises the head of the list of the actual clause line (17), the intermediate result `TSum` (19), and the final result `Sum` (18). The port advice in line (21) accesses those arguments to determine the advice to be added.

A given pointcut description can also be interpreted more procedurally to determine all pointcuts given join point belong to. Let P be a goal or clause corresponding to a join point J and C the context of P. Then $\mathrm{pc}(P, C) := \{(N, A)|\mathrm{pointcut}(P, C, A, N)\}$ denotes all pointcuts containing J represented by pairs of their names together with the name of the aspect they are related with. (Patterns are possible.) This interpretation is the basis for the weaving process.

7.4.3 Pointcut Context

The pointcut context of a goal contains pointcuts which address goals preceding (and including) the actual goal and the surrounding clause; that of a clause contains pointcuts of goals in the body and that of the addressing clause. As pointcuts are described based on goals and clauses, it is also the pointcut context of their corresponding join points.

Context specification can be used to restrict the set of join points belonging to a certain pointcut or to having a desired pointcut in their context. Much more important, the context is necessary to establish communication between several pointcuts, e.g., to have access to intermediate results of a preceding goal in the computation. Each given clause to specify a pointcut influences the context of the addressed goal, the context of goals following the goal addressed, the context of a clause which contains the addressed goal or which is addressed itself. As depicted in Figure 7.12 for goals, the context C of a program point P (a goal or a clause) consists of the parallel context, the parent context, and the left context, i.e., $C = (\mathrm{context}_{||}(P, C), \mathrm{context}_p(P, C), \mathrm{context}_l(P, C))$. Note that the definition is a recurrent one. The determination of the context is a task to be performed by the weaver. We represent contexts as lists. This allows the introduction of a 'kind of distance' between join points in the context (hence, between goals), which can be used for searching the context later on in accordance with operational semantics of Prolog.

Parallel context.

The set of pointcuts addressing the same program point P (i.e., goal or clause) we name the parallel context of P, denoted by $\mathrm{context}_{||}(P, C) := \mathrm{pc}(P, C)$. The parallel context is used, for example, to combine information of pointcuts addressing the same goal.

In the clause for the empty list (pointcut `init_clause`) of Figure 7.10 (a), we want to initialise a variable. The variable has to be identical to the one added for `sum` at the

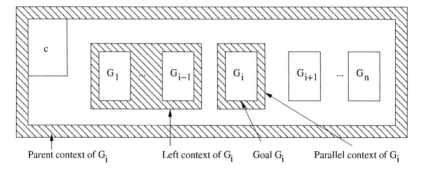

Figure 7.12   Parallel, parent, and left context of a goal G_i in a clause c

same clause. Here, sum is in the parallel context of the clause,
i.e., [(sum(Sum),sumlist),(init_clause(Sum),sumlist)].

Parent context.

Sometimes it is necessary to consider the clause, which surrounds the actual goal, e.g.,
to inspect whether a recursive goal is denoted. Pointcuts, which address boxes enclosing the actual goal form the parent context. Let $c : H \leftarrow G_1, \ldots, G_n$ be a clause of
a Prolog program, G_i an arbitrary atomic goal occurring in the body of c. The par-
ent context of c is denoted by $\mathrm{context_p}(c, \_) := []$, and for G_i by $\mathrm{context_p}(G_i, C) :=$
$[\mathrm{context_{||}}(c, C)]$. If the whole clause is addressed there is no parent context as there is no
information about the dynamic context of this clause. Otherwise, the context is formed
by the parallel context of the clause. For example, for the recursive goal list/1 it
is [(sum(Sum),sumlist),(rec_clause(Sum),sumlist)] (though it is un-
needed for the example).

Left context.

The left context of a clause is determined by all contexts of all goals in a clause. The
left context of a goal is determined by all contexts of all goals left of the addressed goal.
Let $c : H \leftarrow G_1, \ldots, G_n$ be a clause of a Prolog program, G_i an arbitrary atomic goal
occurring in the body of c. The left context of c respectively G_i is defined as

$$\mathrm{context_l}(c, C) := \begin{cases} [] & , \ n = 0 \\ \mathrm{context_{||}}(G_n, C).\mathrm{context_l}(G_n, C) & , \ n > 0 \end{cases}$$

$$\mathrm{context_l}(G_i, C) := \begin{cases} [] & , \ i = 1 \\ \mathrm{context_{||}}(G_{i-1}, C).\mathrm{context_l}(G_{i-1}, C) & , \ 1 < i \leq n \end{cases}$$

Here, · represents list concatenation. The organisation in lists allows the specification of
the distance to the actual goal. The context is left-oriented due to the operational semantics

of Prolog. A right context is not necessary, as the reference between the actual goal and one rightwards could be achieved by using the left context of the goal to the right. The left context allows the reuse of intermediate results of already evaluated goals in predicates.

In the example of Figure 7.10, we want to add the summation `Sum is TSum + H` in the neighbourhood of the recursive call `list(T,TSum)` (up to renaming, which is also done using `sum`). The recursive goal is denoted by a join point contained in `sum`. This pointcut can be found by searching the left context (`[(sum(TSum),sumlist)]`). Note, the order of pointcuts is relevant for determination of certain pointcuts.

The use of context in pointcut specifications.

Context can be given explicitly as a term. For example, (`[[(a,m),(b,n)],[],[]]`) denotes a context which contains two pointcuts a and b addressing the same join point shadow (parallel context). However, using terms is very difficult and very restrictive. Note that the context possibly contains many pointcuts not known to the programmer, e.g., through adding aspects from a library. Hence, the context is investigated using the predefined predicate $context(+C, +K, -A, -N)$, where C is the context, K specifies the kind of context, which has to be investigated, A is the name of the aspect the pointcut belongs to, and N is the name of the pointcut. Possible values for K are `parallel` for the parallel context, `inside` for the parent context, and `left` for the left context. The depth of the search can be controlled with arguments to K (not for parallel contexts). For example, `first` looks for the next pointcut in the context, `near` searches until the first matching pointcut, and `all` looks for all alternatives. There is no restriction for further arguments. The predicate has to be provided by the weaver and allows to abstract from uninteresting pointcuts in the context.

The example in Figure 7.11 uses a specification of pointcuts for describing an aspect `sumlist` to sum up all elements of a list. First, the pointcut `sum` is described, which covers clauses and goals of the predicate `list/1` (2,3). The pointcut has the argument *Sum*, which serves as a temporary variable to contain the sum. Next, the pointcut `init_-clause` gathers nonrecursive clauses of `list/1`, where it will be necessary to perform the initialisation of the sum (10). Therefore, the argument *Sum* is required for the pointcut description. Applying predicate `context/4` we get the *Sum* from the parallel context, namely from pointcut sum(*Sum*). Finally, pointcut `rec_clause` covers the recursive clause of `list/1` (17). Furthermore, it has arguments *H* (which is the actual list element), *TSum* for the result from the recursive call, and *Sum*, the sum to be computed. *Sum* is taken from the parallel context, *TSum* comes from the left context.

This shows the general concept of the context. However, the definition can be refined. Also, `context/4` can be extended to support other kinds of searching.

7.4.4 Advice

Advice is program code to be added at join points specified by pointcut descriptions. The definition of advice is based on the procedural interpretation of Prolog programs and the port model as given in Figure 7.1 and described in Section 7.4.1. We suggest three kinds of advice.

A *port advice* is an additional (possibly compound) goal to be resolved at a port. A port advice declaration is of the form port_advice(A, N, P) ← $G_1, \ldots, G_n$. where A is a term denoting the aspect the advice belongs to, and N is a term denoting a pointcut containing join points affected by the advice, P is a term denoting the port the advice is placed on (e.g., before proving a goal, at redoing the goal etc.), and G_i are goals constituting the advice itself. The possible ports are specified in the port model in Figure 7.1.

Around advice are pieces of code to be used instead of a goal or body of a clause. It also allows to place code around a goal respectively clause body. Due to the similarity of the effect to that of port advice they are specified as port advice to be attached to a virtual port *around*.

Term advice describe a transformation of the term representation of a goal or clause. For a goal goal(G) the term affected is G, for a clause clause(H, B) the term affected is H. A term advice is specified by term_advice(A, N, T) ← $G_1, \ldots, G_n$. where A is a term denoting the aspect the advice belongs to, N is a term denoting a pointcut containing join points affected by the advice, T is a term denoting the advice (a term transformation), and G_i auxiliary goals computing arguments used by the advice. Possible values for T are rename/1 and extra_args/2 for renaming of predicates and introduction of extra arguments. Term advice in general is not limited to those. In Figure 7.11, term advice is used to perform a renaming (6) and to add an extra argument at the last position of the actual goal (7).

Similarly to around advice, term advice could have been provided by virtual ports serving as join points for components of the term representation. However, term transformations simplify the application of term advice.

7.4.5 Aspects

Simple aspects.

An aspect is a language construct which contains all advice needed to implement a particular concern together with the corresponding pointcut descriptions. In our setting aspects are a grouping mechanism for pointcuts. The description of a pointcut by pointcut/4 contains the name of an aspect the pointcut belongs to. Advice specify the pointcut they are associated to, as well as the aspect they belong to. For example, Figure 7.11 shows a complete aspect to sum up the elements of a list.

A weaver takes the aspect and the original program and creates a program with the advice woven in. For the given aspect and the skeleton of the list traversal in Figure 7.10 the weaving leads to the result shown in Figure 7.13, which is actually (and intentionally) the same as sumlist/2 in Figure 7.10.

Aspects can depend on other aspects. Cyclic dependencies can exist, e.g., a group of aspects only makes sense together, while their descriptions remain separated. The weaver can determine the dependencies and weave in all required aspects.

```
sumlist([], Sum) :- Sum is 0.
sumlist([H|T], Sum) :- sumlist(T, TSum), Sum is TSum + H.
```

Figure 7.13 Result of weaving the `sumlist` aspect to `list/1` of Figure 7.10

```
pointcut( Pattern, Context, rename(Name/Arity, NewName), rename):-
    ( Pattern = goal(Goal) ; Pattern = clause(Goal, _) ),
    nonvar(Goal), functor(Goal, Name, Arity).

term_advice(rename(Name/Arity, NewName), rename, rename(NewName)).
```

Figure 7.14 Generic Aspect `rename/2` for renaming predicates

Generic aspects.

If aspect names are parameterised, those arguments can be used in pointcut descriptions and advice in a generic way. An example is aspect `rename/2` for renaming predicates given in Figure 7.14. The first argument contains the symbol and arity of the predicate to be renamed, the second one contains the new name. Due to the static weaving, generic arguments have to be instantiated at weave-time. This can be done by delivering concrete values at weaver execution or by aspects depending on the generic aspect. For example, generic aspects can be used to describe techniques from the field of stepwise enhancement.

7.4.6 Weaver

The weaver is a meta-program which takes the original source program and the aspects (pointcut descriptions and advice) and transforms them to a source program with the aspects woven in. We decided in favor of a static weaver. This has the advantage that the effect of the aspect specification can be studied in the source code produced by the weaver.

For the transformation, the weaver needs to investigate each possible clause and goal in the source (simple traversal), to determine all pointcuts containing join points associated with the clauses and goals examined (usually includes context analysis), and to insert the corresponding advice in the source in a way that its effect seems to appear at the desired port. Figure 7.15 shows the weaving transformations. For example, for a port advice at port `call`, the goal *Goal* is replaced by the compound goal, consisting of the attached advice *Advice* followed by *Goal*. Considering the operational semantics of Prolog, the advice is evaluated in the transformed program before the original goal is tried. Hence, the desired effect of an added goal at a call port is yielded.

Additionally, the weaver makes information provided by possible arguments in pointcut names accessible for an advice, which then uses it to access to data from the goal and clause corresponding to the join point and to exchange data between advice. The weaver takes into account only pointcut descriptions, which belong to the aspects to be woven. Thus, aspects can be used to summarise pointcut descriptions and advice. This allows for

131

a separate description of aspects and increases their reuse. From this point of view, an aspect summarises the implementation of a concern.

$Goal$	$\overset{\text{call}}{\leadsto}$	$Advice, Goal$
$Goal$	$\overset{\text{exit}}{\leadsto}$	$Goal, Advice$
$Goal$	$\overset{\text{error}(Error)}{\leadsto}$	$catch(Goal, Error, Advice)$
$Goal$	$\overset{\text{fail}}{\leadsto}$	$(true; Advice), Goal$
$Goal$	$\overset{\text{redo}}{\leadsto}$	$Goal, (true; Advice)$
$Goal$	$\overset{\text{around}}{\leadsto}$	$Advice$
$p(X_1, \ldots, X_n)$	$\overset{\text{rename}(q)}{\leadsto}$	$q(X_1, \ldots, X_n)$
$p(X_1, \ldots, X_n)$	$\overset{\text{extra\_args}([Y_1, \ldots, Y_m], i)}{\leadsto}$	$p(X_1, \ldots, X_i, Y_1, \ldots, Y_m, X_{i+1}, \ldots, X_n)$
$p(X_1, \ldots, X_n) \leftarrow Body.$	$\overset{\text{trymatch}}{\leadsto}$	$p(Y_1, \ldots, Y_n) \leftarrow Advice,$ $\quad X_1 = Y_1, \ldots,$ $\quad X_n = Y_n \rightarrow Body.$
$p(X_1, \ldots, X_n) \leftarrow Body.$	$\overset{\text{enterbody}}{\leadsto}$	$p(X_1, \ldots, X_n) \leftarrow Advice, Body.$
$p(X_1, \ldots, X_n) \leftarrow Body.$	$\overset{\text{exitbody}}{\leadsto}$	$p(X_1, \ldots, X_n) \leftarrow Body, Advice.$
$p(X_1, \ldots, X_n) \leftarrow Body.$	$\overset{\text{failmatch}}{\leadsto}$	$p(Y_1, \ldots, Y_n) \leftarrow (true; Advice),$ $\quad X_1 = Y_1, \ldots,$ $\quad X_n = Y_n \rightarrow Body.$
$p(X_1, \ldots, X_n) \leftarrow Body.$	$\overset{\text{failbody}}{\leadsto}$	$p(X_1, \ldots, X_n) \leftarrow (true; Advice), Body.$
$p(X_1, \ldots, X_n) \leftarrow Body.$	$\overset{\text{redobody}}{\leadsto}$	$p(X_1, \ldots, X_n) \leftarrow Body, (true; Advice).$
$p(X_1, \ldots, X_n) \leftarrow Body.$	$\overset{\text{around}}{\leadsto}$	$p(X_1, \ldots, X_n) \leftarrow Advice.$

Figure 7.15 Transformations implementing advice

If dependencies between aspects are specified, required aspects can be loaded during weaving. Cyclic dependencies can be handled based on set semantics. The weaver can be provided as a simple library applied at load-time using `term_expansion/2`, thus making a separate preprocessor unnecessary.

7.4.7 A Note on the Implementation

Some Prolog implementations such as [Wie06] allow to customise loading of Prolog programs by providing a predicate `term_expansion(+C1,-C2)`, which replaces each clause `C1` by `C2`. Then, weaving is done at load-time, if the weaver is called in the definition of the predicate.

Due to the operational semantics of Prolog, the order in which the aspects are woven in is significant. In our current implementation, renaming the same predicate by several aspects renames the predicate to the name determined by the last aspect added. Adding extra arguments twice results in adding two arguments. This is used in Section 7.2 to add extra arguments for the AST with the `ast`-aspect and to add extra arguments for the AST without free variables with the `free`-aspect. Here, the use of `term_advice` to add extra arguments is hidden in the `build`-aspect. While weaving advice code, fresh variables are introduced and corresponding variables are unified.

We provide a predicate `require_aspects/2` to read all necessary aspect definitions and to determine circular dependencies. The use of side effects in Prolog code, such as the ! or \+ (negation) can lead to infinite loops when used in pointcut expressions.

7.5 The Aspect Library - Level 2

The aspect library comprises reusable aspects to support language processing. Most important, a set of generic aspects formalise generalised techniques in a skeleton (i.e., grammar) independent manner. For example, Section 7.2 applied the generalised technique `build` to create ASTs in combination with the generic `parser` aspect. Besides, these aspects support incremental development of Prolog programs in general.

The aspect `sumlist` in Section 7.3 modularises a particular application of the `calculate` technique. In this section, we will discuss generic techniques and demonstrate by the example of `calculate` how we can make it reusable and independent from a concrete skeleton.

7.5.1 Stepwise Enhancement, Skeletons, and Techniques

Adapting Wirth's *stepwise refinement* to Prolog the method of *stepwise enhancement* [JS94] specifies an incremental process to develop Prolog programs. In a first step a *skeleton* constituting the control flow of the program is identified. Parser, meta-interpreter, or traversals are typical skeletons. In a further step, applications of standard programming *techniques* place additional computations around the skeleton's control flow and yield *enhancements* of the skeleton.

Techniques, e.g., [SK93], constitute standard programming practices in Prolog and can be considered as design patterns, i.e., they are generic and frequently used. Techniques define the computations along the control flow determined by the skeleton. It extends the structure of a skeleton by adding arguments and goals. Then those enhancements are combined to a program including all additional computations. This program can be considered as a new skeleton. The final program is obtained by repetitive application of techniques. The authors argue in [JS94, JKS94] that a proof of correctness of the final program can be leveraged from the development history. Furthermore, skeletons and techniques offer a high degree of reuse.

A technique can be applied to different skeletons. It can be considered as a structural mapping between a skeleton and an enhancement [JS94]. In general, application of a technique adds an extra argument to the predicate carrying the result of the calculation. Furthermore, initial values and arithmetic functions computing new values out of values from preceding calculations are specified.

7.5.2 Generalised Techniques

Using the first level discussed in Section 7.2, it is now possible to describe and use the application of a technique such as the *build-*, *accumulator-*, and the *calculate*-techniques. For example, the application of the `calculate`-technique to Figure 7.10 (a) to achieve Figure 7.10 (b) in Section 7.3 is described by aspect `sumlist` (cf. Figure 7.11). Techniques, too, can be described by generic aspects. We will demonstrate this in the following. Generic aspects need good user documentation to be beneficial.

Formal parameters of the generic aspect make the description of a technique independent of particular skeletons. Generic pointcut descriptions use the parameters to classify clauses and goals in terms of the technique. Aspects describing the application of a technique instantiate the formal parameters with a list of concrete predicates in the skeleton affected by the application. The application aspect can then use pointcuts described by the generic aspect. In a next step pointcuts described by the generic aspect can be used by the application aspect to place individual advice. We will illustrate this in the following example.

7.5.3 Formalising Techniques as Generic Aspects: Calculate

While explaining the representation of concepts in Prolog, we showed that an application of the `calculate`-technique could be modularised by the `sumlist`-aspect. However, those pointcut descriptions rely on the `list/1`-skeleton. Here, we illustrate by the example of the `calculate`-technique how techniques themself can be described in a formal way by generic aspects (cf. Figure 7.16). The approach is an example for providing new generic aspects for the aspect library. We use the Laola (Prolog) syntax for its compactness. At the end, `sumlist` is described in Figure 7.17 based on `calculate`. Note that term structures such as an AST could be constructed using this technique, too.

The `calculate`-technique is employed for additional calculations along the control flow of a skeleton. Applications of the technique add an extra argument to predicates involved in calculation. Furthermore, an extra arithmetic goal is added to the body of each recursive goal to relate the calculation from the body with the final result in the head of the clause. The technique can be represented as a generic aspect `calculate(+N, +Preds)`, as illustrated in Figure 7.16. Here, the first generic parameter N specifies a unique name to distinguish different applications of the technique. The second generic parameter `Preds` contains a list of predicates involved in calculation. Each predicate is represented by a term `Pred/N/Pos`, where `Pred` is the predicate symbol, N its arity, and `Pos` the position to insert the extra argument carrying the structure to build.

Involved predicates. Clauses and goals of predicates involved in calculation are addressed by a generic pointcut `val/2` (Lines 1-2 for addressing clauses, lines 3-4 for goals). For a given clause or goal the predicate symbol `Pred` and its arity N are determined. If corresponding information is found in the list of involved predicates, the corresponding join points are included in a pointcut `val(Pred/N, V)`, where V is a free variable intended to carry the result of calculation. Term advice is placed at the pointcut to add the extra argument to all occurrences of involved predicates (6-7).

```
1   pointcut(clause(Head, _), _, calculate(Name, Preds), val(Pred/N, _V)):-
2       functor(Head, Pred, N), memberchk(Pred/N/_, Preds).
3   pointcut(goal(Goal), _, calculate(Name, Preds), val(Pred/N, _V)):-
4       nonvar(Goal), functor(Goal, Pred, N), memberchk(Pred/N/_, Preds).
5
6   term_advice(calculate(_, Preds), val(Pred/N, V), extra_arg(V, Pos)):-
7       memberchk(Pred/N/Pos, Preds).
8
9   pointcut(clause(_, _), C, calculate(Name, Preds), Pointcut):-
10      context(C, parallel, calculate(Name, Preds), val(Pred/N, V)),
11      \+ context(C, left(all), calculate(Name, Preds), val(_, _)),
12      ( context(C, parallel, N, elem(Elem)) ->
13          Pointcut = init_clause(Pred/N, Elem, V) ;
14          Pointcut = init_clause(Pred/N, V) ).
15
16  pointcut(clause(_, _), C, calculate(Name, Preds), Pointcut):-
17      context(C, parallel, calculate(Name, Preds), val(Pred/N, V)),
18      context_all(Pattern, C, left(all),
19              calculate(Name, Preds), val(_, Pattern), Bag),
20      \+ Bag = [], reverse([V|Bag], Vs),
21      ( context(C, parallel, N, elem(Elem)) ->
22          Pointcut =.. [calc_clause, Pred/N, Elem|Vs] ;
23          Pointcut =.. [calc_clause, Pred/N|Vs] ).
24
25  pointcut(goal(_), C, calculate(Name, Preds), calc_goal(Pred/N, V)):-
26      context(C, parallel, calculate(Name, Preds), val(Pred/N, V)),
27      context(C, inside(first), calculate(Name, Preds), val(_, _)).
28
29  pointcut(goal(_),C,calculate(Name,Preds),client_goal(Pred/N,V)):-
30      context(C, parallel, calculate(Name, Preds), val(Pred/N, V)),
31      \+ context(C, inside(first), calculate(Name, Preds), val(_,_)).
```

Figure 7.16   The `calculate`-technique can be described as a generic aspect

Initialisation clauses.   Clauses of involved predicates are classified into *initialisation clauses* and *calculation clauses*. Bodies of initialisation clauses do not contain goals of involved predicates. During the calculation process results are initialised in these clauses possibly using elements provided by the clause. More formally, consider (9-14). Firstly, the parallel context must contain a pointcut `val/2` because initialisation clauses are clauses of involved predicates. Secondly, no pointcut `val/2` is allowed in the left context of the clause since initialisation clauses do not contain involved goals. Finally, an extra element needed to initialise a result can be provided by a pointcut `elem/1`. If there exists such a pointcut in the parallel context of the clause, the corresponding join points belong to a pointcut `init_clause(Pred/N, Elem, V)`. Here, `Pred/N` denotes the symbol and arity of the predicate the clause defines. Elem forms the extra element provided by the clause. V is a variable carrying the result to initialise. If the clause provides no extra element there will be no pointcut elem/1 in the parallel context of the clause. The join points corresponding to the clause are part of a pointcut init_clause(Pred/N, V).

Bodies of calculation clauses contain goals involved in the calculation. Results calculated by these goals are used to calculate a new result in the head of the clause. As in initialisation clauses, an extra element can be provided by the clause. Pointcuts addressing calculation clauses can be described as illustrated by (16-23). As calculation clauses define involved predicates the parallel context must include a pointcut val/2. Furthermore, all substructures provided by involved goals in the body of the clause are collected from the left context of the clause (right to left). If there exists at least one such substructure, the clause is a build clause addressed by a pointcut calc_clause. The pointcut refers the predicate symbol Pred, its arity N, a possibly offered element Elem, temporary results ordered from left to right, and the result to calculate by the clause.

Calculation goals. Similarly, involved goals can be classified. *Calculation goals* calculating temporary results occur in the body of calculation clauses. This is formalised by the description of the pointcut calc_goal/2 in lines (25-27). Firstly, the parallel context again needs to contain a pointcut val/2 expressing the goal is involved in calculation. Secondly, the parent context must contain another pointcut val/2 covering an involved clause the goal belongs to. The goal then is addressed by a pointcut calc_-goal/2. Arguments of the pointcut are taken from the pointcut val/2 in the parallel context.

Client goals. In contrast to calculation goals, *client goals* occur only in clauses not involved into the building process. These goals offer an interface to use calculated values outside involved predicates. The description of the pointcut client_goal/2 is similar to the one of calc_goal/2 discussed earlier (29-31).

Representing sumlist/1. In Section 7.3.2 we modeled the stepwise enhancement of Figure 7.10 (a) to achieve (b) using aspect-oriented means. Using the generic aspects calculate/2 and rename/2 (from the example Figure 7.14, Section 7.4.5), it is now possible to modularise the application of the calculate-technique to the skeleton list/1 to a more compact aspect, as shown in Figure 7.17. To calculate the sum of elements in a list the actual element is needed, which is expected to be addressed by the pointcut elem/1 (cf. Figure 7.16,(12)). This element expands to the pointcut calc_-clause. Thus, port advice describes the calculation.

7.6 A DSL - Level 3

The Laola notation in Section 7.4 provides the AOP concepts in a very Prolog-like way. Describing aspects is just writing logical programs, a weaver implemented in Prolog can immediately reuse the pointcut descriptions for the weaving process.

```
1   :- require_aspects(sumlist, [calculate(sumlist, [list/1/last]),
2                               rename(list/1, sumlist)]).
3
4   pointcut(clause(list([X|_]), _), _, sumlist, elem(X)).
5
6   port_advice(sumlist, init_clause(list/1, Sum), exitbody):- Sum is 0.
7   port_advice(sumlist, calc_clause(list/1, X, TSum, Sum), exitbody):-
8           Sum is TSum + X.
```

Figure 7.17   sumlist can be described based on calculate and rename

```
aspect = "aspect" a_id  [requirements]
             (pointcut_definition | term_advice | port_advice)*
requirements = "requires"  a_id ( "," a_id) *
pointcut_definition =
      "Define" "Pointcut" pc_id ":"
               source_pattern  ( "," source_pattern )*
      [ "where"  (property | context)+ ]

context = (parallel_context |  left_context  | parent_context)
           "of" "aspect" a_id
parallel_context = "parallel" "context" "contains" pc_id
...
term_advice = ...
port_advice = ..

source_pattern = "Any" | clause_pattern | goal_pattern
property = prolog_goal
pc_id = prolog_term
```

Figure 7.18   Grammar snippet for the DSL

However, that syntax encumbers readability. Pointcut descriptions, term advice and port advice all look very similar. The reader always has to keep in mind the meaning of the arguments. Though the definition of generic aspects of design patterns will remain the task of experts, it should be easy for the user to apply them. This is supported by a relatively straightforward syntax named Swell, increasing the readability while allowing this notation to be translated to the original notation with a simple scheme. The advantage is that the semantics of the DSL is immediately defined by Laola.

We used the following simple method to derive a DSL (also applicable to other Prolog-based prototypes):

Reduce redundancy (of non-keywords) emerging from the use of several facts describing the same category. For example, for specification of term advice for AST construction the predicate name and the associated aspect name can be saved, as shown in Figure 7.7. All advice referring to the aspect ast are grouped into an aspect declaration.

137

Use keywords as comments to describe argument positions. In Laola, keeping the meaning of argument positions is distracting and reduces the understandability. Using their meaning as keyword solves this problem (cf. Figure 7.7), e.g., labeling positions for pointcuts and advice.

Make predefined values to constants to allow simple syntax checking. For example, possible ports for port advice (`exitbody`, `retry`, etc.) form the set of predefined constants, which can be controlled easily.

Use optional constructs for anonymous variables if those might be used frequently. For example, pointcut descriptions may possibly only need their name and patterns for goals, as in Figure 7.5.

Simplify expressiveness to improve readability. Contexts used in pointcut descriptions can be described using patterns on terms. However, in most cases, it will suffice to query the context using the predicate `context/4` as described in Section 7.4.3. Hence, this position can be hidden behind a more readable description of what the user wants.

An extract of the grammar is shown in Figure 7.18. Though the resulting DSL avoids some redundancy, it is more verbose. However, it is more readable. The informal mapping of the DSL to the Laola notation is given by examples in Figure 7.19.

7.7 Related Work

Modular Language Processors

OO world. In compiler construction using imperative implementation languages a shift to object-oriented programming languages can be observed as they are oriented much more towards abstract syntax trees. Initial approaches considered nonterminals as classes containing all compiler phases [Paa95], which generated disadvantages such as tangled code resulting in difficult maintenance. Subsequently, different compiler phases were combined in separate classes for each concern and were added using the visitor design pattern to separate different phases into a visitor class as described in, e.g., [WB00]. For example, JJForester [KV01] generates AST classes and abstract visitor classes for traversal schemes. Recently, the usefulness of AOP in this field has been shown. JastAdd [HM03], e.g., is an aspect-oriented compiler construction system. It is centered around an object-oriented representation of the AST. Name analysis, type checking, code generation etc. can be modularised into aspects. These are woven together using AOP techniques. The similar development can be seen in the construction of language processors based on logic programming.

Logic grammars. LDL (Language Development Laboratory) [Rie92, HLR97] makes use of grammars of syntactical functions (GSF) and supports modularisation into language fragments. In a separate specification the data-flow between modules is defined. Laptob

```
Aspect   let Define Pointcut lexeme :    goal(nat), goal(id)

pointcut(goal(nat), _, let, lexeme).
pointcut(goal(id), _, let, lexeme).
```

```
TermAdvice
    Pointcut: build_clause(exp, "let", Id, Exp1, Exp2, Exp)
    Advice    unify (Exp, let(Id, Exp1, Exp2))

term_advice(ast,build_clause(exp,"let",Id,Exp1,Exp2,Exp),unify(Exp,let(Id,Exp1,Exp2))).
```

```
PortAdvice
    Pointcut: build_clause(exp, "let", id(Id), Free1, Free2, Free)
    Advice at exitbody
        ( select(Id, Free2, Free3); Free2=Free3) , union(Free1, Free3, Free).

port_advice(free,build_clause(exp,"let",id(Id),Free1,Free2,Free),exitbody):-
        ( select(Id, Free2, Free3); Free2=Free3), union(Free1, Free3, Free).
```

```
Aspect edl
    requires  [free, build(edl, let, [exp, sexp, uop, bop])]
    Define Pointcut  eliminate(FreeVars, Id, Exp1, Exp2, Exp) :
        AnyJoinPoint
        where
            parallel context contains
                build_clause(exp, "let", Id, "=", Exp1, "in", Exp2, Exp)
                of aspect edl
            first left context contains
                struct(exp, FreeVars) of aspect free

require_aspects(edl, [free, build(edl, let, [exp, sexp, uop, bop])]).

pointcut(_, Context, edl, eliminate(FreeVars, Id, Exp1, Exp2, Exp)):-
        context(Context,parallel,edl,build_clause(exp,"let",Id,"=",Exp1,"in",Exp2,Exp)),
        context(Context, left(first), free, struct(exp, FreeVars)).
```

Figure 7.19   Mapping of Swell to Laola by example

(Language processing toolbox) [LR01], the successor of LDL, focuses on logic grammars to obtain a more light-weight approach to achieve prototype interpreters. Terminals are marked with an operator resulting in a call to a scanner, other goals are considered as nonterminals. Thus, with slight modifications, such grammars immediately provide the user with a recursive descent parser. Additional libraries contain meta-programs on Prolog programs to manipulate this kind of grammars as well as several general traversals on heterogeneous data structures such as fold to collect/compute data. (The close relationship between logic programs and attribute grammars has been discussed in [DM93, RL88, DM85].) Our work simplifies the implementation of those ideas. Creating language processors is now writing and combining reusable aspects.

Modular attribute grammars.   There are attempts to modularise attribute grammars (which form the basis for generation of language processors), e.g., in [Bau92, GG84, Ada91]. However, the modularisation concerns the hierarchical structures, while with using AOP, it is possible to separate a concern distributed to many parts of the hierarchical structure.

Aspects in grammars.   In [LR03b] we examined the addition of new nonterminals through the grammar to formalise whitespace and comments as parts of the grammar and transformation rules on corresponding programs) to support layout preservation. Layout preservation is an aspect in language description. The position of the nonterminals is specified separately and they are woven by a weaver. Join points are nonterminals, terminals, and positions of arguments in semantic rules. Advice are nonterminals and terminals for the syntax and terms for semantic rules.

Aspect G and AspectLISA are examples in a general introduction to aspects for grammars [RMHVP06]. AspectG for weaving crosscutting concerns into ANTLR specifications provides four possible join points (before/ after a semantic action/ a specific action that is inside a semantic action). Weaving is transformation-based. AspectLISA extends the underlying LISA [MvLA99] system. Join points are static points in a language specification, where additional semantic rules can be attached (syntactic production rules or generalised LISA rules). Pointcuts match rules using wildcards on a text basis. Advice are parameterised semantic rules written as native Java assignment statements. No before/after advice is possible to keep grammars declarative (dependencies of attributes determine execution order). We provide a more fine-grained addressing mechanism. Our approach is more general. On the other hand, we do not restrict the result to be declarative.

Modularisation in Prolog

Stepwise enhancement.   Stepwise enhancement with skeletons and techniques has been proposed to reach a higher degree of reuse, to reduce errors and increase maintainability [JS94, SK93, SJK93b]. Typical techniques have been identified and described in a modular way, e.g., such as accumulator pairs, building structures, difference structures, calculations, and context passing [SS97, SK93]. Meta-interpreters and simple traversals on syntax trees are further examples for extendable skeletons. Techniques are usually explained informally or example-driven [SK93, KMS96]. Formal approaches are restricted, i.e., in application to certain skeletons [Rob92] or describing techniques only in combination with a skeleton [JS94, Vas93]. The approach in [Läm99a] allows a formalisation of techniques. In [Rob92] techniques are formalised using a DCG notation. The approach is restricted to skeletons of single predicates.

As a side note, stepwise enhancement in Prolog resembles to stepwise refinement in object-oriented programming. The authors in [BSR04] show how it scales to the simultaneous synthesis of multiple programs and multiple noncode representations written in different languages. A refinement of a base grammar, e.g., is a grammar fragment that defines new tokens, new productions, and extensions to previously defined productions. The authors see AOP as a program refinement technology.

Higher-order predicates. An example for the in-Prolog approach to solve the problem to separate traversals and computations are higher-order predicates, like *fold* and *map* as given in [Nai96, SS97]. The next step is to introduce generic traversals on arbitrary data structures [LR01]. Both of the above techniques and the higher-order approach lead to equivalent results [NS00].

Transformational approach. A very early example for a transformational approach is the predicate `advice/3` implemented for the libraries of DEC-10-Prolog by Richard O'Keefe [O'K84], which can be seen as an early root for aspect-orientation in Prolog. It already allows adding advice to ports of a goal. Also, the author in [Kul99a, Kul99b], presents port annotations for debugging. The above approaches restrict to semantics preserving addition of code. Other transformation frameworks are presented in [Läm99a, LRL99] for complex program manipulations such as the introduction of context passing. Aspects are represented as transformations. Positions are addressed by unique selectors.

AOP can be seen as a generalisation of these approaches above. It allows a formalisation of techniques (e.g., Sec. 7.5 or [Läm99a]) and, thereby, a disciplined way of doing stepwise enhancement. Higher-order predicates and transformations can be simulated, too.

Other AOP in Prolog

We are aware of another implementation of AOP for Prolog [Auc05]. It provides aspect declarations (`aspect(+before/after/around, +ForGoal, +Aspect)`) to be used as immediates (they are called when loading the Prolog program). They demonstrate the use of the directives by example of debugging and profiling an interpreter. They do not explain the implementation and have no relation to modular grammars. Only `before`, `after`, and `around` advice for goals are provided. Weaving generates three files: one rewrites all modules to be affected, a file with assertions, which redirect direct predicate calls to their corresponding aspect-managed predicates, and a translation of aspect declarations to normal predicates.

We derive our approach from the established port model, and thus provide a good foundation for AOP in Prolog. We provide a much more fine-grained addressing and control over points in the execution, e.g., it is possible to react to failed matching of a certain alternative clause. This is useful, e.g., for debugging grammars.

AOP and Logic

In AOP, usually pointcuts are defined as predicates, which quantify over join points. Pointcut descriptions often test logic expressions, as in the most popular AOP language AspectJ [KHH+01]. The authors in [RK04] extend AspectJ by uniform genericity, that is mainly, the uniform use of logic meta-variables and logic list meta-variables, which cannot be manipulated by side-effects and range over syntactic entities instead of strings. The extension of the pointcut language allows generic pointcuts in the sense that logic meta-variables generalise wildcards provided by AspectJ. Predicates are added to work on different syntactic entities. The use of meta-variables from generic pointcuts allows generic advice.

Pointcuts in [KO05] can be used to describe temporary relations between join points. They are Prolog queries embedded in a small object-oriented language, which are sent to a Prolog engine to examine execution traces stored during execution.

In aspect-oriented logic meta-programming [DVD99], input programs are represented indirectly by means of a set of logic propositions on quoted pieces of Java code. Aspect declarations are logic assertions expressed in a logic language, which is also usable to express queries about aspect declarations, and declare rules which transform aspect declarations. A set of logic rules describe how code is added to that representation, which can finally be exported as Java source code. This approach allows extension of the aspect language without being concerned with the weaver's implementation. Description of aspects, pointcuts and weaving is separated (TyRuBa) from the language it is applied to (Java).

In [KMBG06] the authors use CARMA, an aspect-oriented extension to Smalltalk with a logic pointcut language. Pointcuts are logic queries expressing structural and dynamic conditions over the join points addressed by the pointcut. The authors propose model-based pointcuts, which are defined in terms of a model of the program that is more robust to evolution of the base program the aspects were added to.

In [Läm99a, Läm99b] a framework is provided for meta-programming and achieving aspect-oriented programming for declarative languages. Due to its abstraction, it can be applied to Prolog too, but at the same time, the abstraction makes integration and Prolog-typic usage difficult. Instead of pointcut descriptions, interesting places are identified using selectors. Aspects are represented by functional transformations. In [Läm04b], the aspect-oriented view is emphasised, but it is closely oriented to stepwise enhancement and does not provide a port model.

A framework for functional meta-programming [Läm00, Läm99a, Läm99b] was developed, in which AOP on several kinds of declarative language specifications such as attribute grammars or inference rules can be achieved. Aspects were represented in the form of functional transformations.

Our approach extends Prolog with AOP abilities, which gives us advantages of logic programming including logic variables for free. We provide explicite pointcut descriptions and use a join point model based on a port model. The integration is smoothly, as the language extension is embedded and uses Prolog syntax, e.g., pointcut descriptions are simple Prolog predicates, which are executed by the weaver to determine places to weave in advice, which again is ordinary Prolog. The weaver is itself a logic program. The extension can be provided as a simple library applied. Instead of explicite selectors, the more general concept of context is used to refer to interesting points in the program based on patterns and properties.

7.8 Concluding Remarks

Summary. In this chapter we argued that logic grammars and language processors written in Prolog can benefit from AOP. We illustrated how aspects can be used to modularise a logic grammar. We explained how the concepts of AOP can be represented in Prolog and introduced the general concept of contexts of join points for communications of aspects, relations between join points, and selection of join points. We used a join point model based on a port model and provided explicit pointcuts. A prototype weaver has been implemented as a logic program, which takes the original program, descriptions of pointcuts (predicates), and advice and produces a program with the desired behaviour. The weaver can be used as a preprocessor or integrated into Prolog to weave at load-time of programs. Integration is smooth due to the Prolog-like form of description. Furthermore, we illustrated how common programming techniques can be formalised as generic aspects. A library of generic aspects is provided to support definition of language processors. We presented a method to derive a simple DSL and applied it to increase readability.

Programming in Prolog in general benefits from our work. AOP in Prolog increases readability, maintainability, and reusability of Prolog programs as it allows for modular introduction of tangled or crosscutting concerns and for stepwise enhancement. Though the use of AOP in Prolog is based on the operational semantics of Prolog, it can even improve declarativity of Prolog programs. Much use of `assert/1` and `retract/1` is motivated to save another parameter just for context passing, e.g., environments in interpreters, which can now be described in a modular way as aspects. Our work maps AOP concepts to Prolog in a systematic way and defines pointcut descriptions explicitly. It is very near to Prolog due to the use of the port model. Moreover, AOP for Prolog provides interesting new ideas, e.g., the concept of backward directed advice, advice on error and failure ports, or advice and clauses not matching.

Future work. The join point model and the concept of pointcut concepts could be extended to support dynamic join points. Furthermore, more theoretical investigations are needed, e.g., on application of techniques of modularised logic programming, or on relations between skeleton and aspect as well as relations between aspects themselves. A further level of abstraction is needed to simplify the composition of aspects. Also, aspect-oriented programs introduce new problems (also for maintenance). Changes in the base program can lead to unexpected effects caused by aspects. A new kind of debugging support is necessary, e.g., debuggers need to distinguish advice from base code or the benefit of readability and maintainability cannot be used to its full extent.

Chapter 8

A Lightweight Infrastructure to support Experimenting with Heterogeneous Transformations

We report on a class library called Trane, which provides an infrastructure to support experimenting with transformations interactively. The base is an object-oriented combination model for transformations. Transformation here means algorithm that take software artefacts as input and produce manipulated artefacts as output. Trane simplifies the combining of transformations available in different languages, libraries and tools. Several combinations can be presented at the same time, parameters can be visually changed, and results can be compared. New transformations can be easily added. Generated transformations from experiments can be integrated into the experiments at run-time.

The chapter presents the general model of the class library. We show how the class library profits by the features provided by .NET, such as language interoperability, foreign language interface, shell access, reflection, and web services by demonstrating five variants to integrate new transformations.

8.1 Introduction

We report on a lightweight infrastructure developed to support experimenting with transformations interactively. The basic idea is to define an object-oriented combination model for transformations. Here, transformation means algorithm that take software artfacts as input and produce manipulated artefacts or results of an analysis. We use .NET, as it facilitates integration and combination of heterogeneous transformations, i.e., transformations available as programs in different languages, existing command line tools, web services, libraries through a foreign language interface, and dynamic compilation and loading of DLLs resulting from a transformation.

8.1.1 Experiments with Transformation Nets

Some kinds of complex transformation are developed in an explorative way, where they are extended after a test with representative examples shows that the development might be on the desired way. Examples vary from combinations of UNIX command line tools such as sed, awk and grep to extract and manipulate information in text files to more sophisticated examples, such as refactoring, where there are many ways to achieve an improvement of the source code, or to achieve software evolution by transformations [Läm04b, HM05]. Another example is the collection of individually changes for maintenance in batch files for later reuse in [KLV05b].

We intend to use Trane to experiment with transformations on language components, e.g., grammars, semantic descriptions, and language processors, though it is not restricted to those applications. We want to extend languages stepwisely during their development. Also, we want to explore several possibilities how a grammar could be changed, compare the variants, extract parts of existing grammars and adapt them to form a sublanguage DSL, and directly connect the generated output to front end generators to test example programs. Existing (transformation) tools can not always be combined easily, as they are available in different forms, e.g., command like tools like YACC and GDK [KLV02], left-recursion removal for attributed grammars in Prolog and TXL (cf. Chapter 4), grammar representations in XML, BNF etc.

However, to the user, it should not matter, whether a transformation is a command line tool like YACC, or an analysis written in Prolog, and it should be represented uniformly modulo their parameters.

8.1.2 Using .NET

We were interested in an implementation on .NET mainly because it comes with the promise of language interoperability and cross-language inheritance. With C# as main implementation language, we could make use of properties, generics, delegates, reflection, and web services. The implementation was also an experiment in platform independence wrt. the availability of .NET on Linux as well as Gtk# on Windows.

8.1.3 Resulting Prototype

We designed a simple class model. Transformations are represented by automatically generated or self-designed boxes to be placed on a workspace, which is itself part of an hierarchical box. The boxes have typed input and output ports, which can be connected using converters to describe dataflow. Converters are special transformations. Boxes can provide facilities to control transformation parameters. Several sequences of transformations can be presented simultaneously, parameters are visually changeable, and results can be compared.

Trane can be extended easily with new transformations. New boxes can be any program, a web service, an encapsulated command on shell level, etc., written in any .NET language, as long as the box interface is implemented. No configuration files are required for new kinds of boxes, as all information (e.g., number and type of input/output positions) can be extracted from the box implementation via reflection. Thus, the user creates transformation nets without paying attention to the implementation of a transformation. Trane can also be seen as a wrapper architecture or an interpreter for call graphs of complex functions. It is a lightweight implementation, because .NET already encapsulates much work for the integration of transformations.

Remainder of the chapter. In Section 8.2 we present the concept of Trane. In Section 8.3 we discuss the model and the computation strategy. In Section 8.4 we show five categories of transformation and how they are integrated. Section 8.5 discusses some related work. Finally, the chapter finishes with concluding remarks.

8.2 Trane Concept

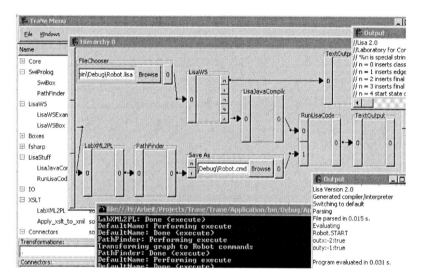

Figure 8.1   Trane in action

Trane provides facilities to model *Tra*nsformation *ne*ts with heterogeneous transformations. In Figure 8.1, for example, an attribute grammar of a robot move language is sent to the Lisa web service (available at web site of university of Maribor, hidden inside the `LisaWS`-Box). The web service is connected to the Lisa compiler-compiler, which generates a compiler for the language sent to the web service. Using `LisaJavaCompile` (wrapper for Java at command line), the code generated by the Lisa compiler-compiler and delivered via the web service is compiled. In the second sequence, a description of a maze in XML is converted to Prolog by an XSLT based transformation (`LabXML2PL`). A Prolog-based transformation (`PathFinder`) now analyses the inherent graph and generates a program for robot moves to control its way through it. The program is saved, the filename is combined with the generated compiler for the robot language using `RunLisaCode`. The result of the execution, namely the final position of the robot relative to start position $(0, 0)$, is delivered to the `TextOutput`.

The underlying structure is a directed graph with nodes representing transformations. Nodes have input and output ports, which possess types, and correspond to input and output positions of the transformations. Output ports can be connected to input ports of other nodes by directed edges, assumed the types associated to the ports are equal. This way, the call graph of a composite transformation is modelled.

Connections between ports of different types can be obtained indirectly by converters. These are special transformations, which map values of a given type onto values of a related type. In the graphical representation, they are hidden behind connections to allow a simplified view on the net. For example, it should not matter that the result of a transformation is a grammar in XML format, but the next transformation expects it in a BNF style. An XML2BNF connection can transport the grammar and hide the necessary format conversion. The user simply chooses the connector with the desired type combination. Data transported can be text as in UNIX-pipes, structured data such as grammars, or file names for results in files.

Transformations can be added at run time, e.g., transformations created with Trane. Providing a new transformation means to embed a transformation into a node such that input and output ports are provided with data. To create a new converter means to provide a new transformation, which implements the desired type mapping. This requires knowledge about the structure of data.

The order of computations is determined by the dependencies between transformations in the graph. Cycles are not considered, as their role is not clear in this setting. The computations are performed always once, when a result is demanded and the required input data for the transformation is available. Results can be queried at any output port at any transformation. Consequently, comparing the values of different transformations is possible. The intermediate results can be investigated, which is helpful, if the result of a transformation delivers unexpected values.

8.3 Object-Oriented Model

Figure 8.2 shows the UML class diagram of the infrastructure, which largely mirrors the concept.

8.3.1 First Level: Combination Infrastructure

The class *Transformation* defines minimal requirements of transformation nodes. As can be seen in the class diagram, it provides lists for input and output ports. These ports manage edges connected to ports of other transformations, data, and a type annotation, which constrains data accepted. Data is packed in a separate object, which provides its value and a type. This allows for a subtype concept, i.e., the value has to be a subtype of the type of the port. The values are used as input and output values for a transformation and the object representing the transformation. To define the port lists of a special transformation, it has to override method *init_port_lists* to configure the ports (e.g., with type annotations). Port lists are extendable dynamically at run-time. Ports of transformation objects

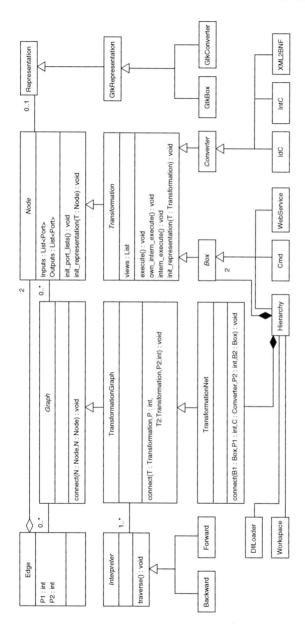

Figure 8.2 Class model of Trane

are connected using the method *connect/4* of *TransformationGraph*, which tests on type conformance, creates an edge between the ports, and keeps track of transformation objects and their connections. Edges store the nodes and indices of the ports connected.

A subclass has to override *execute*, where the actual mapping from values of input ports to values of output ports is defined or the embedded transformation is called. The computation can depend on several conditions, such as the actual computation strategy, or lazy computation (do not compute if input values have not changed). To save the user from uninteresting management work, *execute* is wrapped by methods *intern_execute* and *own_intern_execute* that take care of the conditions, and at a suitable point in the computation call *execute*. *init_representation* associates a representation to an instance of *Transformation*.

The difference between common kinds of transformation nodes and converters is expressed by classes *Box*, which box a desired transformation, and *Converter*, whose main task is to provide some kind of type conversion. The provider of a converter will find it nice to implement it like any other transformation. They only differ from boxes through their representation and arity. This enables converters of all kinds, simple converters or arbitrary complex computations, from which the user would like to abstract in a model.

The *TransformationNet* provides a method *connect* to connect two objects of type *Box* using a *Converter* at the ports specified with the port index each.

We decided for overriding of some init-methods over configuration inside of a constructor, because in the chosen implementation language C# constructors of super classes are evaluated first before that of the actual class. For some tasks provided in the super class, e.g., for the generation of graphic representations, it is necessary that the actual class is configured already at least partially.

8.3.2 Second Level: Interactivity and Views

The second level provides graphical representations for transformations. In the standard representation, rectangular boxes are generated for transformations (e.g., most representations in Figure 8.1 are generated). Lists of buttons, which also activate the execution of the associated box, represent input and output ports. Converters are represented as a line, which connects two boxes. This simplifies the view on the transformation net.

If desired, the provider of the transformation can create own representations for boxes and converters by inheriting *GtkBox* and *GtkConverter* respectively. Their instances are associated to the specific transformation class by overriding *init_representation*. Objects of class *GtkBox* can be provided with additional buttons, fields, sliders, and other kinds of input/ output support for users to control the transformation.

Objects of transformation nodes can provide several views at them. The first level can already be considered as the most basic view. The main view used is the graphic representation on a workspace to combine them. In addition, more information and controlling facilities are possible, e.g., a description of the transformation represented by the object, a description of its input/output, complex tables for the user to describe or influence the way the transformation is working, status messages, and logs. Note, the workspace in Figure 8.1 is just another view on a special box, allowing to create a hierarchical subnet interactively.

8.3.3 Providing a New Box

To create a new box, the following steps are required:

1. Choose a box to inherit from.

2. If desired, override *init_port_lists* to redefine input and output ports by simply adding new ports to a generic list.

3. Override *execute* to describe how values of input ports are used by the transformation to compute values and copy them into output ports.

4. If a new representation is desired create a new subclass of *GtkBox* and redefine components or add new features to the inner frame, e.g., a button to show a new view, which can be any graphical object. Override *init_representation* in the box to assign it to the box.

8.3.4 Computation Strategy

There are several variants to initiate computation of the transformation net: backward and forward computation (similarly to demand-driven vs. data-driven) and direct vs. indirect data transport. The choice is realised through an instance of *Interpreter* that performs/initiates the traversal.

With direct data transport, a transformation itself informs its successors / predecessors about results/ required results and calls their *own_intern_execute*. With indirect data transport a separate object of class *TransformationNet* controls the traversal process, e.g., calls *intern_execute*. Note that by *connect/5* the object keeps book about created transformations and connections. This allows intercepting and changing values for experimenting.

Backward computation is initiated by requesting the output port of the last transformation of a chain by initiating *own_intern_execute / intern_execute*, which then determine missing input values for the computation of the embedded transformation, and activate the preceding transformations. When all values are available, the wrapped *execute* is called. This strategy will be used mostly to compare several transformations at the end of a common sequence.

The forward computation strategy is thought for experiments to investigate the effect of a changed input. E.g., a composite transformation can be attached to a text editor, and show the results of a transformation chain immediately while typing e.g., a new part of a grammar (or delay start until a save-command is fired). Forward computation is simulated on top of the backward computation by calling the output ports of following transformations. This can be very expensive, though. Cycles are not allowed in the computation though we have not included a check to avoid them yet (we could think of a graph analysis based on a term generated from the net).

8.4 Variants of Boxes

Many transformations will only inherit from the common box type, configure the input and output ports, and define a mapping between them to create different kinds of boxes. However, using .NET, several different kinds of special box categories are viable, e.g. hierarchy boxes (to provide subnets and workspaces), web service boxes, command line tool wrappers, compilers, foreign libraries wrappers, or DLL loaders. Here we show five variants to integrate different transformations in boxes.

8.4.1 Web Services

As an example for a web service transformation we show in Figure 8.3, how to implement the compiler generator box *LisaWS* used in Figure 8.1. Lisa [MvLA99] is a compiler generator system also available as web service. When sending an attribute grammar, it generates and delivers Java code of a compiler. The code can be compiled and the resulting compiler can be used for the programs of that language.

LisaWS gets an input port for a string value, the attribute grammar. An output port is configured to provide a string for a path (to store the generated files), and further ports, where the generated lexer, scanner, parser, and evaluator can be requested separately.

We find it especially charming to integrate remote applications into transformation nets from locally existent algorithms. Problems might be that connections are unavailable or slow. Depending on the kind of service boxed, the transformation could require to re-compute always, even if no input values have changed.

8.4.2 Hierarchical Transformations

Hierarchy in transformation nets means to hide a transformation subnet TSN behind a box B_H, which looks and behaves like other boxes with input and output ports. Note, there are different types of hierarchy boxes. They can differ in the number of input/ output ports, or in the way they are to be used. Hiding requires mapping inputs and outputs of B_H to inputs and outputs necessary for TSN. This can be easily done by providing two identity boxes B_I and B_O as interface for inputs and outputs, between which TSN is constructed. Since transformations use properties to connect to ports, .NET helps to redirect port access to the input ports of B_H to input ports of B_I as well as output ports of B_H to those of B_O by simply overriding the definition of the properties (see Figure 8.4). The graphical representation is extended by a button, which when pressed provides a second view, namely the workspace of the hierarchy box. Figure 8.1 shows the inner view of a hierarchical box. We additionally added a transformation browser for choosing boxes and converters. This browser makes use of reflection to analyse DLLs in a chosen directory and to create instances of provided classes.

8.4.3 Use of Native Libraries

As an example for the use of existing DLLs outside of .NET we choose SWI-Prolog [Wie07], mainly because we want to use Prolog for experiments with transformation tasks

```
public class LisaWSBox : Box {

  public override void init_port_lists(){
    Inputs.Add(new Port("String"));
    Inputs[0].data = new ValueData(null, "String");
    Outputs.Add(new Port("String"));
    Outputs[0].data = new ValueData(null, "String");
      ... // some more output ports
  }

  public override void  execute(){
    CServiceBeanService lisaService = new CServiceBeanService();
    System.Net.CookieContainer container =
                           new System.Net.CookieContainer();
    lisaService.CookieContainer = container;
    lisaService.mkdir("wlohmann");

    // read file with lisa specifications
    String path = Inputs[0].data.value;
    FileStream fs = File.OpenRead(path);
    StreamReader r = new StreamReader(fs);
    String Spec = r.ReadToEnd();
    lisaService.clearError();

    // compile and save specifications
    bool OK = lisaService.compile(Spec);
    if (!OK) { /* error */ } else {
        String scanner = lisaService.getScanner();
        Outputs[0].data.value = scanner;
        }
  }
}
```

Figure 8.3 A web service box

similar to Chapters 4, 5, 6, and 7. In Figure 8.1, the *PathFinder*-box is based on Prolog. It determines a path through a labyrinth and generates a control program in the Robot language for it.

.NET offers the attribute *DllImport* to define access to foreign libraries. We created a DLL based on *SwiCs.cs* (cf. [Les03]) where for each exported function in the library its name is declared after the attribute (Figure 8.5). The DLL provides .NET programs with methods and types to model Prolog terms and to query a SWI-Prolog engine; and is used by the box.

Figure 8.6 shows how to interpret a string input as Prolog term directly and to call it. Combined with text boxes it can serve as interactive Prolog interpreter. Also, a Prolog box can provide programs that are more complex or initiate loading of a rule base.

```
public class HierarchyBox  : Box {
  public IdBox InputBox  = new IdBox();
  public IdBox OutputBox = new IdBox();

  // Hide Inputs of this box by pointing
  // to corresponding interface box
  public override  List<Port> Inputs {
      set { InputBox.Inputs = value; }
      get { return InputBox.Inputs;  }
  }

  public override List<Port> Outputs{ ... }

  public override void init_port_lists(){
      base.init_port_lists();
      InputBox.Double_PortLists();
      OutputBox.Double_PortLists();
  }

  public override void execute() {
      OutputBox.ownInternExecute();
      // Input execute not necessary
  }
  // save hierarchy in a separate subnet
  private TransformationNet _TraNe = new TransformationNet();
  public TransformationNet TraNe {
      get { return _TraNet; }
  }
  public override void
        init_representation() {
      this.Representation = new  Gtk_HierarchyBox_Representation(this);
  }
}
```

Figure 8.4 A plain hierarchy box

A problem is, in our opinion, that the attribute *DllImport* expects a static string, which has to be known at compile-time. This makes replacing different versions of the Prolog DLL impossible without recompilation of the interface DLL *SwiCs.cs*, thus, reducing platform independence (the name of the dynamic libraries differ between, e.g., Windows and UNIX systems).

8.4.4 XSLT Boxes

.NET comes with good XML and XSLT support. This offers a good basis to provide boxes to transform XML documents. Figure 8.7 gives an example for the contents of *execute*.

The example takes some XML data from an input port and delivers transformed data to the output port. Note that the XSLT script in this case is provided by a return value of

```
[DllImport(DllFileName)]
internal static extern uint
PL_new_term_ref();
     ...
// make a PlTerm from a C# string
public PlTerm(string text) {
  m_term_ref = libpl.PL_new_term_ref();
  libpl.PL_put_atom_chars(m_term_ref,text);
} // SwiCs.cs by Uwe Lesta
```

Figure 8.5 DLL Import

```
public override void execute(){
  String[] param = { @"H:\\ Projects" +
            ... "\\Application.exe"};
  PlEngine e = new PlEngine(1, param);

  // Get query as Text, call it, e.g.
  // (tell('log'),write('HiWorld'),told);
  string goal = (string) (Inputs[0].data.copy().value);
  PlQuery q = new PlQuery("call", new PlTermv(new PlCompound(goal)));
  bool b = q.next_solution();
  q.free();
}
```

Figure 8.6 Providing direct Prolog access

Xslt_Script, a method to be overridden by subclasses to specify a concrete transformation. Other variants of XSLT boxes might expect the script itself, or a filename for the script as input at a port or configured in another box view. A subclass of this box is used in Figure 8.1 to transform the description of a labyrinth into Prolog notation.

8.4.5 Command Line Tools

Many transformations are available as command line tools. Examples are compilers, but also yacc, lex and awk. Additionally, there are tools like grammar deployment kit [KLV02], which could be made available through the integration in Trane. Figure 8.8 shows how to use the Java-compiler for Lisa-generated code (cf. Figure 8.1). Here, the tool represented is hard coded into the box, but could also be provided through extra views with input fields or from input strings as part of the transformation.

The problem with this kind of boxes is that platform independence is restricted to the availability of the integrated tools on the platform.

155

```
String xml_input = (String)((Inputs[0].data.copy()).value);
StringReader xml_reader =  new StringReader(xml_input);
XPathDocument xpath_document  = new XPathDocument(xml_reader);
XslCompiledTransform transformation =  new XslCompiledTransform();
StringReader xsl_script_reader = new StringReader(Xslt_Script());

XmlTextReader xsl_script = new XmlTextReader(xsl_script_reader);
transformation.Load(xsl_script);
StringWriter xml_output_writer = ...
XPathNavigator document_navigator = xpath_document.CreateNavigator();

transformation.Transform(document_navigator,null, xml_output_writer);
Outputs[0].data.value = xml_output_writer.ToString();
```

Figure 8.7   Apply XSLT script to input

8.4.6 Dynamic Compilation and Integration

The command line tool approach can be used to compile a transformation for Trane and make it usable at run-time. Depending on given options, the resulting executable can be started as command (maybe again wrapped in a box, as in Figure 8.8) or the DLL can be examined/loaded and classes instantiated using reflection, if it is written in a .NET language. If the compiler generates .NET code itself the resulting class can be directly instantiated instead of generating a DLL first.

8.4.7 F# and Other Languages

Though the above examples can use transformations written in other languages, the boxes themselves, however, have been specified using C#. It is better to use the language of choice itself to define a box, especially, if a new transformation is created. This requires that the language is implemented on .NET. The resulting DLL can be used in Trane, as if C# had been used due to cross-language inheritance. Only then the *real benefit* of .NET occurs in our opinion, because the still existing problems of data conversion during the integration of transformations provided as command line tools or foreign libraries could be avoided.

With F# [Mic06] we were able to inherit from C# classes of Trane (the box) to create a new box (written in F#) and to instantiate from it in Trane again. F# is functional, and thus it issimilar to Prolog suitable to describe transformations.

Several languages on .NET are differently suitable. We were not successful using P#. With Eiffel# it is necessary to take care of the naming scheme during compilation. J# is not portable on Linux as it requires DLLs available on Windows only. We would be interested in a smooth integration of Haskell. There are some attempts, but there is still a way to go.

```
System.Diagnostics.Process p = new Process();
p.StartInfo.UseShellExecute = false;
p.StartInfo.CreateNoWindow = true;
p.StartInfo.RedirectStandardOutput=true;
p.StartInfo.RedirectStandardInput= true;
p.StartInfo.FileName = "cmd";
p.Start();
StreamWriter sw = p.StandardInput;
StreamReader sr = p.StandardOutput;
sw.AutoFlush = true;
//sw.WriteLine("dir /AD");or any cmd/tool
sw.WriteLine(@"javac -classpath lisa.jar" +path+"*.java");
sw.Close();
p.WaitForExit();
Outputs[0].Data.Value=TextBuffer.Text;
```

Figure 8.8   Wrapping command line tools

8.5 Related Work

Several tools provide a plugin structure and interactive placement of components. They are either large or provide a proprietary language to extend them with new objects. Trane has mainly been inspired by Cantata, the graphical user interface for the Khoros system to analyse and manipulate graphics [YAK95]. Cantata allows to interactively construct such filter pipelines.

[Spi02] considers UNIX tools as components. A GUI builder is used to create the visual programming environment. The placing relation of the components describes dataflow, which is text. UNIX tools have to encapsulate as ActiveX components with much manual work. Connectors are simply a visual encapsulation of the operating system pipe abstraction. Connector and glue-type components still need to be written by hand. Trane is not restricted to one kind of data, though it is intended to be applied mainly to artefacts of language processors, i.e., data are grammars, specifications, rewrite rules, parts of parsers, etc. We provide among others a system call box, which can take the command call directly as string. A new wrapper box for a special command can be easily written on top of the system box, which can take even the options at input ports. Our converters can transport structured data of any kind, they just have to inherit from a general converter class and implement additional treatment.

Stratego/XT [Vis04] uses mainly ATerms [vdBdJKO00] to provide input and output for terms in Stratego, and to exchange terms between transformation tools. New created transformations are wrapped into stand-alone components, which can be called from the command-line or from other tools. Those tools can be used similarly to Unix pipes, but can additionally work on structured data. For compositions of complex transformations they provide the XTC model. A repository registers locations of tools. An abstraction layer implemented in Stratego supports transparent access, allowing to call and use a tool like a basic transformation step in Stratego programs. Additionally, Stratego provides a foreign language interface to call C functions. Trane is designed mainly to reuse and to combine transformations for experiments. The XT tools could be wrapped in boxes, and used for experiments. We cannot generate stand-alone tools from composite transformations.

The Meta-Environment [vdBvDH+01] also allows the combination of different tools, but separates strictly between coordination and computation. Basis is the TOOLBUS coordination architecture, a programmable software bus based on process algebra. Coordination is expressed by a formal description of the cooperation protocol between components, while computation can be expressed in any language. Meta-Environment is used to produce real life products, on the other hand, it is complex, and difficult to adapt a new tool to the tool bus.

In Trane, coordination and computation are tangled. Evaluation of a transformation net is just traversing to each node and computing as given by the inherent dependencies between transformation nodes. Transformations can be added easily by providing a wrapper, where only two methods have to be overridden.

In the Eclipse framework, the Graphical Editing Framework (GEF) allows to create similar models and associate semantics to them. However, for new parts of the model (e.g., similarly to a new box in Trane) it requires a new compilation, while Trane nets are open. We do not need to compile the net. It is directly executable. New transformations can be added dynamically. Like other plugin systems, in Eclipse a plugin needs configuration files to add a new component, while we use reflection to extract necessary information. The language plugins for Eclipse are Java classes in a JAR archive. Transformations in Trane do not need to be written in one specific configuration language, as long it is supported by .NET.

[SdPL99] also try to spread transformation system technology over a set of reusable heterogeneous components. Using Java, CORBA and HTTP, they have instantiated a communication layer. To configure components, a description in a hybrid architecture description language is necessary.

Calling functionality from foreign DLLs is not new. However, usually the calls are determined at compile time. We offer to combine functionality, which might come from different DLLs without recompilation.

Using Trane is similar to programming in dataflow languages. We refer to [WP94] for further reading.

8.6 Concluding Remarks

Summary. We have presented a lightweight infrastructure that allows to provide heterogeneous transformations with a uniform façade to combine and interact with them. The model has been given and the essential classes have been explained. We presented five categories of transformations such as integration of web services, or command line tools. Integration of new transformations is simple. Due to reflection, no extra configuration files are necessary. Trane is lightweight as a large part of the work for integration is encapsulated in .NET. The biggest advantages have languages that are implemented on

.NET directly, but we still wait for more pure .NET languages without name scheme or inheritance problems.

Future work. Trane is rather a proof of concept than a tool yet. The type system is currently very ad hoc. Types are still conceptual. It is still matter of research, what types mean in our context. For example, for some transformations grammars of different languages are of the same type, if they are in the same format such as BNF. On the other hand, grammars can be considered as different types despite their format, if the algorithm using it is language specific. We want to design an extensible type hierarchy.

The Visitor pattern might help with configurable computations on the transformation net; also, to generate command line tools from a net as well as terms describing nets for analysis. As another way to integrate transformations sockets should be examined. The usability has to be increased vastly. It might be interesting to initiate the evaluation of transformations in separate threads. A classification of boxes would be nice. We need more transformations with grammar typical support to perform the experiments. We are new to F# and need more experiments with it and with other .NET languages.

Chapter 9

Concluding Remarks

We summarise the contents of the thesis. The subsequent section lists the achievements in more detail. Finally, we point to future work.

9.1 Summary

The thesis contributes to software language engineering and software maintenance. On an abstract level, the thesis provides insights in

- co-evolution of software languages, software in that language, and software transforming software written in that language,

- support for disciplined meta-programming,

- improvement of maintenance tools,

- layout preservation during source to source transformation,

- aspects in language descriptions,

- usability in transformational programming,

- readability of language descriptions, and

- combination support for arbitrary transformations available in different languages and formats.

We started with an introduction to the context of the thesis being software evolution and co-evolution. We discussed that software language dependency establishes co-evolution. We argued that software language evolution requires maintenance of software written in that language as well as software that transforms software written in the evolving language. We argued therefore, maintenance tools based on language technology, especially language processors, require special maintenance. As application example we discussed that software maintenance factories (SMF) need to be maintained, too, as language processors form the heart of this software. Additionally, SMFs should be extended by SMFs for language descriptions as large portions of an SMF are based on language technology and some necessary maintenance of generators and generated tools are directly related to maintenance of a language description. Next, we introduced seven research questions that were the guideline for the research topics in the core of the thesis.

We described a carefully designed framework for program transformation that can avoid the construction of erroneous software by ensuring desired properties of transformations also applicable to language descriptions. We have identified the basic roles of program manipulation, which allows to introduce a higher degree of disciplined meta-programming. We studied format evolution for XML documents, where the changes of a DTD are described as transformations which induce the migration of existing XML documents. Then, we developed a transformation for left recursion removal in attribute grammars and proved that it is semantics-preserving. The next chapter used the introduction of layout preservation to existing rewriting rules as case study to study the effect of grammar extensions to existing transformation rules. To be able to hide the additional complexity in transformation rules, the migration is derived automatically. For this, we analysed the effect of the transformation rule to layout preservation. We showed that hiding the complexity in transformation rules can be applied more general. Next, we developed a theory for aspect-oriented programming in Prolog to support aspects in language descriptions based on logic grammars and derived language processors. By the example of the `calculate`-technique we demonstrated how techniques from the field of logic programming can be modularised as aspects. We described aspects in language descriptions. A DSL was given to simplify the use of these concepts. Finally, we developed an object-oriented combination model for transformations that allows to experiment with transformations available in different languages and formats in an visual interactive way.

The examples studied support the demand for more research in grammarware or, more generally, in software language engineering.

9.2 Achievements

The detailed results are summarised in the chapters. Here, we list the key achievements ordered according their subject.

Consequences of grammar evolution

- We discussed *format evolution* of DTDs as a special case for *grammar modification and necessary document migration* in Chapter 3. We demonstrated how (partially) XML documents can be migrated automatically by deriving the necessary document migration transformation from the desired transformation describing the evolution of the DTD.

- We discussed left recursion removal in attribute grammars in a grammar evolution context as special case of *consequences of grammar refactoring to transformation rules*. We developed a transformation for left recursion removal in attribute grammars that adapts semantic rules, and proved that it is semantics-preserving (Chapter 4).

- We also studied the *consequences of grammar extension to transformation rules*. A grammar is extended by layout nonterminals, which leads to enriched abstract syntax trees in language processors derived from the grammar. We extended the existing transformation rules on programs (ASTs) for this grammar automatically by a transformation derived from the grammar extension (Chapter 5).

- We discussed that this approach allows users to specify semantics for a grammar that is less obfuscated and less deviated from the original grammar in a language reference than without this approach. It also allows a possible evolution of a grammar without forcing users to readapt all semantics definitions.

Disciplined meta-programming

- In Chapter 2, five basic roles needed for the development of transformations to extend the computational behaviour of programs were presented. They can be used to derive high level abstractions such as techniques known from the field of logic programming. The roles and the derived techniques have been formalised and implemented in a formal and operational framework for meta-programming. The roles are specified in separation. This provides a uniform and similar interface for specification of similar meta-programming tasks for programs in several declarative languages including grammars, natural semantics, logic programs.

- In Chapter 7, the developed support for AOP in Prolog allows for a more systematic way to meta-programming. Applications of techniques in logic programming and techniques themself can now be modularised and provided as aspects in libraries. The approach also provides a defined interface for meta-programming on language descriptions based on logic grammars in Prolog.

Improvement of maintenance tools

- The *layout preservation* case study contributes to the *improvement of maintenance tools* regarding a) the output of source to source transformation, b) the enabling of experiments with several (layout preservation) strategies, and c) the maintainability of maintenance tools. In Chapter 5 and 6, a grammar is extended to formalise layout positions. Existing transformation rules on programs of that grammar are adapted automatically so they do not break when they are applied on the AST enriched by layout information.

- To hide the complexity introduced by layout information, we analyse transformation rules regarding their influence to layout preservation. Based on it, the desired mapping of layout during the transformation is determined automatically and encapsulated in separate modules, making several heuristics possible. The automatic decisions are better than existing work due to a more formal investigation of the problem. The analysis can form the basis to provide algorithms that determine the quality of transformation rules with respect to layout preservation and that can suggest a different implementation to the programmer of the transformation.

Aspects in language descriptions

- The layout aspect is orthogonal to the program source. The grammar can be enriched by the aspect. Then, abstract representations by parsers derived from the grammar carry layout information. Transformation rules on those representations are extended automatically by a layout preservation aspect, which is determined partially by the layout aspect in the grammar (Chapters 5 and 6).

- Aspects in language definitions are discussed in Chapter 7 such as AST construction and program analysis. The logic aspect description language is developed allowing a separate description of the given aspects. This leads to a more readable, better maintainable, and partially reusable language description. A consequence is a better modularisation of derived language processors. This also allows experiments with different variants of language processors/ maintenance tools. Additionally, this allows for a configuration and adaptation of language processors to different variants of a language.

Object-oriented combination model for transformations

- We have defined an *object-oriented combination model for transformations* (Chapter 8) that allows to combine different kinds of transformations in a unified manner as long as they provide certain common properties or can be encapsulated to provide them as subclass. In this model, each transformation has a list of (typed) input and output ports and can be connected using typed connectors that are typed transformations again (especially for the purpose of type/data converters, but not restricted to those). This model forms the base for a tool implementation (see below). Grammars and transformation programs are treated as first class citizens in this context.

Usability in maintenance and language based tools

- Using a framework and transformations based on defined roles as in Chapter 2 allows to automate recurrent tasks. Unified interfaces for meta-programming ease the reuse and understanding of recipes used for program transformation. E.g., a folding operation works similar in several programming languages / formalisms (cf. [Läm02]). Transformations on language descriptions reduce the introduction of errors.

- In Chapter 4, we demonstrate how transformations for refactoring on attribute grammars enable the programmer to work with (specify) on a grammar more near the original grammar in a reference manual despite more restrictive technical requirements. The grammar extension in Chapter 5 together with the given migration relation can be used to hide unnecessary argument positions in rewrite patterns. Therefore, it simplifies specifications and helps to avoid bugs. The AOP approach from Chapter 7 lets the rewriter focus on separated aspects of the language description.

- The DSL described in chapter 7 eases to definition of aspects in language descriptions based on logic grammars and of aspects in Prolog in general.

- With Trane (Chapter 8), we provided an interactive workbench for transformational programming based on the object-oriented combination model for transformations. It provides a simple user interface for combining transformations and data. Explorative programming is supported. For example, different versions of composite refactorings can be compared, but it is not restricted to refactorings. Also, the workbench helps in exerimenting with several layout heuristics. Different kinds of transformations are used similarly, no matter, whether they are simple programs, meta-programs or meta-meta-programs, whether they are written in different languages such as Prolog, F#, whether they are XSLT transformations, simple data mappings, complex computations, generators of parsers from grammars, transformation programs on transformation programs, etc. Grammars and transformation programs are first class citizens. Existing transformation tools, e.g., Yacc and Stratego, can be easily integrated. The output of a transformation T can be used to transform other input, e.g., if T generates a parser from some grammar the resulting parser can immediately used to parse input on the same workbench. Language artefacts can be treated as simple data. It is easy to extend the workbench.

9.3 Outlook

We examined consequences of evolution in a software language setting and pointed out, where conflicts occur and where maintenance support is needed. Automating maintenance here is possible to a certain extent. The experience discussed in the thesis can be used to improve software maintenance factories. The tools are proof of concept prototypes, and are not suitable for real usage yet. Based on the object-oriented combination model for transformations, many different approaches and implementations can be integrated.

The central theme of the thesis has been the consequence of software language evolution. Despite the fact that the publication of some chapters are dated back, recent work on software language evolution and a new established conference with a focus on software language engineering [CFP08]) show that the chosen research topic is actual (e.g., [VV08, PJ07, dGSA07]. Coupled (or co-transformations or two-level transformations) are also used to taggle the format evolution problem of XML documents and the adaptations of XPath expressions [COV06, CV07]. The two-level approach is also related to the work on round trip engineering [AC06, AC08, EEE+07, Ste07].

Interpreter are more tightly bound to the definition of a language. Evolution in interpreters has been investigated in semantics. For example, in Modular Structural Operational Semantics [Mos99, Mos02] the idea is that transition rules for each language construct of a programming language can be given and never need reformulation when further constructs are added to the language. Much more related to our work are [Läm04b, Läm05], where an SOS-based interpreter example is used to illustrate the evolution of rule-based programs. While the consequences of language evolution in our thesis can be simulated with that approach using evolutionary transformations, we are concerned with a two-level approach, where the transformation of one of the levels can be controlled by the transformation of the other.

In future, each of the "hot spots" of the thesis should be investigated more in depth. Some more detailed work could be concerned with the following:

1. The solid basis for general and typeful meta-programming in Chapter 2 for defining and executing techniques has to be integrated into an transformational programming environment such as Trane from Chapter 8 similar to, e.g., JTransformer [KHR07], which provides interactive support for composing composite refactorings based on a well-defined core in the jConditioner framework [KK04]. Only when such systems are easy to use newly introduced restrictions will be accepted. Libraries of meta-programming techniques and recipes of their application are needed. Similar implementations are needed for other languages than Haskell.

2. The study of consequences of software language evolution can save and improve existing software. The relation of language evolution to existing documents was studied using the special case of XML document migration after DTD evolution (format evolution). More extensive work for XML documents has been done, e.g., by [Kle07, COV06].

   Besides the migration of program documents, it is interesting to investigate how much old program texts can benefit from language evolution. This is worked on by, for example, [VV08, PJ07]. In our opinion, it will mainly be possible for language extensions. For example, new language constructs can be made available to old programs, which can be simplified now automatically, for example, the refactoring of classes to generics [KETF07].

3. Chapter 4 examined left recursion removal in attribute grammars. The algorithm should be examined, e.g., for a context-free grammar and separate transformation rules as used in our Prolog examples. Other grammar refactorings should be investigated likewise. The algorithm should be integrated in a software maintenance factory to generate tools.

   Regarding the readability of language descriptions, the algorithm hides changes in a grammar that are necessary due to technical demands. What other (attribute) grammar refactorings are possible to allow the user to work with a version identical to the reference grammar?

4. In Chapter 5 we studied an automatic adaptation of transformation rules according to a grammar extension by layout nonterminals. What other extensions are possible that allow the automatic adaptation of existing transformation rules? Where are the limits? How can tools help with those parts where manual modifications might be necessary, i.e., how can those points be detected in the transformation rules that require the adaptation?

5. The layout preservation problem is a comment preservation problem in the first place. The style of writing rules affects the comment preservation in a logic programming setting. An algorithm has been developed in [Wal07] that examines transformation rules regarding their layout preservation quality based on the analysis in

Chapter 6. It should be integrated in rewriting environments. To improve solutions for the layout preservation problem, we have several suggestions. We believe that the design of a language can help. Firstly, the better a language is designed and the more it is focussed to a certain domain, the more the program text speaks for itself, making many comments dispensable. "Speaking" names for keywords, variable names and abstractions should be enforced. In source to source transformation tools, a mixture of declarative and imperative implementation techniques as well as with regular expression based tools can help in transformation tools. The regular expression based tools leave nearly all the program text unchanged while the former help to identify the places to be changed and provide information through analyse abilities.

For the case study of Chapters 5 and 6, bayesian techniques can help to reason about the relations of comments and language constructs in program texts and improve heuristics for automatic comment preservation. The programmer of transformation rules should be bothered as little as possible with the comment aspect (additional argument positions in our case). Overriding an automated decision of comment preservation is sometimes necessary, but should be made in separate modules. This also allows to experiment with a layout preservation strategy without risking the introduction of bugs into the real programming task. Several heuristics should be determined. To measure the degree of layout preservation, a metrics is desirable to compare different heuristics, or simply to inform the rewriter how much the impact of a transformation rule regarding layout preservation is.

6. The DSL presented in Chapter 7 can be improved. The user needs simple means of composing aspects from a library, which should be supported by the language. User guides and more examples are required. Also, the usage of the pointcut context is probably too difficult and should be hidden behind some language constructs. The introduction of AOP to Prolog brings also new challenges. For example, debugging/tracing for logic grammars can now be implemented on a higher level. However, maintaining aspect-oriented programs themselves is not trivial. How can the programmer informed, when aspect specifications are too expressive (capture more/too little join points). When the base programs are changed, some aspects may have to be adapted, especially the determination of pointcuts. How can one ensure the consistency during maintenance?

Several aspects are known in language descriptions, such as the layout aspect mentioned earlier. The debugging aspect [WGRM05], and the aspects used to derive a language processor are very implementation related. Are there more pure aspects in language descriptions?

7. Trane, as described in Chapter 8 provides a (proof of concept) platform for visual transformational programming. Together with the work from the earlier chapters it can form the basis of a software maintenance factory with a software language factory as a subpart. The desire to maintain the system itself is not supported, though

higher level functionality (non-core) based on DLLs can be maintained and replaced by the system.

There is a long list which could be done. Many technical weaknesses could be removed (missing save/load for many transformations). It was planned to connect Trane to MonoDevelop [WWW08]. The plan has been suspended for several problems. Trane needs a library concept how different or similar transformations for different or similar languages are stored and presented to the user of the system are necessary. The implementation of the forward strategy is not completed. Many transformations are desirable, especially grammar converters.

Vision

We think that techniques from the design, construction and maintenance should adhere. The far vision would be that software constructed should contain the tools constructing them, including maintaining features. Software should be made a bit harder to get it softer, like a tibetian wired mandala, which has movable rings arreted at special positions. It is flexible in some ways, so that new forms can be created by pushing and moving parts around, and the fixed points ensure that the whole figure is always consistent.

Appendix A

Left Recursion Removal

A.1 Algorithm for Simple Multi-pass AG

Input: $AG = (G, SD, AD, R)$, $G = (V_N, V_T, P, S)$ without ϵ-productions and cycles; without loss of generality let $V_N = \{A^1, \ldots, A^N\}$

Output: $AG' = (G', SD, AD', R')$, G' without left recursion and R' such that attribute values at root and at leaves are preserved.

for $i := 1$ to N **do**

    {Removal of indirect left recursion}

    for $j := 1$ to $i - 1$ **do**

        replace productions of pattern $A^i \to A^j \beta$ by $A^i \to \alpha_1 \beta \mid \ldots \mid \alpha_k \beta$,

        where $A^j \to \alpha_1 \mid \ldots \mid \alpha_k$ are current productions of A^j

        adapt semantic rules according (A.5)

    end for

    {Removal of direct left recursion}

    if replace productions of pattern $A^i \to A^i \alpha_1 \mid \ldots \mid A^i \alpha_n \mid \beta_1 \mid \ldots \mid \beta_m$

    (where no β starts with A^i) **then**

        introduce new nonterminal $A^{i'}$ *with attributes corresponding to (A.1)*

        for $k := 1$ to n **do**

            replace $A^i \to A^i \alpha_k$ by $A^{i'} \to \alpha_k A^{i'}$

            and adapt semantic rules according to (A.2)

        end for

        for $k := 1$ to m **do**

            replace $A^i \to \beta_k$ by $A^i \to \beta_k A^{i'}$

            and adapt semantic rules according to (A.3)

        end for

        add a production $A^{i'} \to \epsilon$ *with semantic rules according to (A.4)*

    end if

end for

for each nonterminal A' newly introduced during transformation holds:

$$
\begin{aligned}
A_S(A') &= A_S(A) \cup \{a' \mid a \in A_I(A)\} \quad \text{mit } TYPE(a') = TYPE(a) \\
A_I(A') &= A_I(A) \cup \{a' \mid a \in A_S(A)\} \quad \text{mit } TYPE(a') = TYPE(a) \quad (A.1)
\end{aligned}
$$

During transformation of production $p : A_0 \rightarrow A_1\alpha$ to $p' : A'_0 \rightarrow \alpha A'_1$

$$
\begin{aligned}
R(p) \;=\; & \{A_0.a := f_a(X_1^p.a_1, \ldots, X_{n_a}^p.a_{n_a}) \mid a \in A_S(A)\} \;\cup\; \\
& \{X_0^p.a_0 := f_a(A_0.a_1, \ldots, A_0.a_{n_a}) \mid X_0^p.a_0 \in DO(p),\ a_0 \in A_I\} \\
\Longrightarrow & \\
R(p') \;=\; & \{A'_1.a' := f_a(X_1^{p'}.a_1, \ldots, X_{n_a}^{p'}.a_{n_a}) \mid a \in A_S(A')\} \;\cup\; \\
& \{X_0^{p'}.a_0 := f_a(A'_1.a_1, \ldots, A'_1.a_{n_a}) \mid X^p.a \in DO(p),\ a_0 \in A_I\} \;\cup\; \\
& \{A'_0.a := A'_1.a \mid a \in A_S(A)\} \;\cup\; \{A'_1.a := A'_0.a \mid a \in A_I(A)\} \\
& \text{where}
\end{aligned}
$$

$$
X_i^{p'}.a_i = \begin{cases} A'_0.a'_i, & \text{if } X_i^p = A_1 \\ X_i^p.a_i, & \text{otherwise} \end{cases} \tag{A.2}
$$

For translation of a production $p : A^p \rightarrow \beta$ to $p' : A^{p'} \rightarrow \beta A'$

$$
\begin{aligned}
R(p) \;=\; & \{A^p.a := f_a(X_1.a_1, \ldots, X_{n_a}.a_{n_a}) \mid a \in A_S(A)\} \;\cup\; \\
& \{X^p.a := f_a(A^p.a_1, \ldots, A^p.a_{n_a}) \mid X^p.a \in DO(p),\ a \in A_I\} \quad \Longrightarrow \\
R(p') \;=\; & \{A'.a' := f_a(X_1.a_1, \ldots, X_{n_a}.a_{n_a}) \mid a' \in A_I(A')\} \;\cup\; \\
& \{X^{p'}.a := f_a(A'.a_1, \ldots, A'.a_{n_a}) \mid X^p.a \in DO(p),\ a \in A_I\} \;\cup\; \\
& \{A^{p'}.a := A'.a \mid a \in A_S(A)\} \;\cup\; \{A'.a := A^{p'}.a \mid a \in A_I(A)\} \tag{A.3}
\end{aligned}
$$

While adding a new production $p : A' \rightarrow \epsilon$ add

$$
R(p) = \{A'.a := A'.a' \mid a \in A_S(A)\} \;\cup\; \{A'.a' := A'.a \mid a \in A_I(A)\} \tag{A.4}
$$

During transition of a production $p : Y^p \rightarrow X^p\beta$ to $p' : Y^{p'} \rightarrow \alpha\beta$ by inserting $q : X^q \rightarrow \alpha$ with

$$
\begin{aligned}
R(q) \;=\; & \{X^q.a := f_a^q(\ldots) \mid a \in A_S(X)\} \;\cup\; \\
& \{A^q.a := f_a^q(X^q.a_1, \ldots, X^q.a_{n_a}) \mid A^q.a \in DO(q),\ a \in A_I\} \qquad \text{and} \\
R(p) \;=\; & \{Y^p.a := f_a^p(X_1^p.a_1, \ldots, X_{n_a}^p.a_{n_a}) \mid a \in A_S(Y)\} \;\cup\; \\
& \{X^p.a := f_{Xa}^p(\ldots) \mid a \in A_I(X)\} \;\cup\; \\
& \{B^p.a := f_{Ba}^p(\ldots) \mid B^p.a \in DO(p)\backslash\{X^p.a \mid a \in A_I(X)\},\ a \in A_I\} \\
\Longrightarrow & \\
R(p') \;=\; & \{Y^{p'}.a := f_a^p(X_1^{p'}.a_1, \ldots, X_{n_a}^{p'}.a_{n_a}) \mid a \in A_S(Y)\} \;\cup\; \\
& \{A^{p'}.a := f_a^q(f_{Xa_1}^p(\ldots), \ldots, f_{Xa_{n_a}}^p(\ldots)) \mid A^q.a \in DO(q),\ a \in A_I\} \;\cup\; \\
& \{B^{p'}.a := f_{Ba}^p(\ldots) \mid B^p.a \in DO(p)\backslash\{X^p.a \mid a \in A_I(X)\},\ a \in A_I\} \\
& \text{where}
\end{aligned}
$$

$$
X_i^{p'}.a_i = \begin{cases} f_{a_i}^q(\ldots), & \text{if } X_i^p = X \\ X_i^p.a_i, & \text{otherwise} \end{cases} \tag{A.5}
$$

```
:- op(10,xfx, :=).    %    X := Y :- apply(Y,[X]).

% Unify, if it is variable, an atom or a list
X := Y :- ( var(Y); atomic(Y); functor(Y,(.), _) ), !, X = Y.

% else, we have a term structure, which might be
% a predicate call or a term
X := Y :-  Y =.. [F| Args], append(Args, [X], NewArgs),
           G =.. [F| NewArgs],
           (  % it is a predicate
              functor(G, F, N), current_predicate((F)/N),
              call(G)
           ;  % it will be a term without semantics
              X = Y
           ).
```

Figure A.1   Simulation of computation of an attribute by function application

A.2 The Practical View

Here we will present the attribute grammar we used and report on two implementations of the given transformation.

A.2.1 An AG-like Notation in Prolog

As mentioned earlier, our aim is to decrease the gap between a grammar specification and it use in an implementation. This means the grammar the programmer uses should not differ too much from the grammar, which serves as a reference. We are using grammars in a Prolog setting for prototypes and small transformation tasks. A pure attribute grammar specification is not desired as we want to reuse software already written in Prolog. Our experiments are done with Laptob [LR01], hence we considered, how we could support a more attribute grammar-like notation without leaving Prolog.

Laptob supports the metaphor: *Prolog is the grammar already*. This means that grammar adaptations are simply meta-programming on Prolog programs. Basically, a grammar in Laptob looks as follows:

```
exp(exp(plus,T,T2))  :- term(T), @"+", term(T2).
term(num(N))  :- num(N).
```

Each predicate stands for a nonterminal. Bottom-symbols, like num (not defined elsewhere) are interpreted as tokens from a scanner. @ is an operator, which interprets its argument as a keyword token. Arguments enable computation for example to construct syntax trees. Thus, the logic program immediately implements a recursive descent parser. Actually, it is already a kind of attribute grammar.

It is now not difficult to achieve an even more AG-like look of Prolog programs. We introduced an operator, which implements a sort of function application (see Fig. A.1). If the operator :=/2 finds that Y is a term, it adds X as argument and interprets it as

predicate. So, for example, it is possible to write X := plus(1,2). resulting in a call
to plus(1,2,X). If there is no such predicate, := works as term construction.

```
% delayed evaluation for
% strict operations, here for 'is/2'
eval(Argument, Result) :-           % eval a delayed argument
   ( ground(Argument)               eval_(eval(Argument), Result) :-
       -> % buttom up apply in term     eval_(Argument,Result).
         bu(eval_, Argument, Tmp),
         Result is Tmp,             % special cases, e.g. lists, strings..
   ;                                ....
         Result = eval(Argument)
   ).                               % Unify atoms
                                    eval_(Arg, Res) :- atomic(Arg), !, Res = Arg.

                                    % finally determine arithmetic values
                                    eval_(Arg, Res) :-  Res is Arg.
```

Figure A.2   Delayed evaluation of attribute values

Furthermore, we defined a special predicate eval/1, which implements delayed evaluation (Fig. A.2). Some operators require terms to be ground, for example is/2. This
is often not possible due to the evaluation strategy of Prolog (only for L-attributed grammars). If eval finds its arguments non-ground, it returns the term eval enveloping the
arguments. If at any other place the computation of an attribute is based on the delayed
computation, the := operator tries to interpret the term (now eval) as predicate to be
called, and if its arguments are ground meanwhile, the evaluation can take place (e.g. is),
or it is returned unchanged. Once ground, the term is replaced by its result, hence there
is no further computation overhead in later uses of the attribute. The predicate can easily
be extended to react on user defined predicates in the same way as the case for atoms is
handled (see Fig. A.2).

For an example, see the unfamous knuthian example to convert binary to decimal numbers: As can be seen from the example, in the rule for b the attribute value would be

```
bn(BN) :- n(V),
   BN := eval(V).

n(V) :- l(V0,L0,S0), @".", l(V1,L1,S1),        l(V0,L0,S0) :- l(V1,L1,S1), b(VB,SB),
   V := eval(V0+V1),                               V0 := eval(V1+VB),
   S0 := 0,                                         SB := S0,
   S1 := eval(0-L1).                                S1 := eval(S0+1),
                                                    L0 := eval(L1+1).
n(V) :- l(VL,LL,SL),
   V := VL,                                      l(V,L,S) :- b(VB,SB),
   SL := 0.                                         V := VB,
                                                    SB := S,
b(V,S) :- @"0",                                     L := 1.
   V := 0.
b(V,S) :- @"1",
   V := eval(2^S).
```

Figure A.3   Example of Knuth: Converting binary to decimal numbers

computed using an uninstantiated variable, and thus it would raise an exception. Addition-

```
TXL v10.3a3 (29.10.03) (c)1988-2003 Queen's University at Kingston
Compiling ag.Txl ...
Parsing samples/knuth.ag ...
Transforming ...
bn(BN) :- n(V), BN:=eval(V).
n(V) :- l(V0,L0,S0), @".", l(V1,L1,S1), V:=eval(V0+V1), S0:=0, S1:=eval(0-L1).
n(V) :- l(VL,LL,SL), V:=VL, SL:=0.
l(V,L,S) :- b(VB,SB), ll(V,L,S,V4,L4,S4), V4:=VB, SB:=S4, L4:=1.
ll(V0,L0,S0,V5,L5,S5) :- b(VB,SB),ll(V0,L0,S0,V6,L6,S6),V6:=eval(V5+VB), SB:=S6, S5:=
eval(S6+1),L6:=eval(L5+1).
b(V,S) :- @"0", V:=0.
b(V,S) :- @"1", V:=eval(2^S).
ll(V,L,S,V,L,S).
```

Figure A.4 Output of the TXL prototype for the Knuth example

ally, at 1, Prolog would run into infinite recursion due to the evaluation strategy. Here, the forementioned transformation algorithm offers help (Remark: infinite recursion could be avoided in the example by a change of the order or rules, too).

A.2.2 Prototypes

The given transformation has been implemented twice for the given kind of attribute grammar. In a first proof-of-concept prototype for multi-pass attribute grammar we used TXL [CDMS02]. In Figure A.4 the output of the transformation for Knuth's example grammar generated by the TXL prototype is given.

The prototype was reimplemented in Prolog for S-AGs (thus being able to parse a yacc-like grammar), because it better integrates in our Prolog-based setting. We used SWI-Prolog [Wie03], with some traversal predicates taken from Laptob [LR01].

The transformation scheme is sufficient to implement the adaptation of semantic rules during left recursion removal. However, there were technical issues, which we will mention here. First, in our chosen AG notation we could not address attributes by name. Rather, we had to find a mapping of attributes to positions. From the semantic rules we derived which of the attributes are synthesised or inherited: Used occurrences of variables on the right hand side of the semantic rule are synthesised, if they do not appear in the head of the predicate on the left hand side of the Prolog rule, otherwise they are inherited. This requires that each attribute name is used once only in the part of the Prolog rule representing the context-free part (which could be achieved by a separate transformation on the rule).

Replacements of attributes of one rule in another (e.g. in the case where equation 4.11 has to be applied) are done by constructing a substitution from the predicate occurrence on the right hand side and the left hand side of the rule to be inserted (after refreshing all variable names). Then, the substitution is applied to the attributes of the rule to be inserted including the semantic rules.

The most difficult part was to specify the correct traversals. The algorithm in Figure 4.2 (page 67) gives **for**-loops only explicitly, where necessary. For an implementation, it was necessary, also to iterate on all alternatives for rules of the form $A_i \rightarrow A_j \alpha_1 \mid \ldots \mid A_j \alpha_n \mid \beta_1 \mid \ldots \mid \beta_m$. The extension of the algorithm is set-based, too, requiring traversals again, (e.g., for all attributes, for all semantic rules, for all alternatives, etc.). While there are typical traversal patterns like map for lists, or td for a top down traversal, one has to pay attention, that each step is continued using the actual intermediate result of the transformation.

We used a side effect to reduce the amount of parameters passed around by inserting information about new introduced nonterminals and attributes as well as indexing information into the knowledge base of Prolog.

A more Prolog style to implement the transformation would have been to use set-predicates or to insert a representation of the attribute grammar transformed so far into the knowledge base and to let Prolog do the searching. However, the deterministic traversals restrict the amount of backtracking.

The Prolog prototype changes the order of definitions for the nonterminals. This should, however, not influence the evaluation of the derived parser, but might be unexpected for someone using the generated grammar later on.

A.2.3 Scalability

We have not prepared real life measurements yet. For the small examples, the TXL-prototype shows no delay (on a 800 Mhz Linux computer). The Prolog interpreter is considerably slowlyer, which might be due to numerous uses of =../2 to construct terms from lists or to analyse them, the use of meta-predicates call, and many logging messages to follow the process of the transformation. There is certainly potential to increase the speed. As we want to use this approach to quickly create transformations for programs of such grammar, slow speed might be a problem for the development cycle.

The main problem with this approach might be, that with each left recursion to be removed, n new rules have to be introduced, where n is the number of β (alternatives of the nonterminal not starting with the same nonterminal). Furthermore, the number of attributes is doubled, and new semantic rules are added. Though they are copy rules mostly, and in Prolog variable references are fast, it might become a time factor due to the introduced :=/2. Removing indirect left recursion also adds a rule for each alternative of the nonterminal unfolded. However, trading translation time against space and complexity, one could imagine an analyse whether the nonterminal is really part of a indirect recursion. [Rob00] gives some values we can use to compare. The application of this approach to real grammars still remains to be examined.

Bibliography

[AC06]   Michał Antkiewicz and Krzysztof Czarnecki. Framework-specific model-
            ing languages with round-trip engineering. In *Model Driven Engineering
            Languages and Systems*, volume 4199 of *Lecture Notes in Computer Sci-
            ence*, 2006.

[AC08]   Michał Antkiewicz and Krzysztof Czarnecki. Design space of heteroge-
            neous synchronization. In *Generative and Transformational Techniques in
            Software Engineering (GTTSE'07)*, Lecture Notes in Computer Science,
            2008. To appear.

[Ada91]   Stephen Robert Adams. *Modular Grammars for Programming Language
            Prototyping*. PhD thesis, University of Southampton, Faculty of Engineer-
            ing, Department of Electronics and Computer Science, Southampton, UK,
            March 1991.

[AFCE04]   Mehmet Aksit, Robert E. Filman, Siobhan Clarke, and Tzilla Elrad, edi-
            tors. *Aspect-Oriented Software Development*. Addison-Wesley, October
            2004.

[AK03]   Colin Atkinson and Thomas Kühne. Model-driven development: A meta-
            modeling foundation. *IEEE Softw.*, 20(5):36–41, 2003.

[Alb91]   Henk Alblas. Introduction to Attribute Grammars. In Henk Alblas and
            Borivoj Melichar, editors, *Attribute Grammars, Applications and Systems
            (SAGA 1991)*, volume 545 of *LNCS*, pages 1–15, Prague, Czechoslovakia,
            June 1991. Springer.

[ANS]   *ANSI/IEEE Standard. 729-1983; IEEE Standard. 1219-1998.*

[ASU86]   Alfred V. Aho, Ravi Sethi, and Jeffrey D. Ullman. *Compilers: principles,
            techniques, and tools*. Addison-Wesley, Boston, USA, 1986.

[Auc05]   Douglas Michael Auclair. Aspect-Oriented Programming in
            Prolog. `http://cotilliongroup.com/man/aspects/`
            `aspects-man.html`, 2005.

[Aug99]   Lennart Augustsson. Cayenne - a language with dependent types. In
            S. Doaitse Swierstra, Pedro R. Henriques, and Jose N. Oliveira, editors,
            Advanced Functional Programming, Third International School, AFP'98,
            volume 1608 of *Lecture Notes in Computer Science*, pages 240–267,
            Braga, Portugal, September 1999. Springer.

Bibliography

[Bau92]   Beate Baum. Another Kind of Modular Attribute Grammars. In *Compiler Construction, 4th Int. Conf., CC'92, Proceedings*, volume 641 of *Electronic Notes in Computer Science*, pages 44–50, 1992.

[BC00]   Angela Bonifati and Stefano Ceri. Comparative analysis of five XML query languages. *SIGMOD Rec.*, 29(1):68–79, 2000.

[BCN92]   C. Batini, S. Ceri, and S. B. Navathe, editors. *Conceptual Database Design: An Entity-Relationship Approach*. Benjamin/Cummings, Redwood City, CA, 1992.

[Bec94]   Kent Beck. Simple smalltalk testing: With patterns. In *The Smalltalk Report*, volume 4(2), pages 16–18. Oct 1994. http://www.xprogramming.com/testfram.htm.

[Bec00]   Kent Beck. *Extreme Programming Explained: Embrace the Change*. Addison Wesley, 2000.

[BHW97]   James M. Boyle, Terence J. Harmer, and Victor L. Winter. The TAMPR program transformation system: simplifying the development of numerical software. In *Modern Software Tools for Scientific Computing*, pages 353–372. Birkhauser Boston Inc., Cambridge, MA, USA, 1997.

[BK93]   Anne Brüggemann-Klein. Formal models in document processing. Habilitationsschrift. Faculty of Mathematics at the University of Freiburg, 1993. ftp://ftp.informatik.uni-freiburg.de/documents/papers/brueggem/habil.ps.

[BK96]   Jan A. Bergstra and Paul Klint. The toolbus coordination architecture. In *COORDINATION '96: Proceedings of the First International Conference on Coordination Languages and Models*, pages 75–88, London, UK, 1996. Springer-Verlag.

[BKK+01]   Michael G. Burke, Matthew Kaplan, Vincent Kruskal, Harold Ossher, Frank Budinsky, Christina Lau, David Lauzon, and Ed Merks. Xml transformation: Matching & reconciliation. Technical report, IBM, 2001. http://www.research.ibm.com/hyperspace/mr/.

[BKKK87]   Jay Banerjee, Won Kim, Hyoung-Joo Kim, and Henry F. Korth. Semantics and implementation of schema evolution in object-oriented databases. In *SIGMOD '87: Proceedings of the 1987 ACM SIGMOD international conference on Management of data*, pages 311–322, New York, NY, USA, 1987. ACM Press.

[BKN87]   Dan Benanav, Deepak Kapur, and Paliath Narendran. Complexity of matching problems. *J. Symb. Comput.*, 3(1-2):203–216, 1987.

[BKVV06]   Martin Bravenboer, Karl Trygve Kalleberg, Rob Vermaas, and Eelco
             Visser. Stratego/xt 0.16: components for transformation systems. In
             *PEPM '06: Proceedings of the 2006 ACM SIGPLAN symposium on Par-
             tial evaluation and semantics-based program manipulation*, pages 95–99,
             New York, NY, USA, 2006. ACM.

[BM97]   Johan Boye and Jan Maluszynski. Directional types and the annotation
             method. *Journal of Logic Programming*, 33(3):179–220, 1997.

[BMPT90]   Antonio Brogi, Paola Mancarella, Dino Pedreschi, and Franco Turini.
             Logic Programming within a Functional Framework. In P. Deransart
             and J. Małuszyński, editors, *Proceedings of Programming Language Im-
             plementation and Logic Programming*, number 456 in Lecture Notes in
             Computer Science, pages 372–386, London, UK, August 1990. Springer-
             Verlag.

[BMPT94]   Antonio Brogi, Paola Mancarella, Dino Pedreschi, and Franco Turini.
             Modular Logic Programming. *ACM Transactions on Programming Lan-
             guages and Systems*, 16(4):1361–1398, 1994.

[Bos99]   Annalisa Bossi, editor. *Proc. of the 9th International Workshop on
             Logic Based Program Synthesis and Transformation (LOPSTR'99)*, vol-
             ume 1817 of *LNCS*, Venice, Italy, September 1999. Springer-Verlag.

[Bow98]   Anthony Bowers. *Effective Meta-programming in Declarative Languages*.
             PhD thesis, Department of Computer Science, University of Bristol, Jan-
             uary 1998.

[BP89]   Barrett R. Bryant and Aiqin Pan. Rapid Prototyping of Programming Lan-
             guage Semantics Using Prolog. In *Proceedings of the 13th Annual Interna-
             tional Computer Software and Applications Conference (COMPSAC'99)*,
             pages 439–446, Orlando, Florida, September 1989. IEEE Computer Soci-
             ety Press.

[BP96]   Michael Blaha and William Premerlani. A catalog of object model trans-
             formations. In *WCRE '96: Proceedings of the 3rd Working Conference on
             Reverse Engineering (WCRE '96)*, pages 87–96, Washington, DC, USA,
             1996. IEEE Computer Society.

[BP97]   Ira D. Baxter and Christopher W. Pidgeon. Software change through de-
             sign maintenance. In *ICSM '97: Proceedings of the International Confer-
             ence on Software Maintenance*, pages 250–259, Washington, DC, USA,
             1997. IEEE Computer Society.

[BR00]   Keith H. Bennett and Václav T. Rajlich. Software maintenance and evo-
             lution: a roadmap. In *ICSE '00: Proceedings of the Conference on The*

Future of Software Engineering, pages 73–87, New York, NY, USA, 2000. ACM.

[BRV⁺94]   A. Bowles, David Robertson, Wamberto Weber Vasconcelos, Vera M. Vargas, and D. Bental. Applying Prolog programming techniques. *International Journal of Human-Computer Studies*, 41(3):329–350, September 1994.

[BSR04]   Don Batory, Jacob Neal Sarvela, and Axel Rauschmayer. Scaling stepwise refinement. *IEEE Transactions on Software Engineering*, 30(6):355–371, 2004.

[BSVV02]   Mark G.J. van den Brand, Jeroen Scheerder, Jurgen J. Vinju, and Eelco Visser. Disambiguation filters for scannerless generalized LR parsers. In Nigel Horspool, editor, *Compiler Construction (CC'02)*, volume 2304 of *Lecture Notes in Computer Science*, pages 143–158, Grenoble, France, April 2002. Springer-Verlag.

[BV00]   Mark G.J. van den Brand and J. Vinju. Rewriting with layout. In Nachum Derschowitz and Claude Kirchner, editors, *Proceedings of the First International Workshop on Rule-Based Programming RULE'2000*, Sep 2000.

[Byr80]   Lawrence Byrd. Understanding the control flow of Prolog programs. In Sten-Ake Tarnlund, editor, *Proc. of the Logic Programming Workshop*, Debrecen, Hungary, July 1980.

[CDMS02]   James R. Cordy, Thomas R. Dean, Andrew J. Malton, and Kevin A. Schneider. Source transformation in software engineering using the txl transformation system. *Journal of Information and Software Technology*, 44(13):827–837, October 2002.

[CE00]   Krzysztof Czarnecki and Ulrich W. Eisenecker. *Generative Programming, Methods, Tools and Applications*. Addison-Wesley, Boston, San Francisco, New York, 2000.

[CFP08]   Call for papers: - sle 2008, 1st international conference on software language engineering. LDTA mailing list, March 2008. http://planet-sl.org/sle2008/.

[CH87]   Jacques Cohen and Timothy J. Hickey. Parsing and compiling using Prolog. *ACM Transactions on Programming Languages and Systems*, 9(2):125–163, April 1987.

[CH06]   Anthony Cleve and Jean-Luc Hainaut. Co-transformations in database applications evolution. In Ralf Lämmel, João Saraiva, and Joost Visser, editors, *in Proceedings of Generative and Transformational Techniques in Software Engineering, International Summer School, GTTSE 2005, Braga,*

Portugal, July 4-8, 2005. Revised Papers, volume 4143 of *Lecture Notes in Computer Science*, pages 409–421, 2006.

[COV06] Alcino Cunha, José Nuno Oliveira, and Joost Visser. Type-safe two-level data transformation. In Jayadev Misra, Tobias Nipkow, and Emil Sekerinski, editors, *Proceedings of FM 2006: Formal Methods, 14th International Symposium on Formal Methods, Hamilton, Canada, August 21-27, 2006, Proceedings*, volume 4085 of *Lecture Notes in Computer Science*, pages 284–299. Springer, 2006.

[CV07] Alcino Cunha and Joost Visser. Transformation of structure-shy programs: applied to xpath queries and strategic functions. In *PEPM '07: Proceedings of the 2007 ACM SIGPLAN symposium on Partial evaluation and semantics-based program manipulation*, pages 11–20, New York, NY, USA, 2007. ACM.

[DCMS02] Thomas R. Dean, James R. Cordy, Andrew J. Malton, and Kevin A. Schneider. Grammar programming in TXL. In *Proc. Source Code Analysis and Manipulation (SCAM'02)*. IEEE Press, October 2002.

[DCMS03] T.R. Dean, J.R. Cordy, A.J. Malton, and K.A. Schneider. Agile parsing in txl. *Journal of Automated Software Engineering*, 10(4):311–336, October 2003.

[DDVMW00] Theo D'Hondt, Kris De Volder, Kim Mens, and Roel Wuyts. Co-evolution of object-oriented software design and implementation. In *Proceedings of the international symposium on Software Architectures and Component Technology 2000*, 2000.

[Deu96] Arie van Deursen. An overview of ASF+SDF. In Arie van Deursen, Jan Heering, and Paul Klint, editors, *Language Prototyping: An Algebraic Specification Approach*, pages 1–30. World Scientific Publishing Co., 1996.

[dGSA07] Gerardo de Geest, Antoine Savelkoul, and Aali Alikoski. Building a framework to support domain specific language evolution using microsoft dsl tools. In J. Sprinkle, J . Gray, and M. Rossi J.-P. Tolvanen, editors, *Proceedings of the 7th OOPSLA Workshop on Domain-Specific Modeling (DSM'07)*, number TR-38 in Computer Science and Information System Reports, Technical Reports. University of Jyväskylä, 2007.

[DHK96] Arie van Deursen, Jan Heering, and Paul Klint, editors. *Language Prototyping: An Algebraic Specification Approach*, volume 5 of *AMAST Series in Computing*. World Scientific Publishing Co., 1996.

[DKT96] Arie van Deursen, Paul Klint, and Frank Tip. Origin tracking and its applications. In A. van Deursen, J. Heering, and P. Klint, editors, *Language*

Prototyping: An Algebraic Specification Approach, pages 249–294. World Scientific Publishing Co., 1996.

[DM85]   Pierre Deransart and Jan Małuszyński. Relating Logic Programs and Attribute Grammars. *Theory and Practice of Logic Programming*, 2(2):119–155, July 1985.

[DM93]   Pierre Deransart and Jan Małuszyński. *A Grammatical View of Logic Programming*. MIT Press, 1993.

[dV98]   Kris de Volder. *Type-Oriented Logic Meta-Programming*. PhD thesis, Vrije Universiteit Brussels, 1998.

[DVD99]   Kris De Volder and Theo D'Hondt. Aspect-Oriented Logic Meta Programming. In P. Cointe, editor, *Meta-Level Architectures and Reflection, 2nd International Conference, Reflection'99*, volume 1616 of *LNCS*, pages 250–272. Springer Verlag, 1999.

[EEE⁺07] Hartmut Ehrig, Karsten Ehrig, Claudia Ermel, Frank Hermann, and Gabriele Taentzer. Information preserving bidirectional model transformations. In Matthew B. Dwyer and Antónia Lopes, editors, *Fundamental Approaches to Software Engineering*, volume 4422 of *Lecture Notes in Computer Science*, pages 72–86. Springer, 2007.

[Esp95]   David A. Espinosa. *Semantic Lego*. PhD thesis, Graduate School of Arts and Sciences, Columbia University, 1995.

[Fav05]   Jean-Marie Favre. Languages evolve too! Changing the software time scale. In *IWPSE '05: Proceedings of the Eighth International Workshop on Principles of Software Evolution*, pages 33–44, Washington, DC, USA, 2005. IEEE Computer Society.

[FBB⁺99] Martin Fowler, Kent Beck, John Brant, William Opdyke, and Don Roberts. *Refactoring: Improving the Design of Existing Code*. Addison-Wesley, 1999.

[Fuc98]   N.E. Fuchs, editor. *Logic Programming Synthesis and Transformation: 7th International Workshop, LOPSTR'97, Leuven, Belgium. July 10–12, 1997*, number 1463 in Lecture notes in computer science, Berlin, October 1998. Springer-Verlag.

[GG84]   Harald Ganzinger and Robert Giegerich. Attribute coupled grammars. In *SIGPLAN '84: Proceedings of the 1984 SIGPLAN symposium on Compiler construction*, pages 157–170, New York, NY, USA, 1984. ACM Press.

[Gro]   Object Management Group. MDA - Model Driven Architecture. http://www.omg.org/mda.

[Hin00]   Ralf Hinze. A new approach to generic functional programming. In *POPL '00: Proceedings of the 27th ACM SIGPLAN-SIGACT symposium on Principles of programming languages*, pages 119–132, New York, NY, USA, 2000. ACM Press.

[HL94]   P.M. Hill and J.W. Lloyd. *The Gödel Programming Language*. MIT Press, 1994.

[HLR97]   Jörg Harm, Ralf Lämmel, and Günter Riedewald. The Language Development Laboratory. In Magne Haveraaen and Olaf Owe, editors, *Selected papers from the 8th Nordic Workshop on Programming Theory, December 4–6, Oslo, Norway, Research Report 248, ISBN 82-7368-163-7*, pages 77–86, May 1997.

[HM03]   Görel Hedin and Eva Magnusson. JastAdd: an Aspect-Oriented Compiler Construction System. *Sci. Comput. Program.*, 47(1):37–58, April 2003.

[HM05]   Reiko Heckel and Tom Mens, editors. *Proceedings of the Workshop on Software Evolution through Transformations: Model-based vs. Implementation-level Solutions (SETra 2004)*, volume 127,3 of *ENTCS*, 2005.

[HP01a]   Haruo Hosoya and Benjamin Pierce. Regular expression pattern matching for XML. In *POPL '01: Proceedings of the 28th ACM SIGPLAN-SIGACT symposium on Principles of programming languages*, pages 67–80, New York, NY, USA, 2001. ACM Press.

[HP01b]   Haruo Hosoya and Benjamin C. Pierce. XDuce: A typed XML processing language (preliminary report). In *Selected papers from the Third International Workshop WebDB 2000 on The World Wide Web and Databases*, volume 1997, pages 226–244, London, UK, 2001. Springer-Verlag.

[HTJC94]   Jean-Luc Hainaut, C. Tonneau, M. Joris, and M. Chandelon. Schema transformation techniques for database reverse engineering. In *ER '93: Proceedings of the 12th International Conference on the Entity-Relationship Approach*, volume 823, pages 364–375, London, UK, 1994. Springer-Verlag.

[HU80]   J. Hopcroft and Jeffrey D. Ullman. *Introduction to Automata Theory, Languages and Computation*. Addison Wesley, 1980.

[HVP00]   Haruo Hosoya, Jérôme Vouillon, and Benjamin C. Pierce. Regular expression types for XML. *SIGPLAN Not.*, 35(9):11–22, 2000.

[Iro61]   Edgar T. Irons. A syntax-directed compiler for ALGOL 60. *Communications of the ACM*, 4:51–55, 1961.

Bibliography

[ISO]   ISO. *The ISO Standard. 12207-1995.*

[ISO98]   ISO. Guidance on usability. document ISO 9241-11, 1998.

[Jai95]   Ashish Jain. Projections of Logic Programs using Symbol Mappings. In
            Leon Sterling, editor, *Logic Programming, Proceedings of the Twelfth In-
            ternational Conference on Logic Programming, June 13-16, 1995, Tokyo,
            Japan.* MIT Press, June 1995.

[JJ97]   Patrik Jansson and Johan Jeuring. PolyP - a polytypic programming lan-
            guage extension. In *POPL '97: The 24th ACM SIGPLAN-SIGACT Sym-
            posium on Principles of Programming Languages*, pages 470–482. ACM
            Press, 1997.

[JKS94]   Ashish Jain, Marc Kirschenbaum, and Leon S. Sterling. Constructing
            Provably Correct Logic Programs. Technical Report CES-94-04, Depart-
            ment of Computer Engineering and Science, Case Western Reserve Uni-
            versity, March 1994.

[Jon02]   Merijn de Jonge. Pretty-printing for software reengineering. In *Proceed-
            ings; IEEE International Conference on Software Maintenance (ICSM
            2002)*, pages 550–559. IEEE Computer Society Press, October 2002.

[Jon03]   Merijn de Jonge. *To Reuse or To Be Reused: Techniques for Component
            Composition and Construction.* PhD thesis, Faculty of Natural Sciences,
            Mathematics, and Computer Science, University of Amsterdam, January
            2003.

[JS94]   Ashish Jain and Leon S. Sterling. A Methodology for Program Construc-
            tion by Stepwise Structural Enhancement. Technical Report CES-94-10,
            Dep. of Computer Engineering and Science, Case Western Reserve Uni-
            versity, June 1994.

[JVV01]   Merijn de Jonge, Eelco Visser, and Jost Visser. XT: a bundle of pro-
            gram transformation tools. In Mark G. van den Brand and Didier Parigot,
            editors, *Proceedings of Language Descriptions, Tools and Applications
            (LDTA'01)*, volume 44 of *Electronic Notes in Theoretical Computer Sci-
            ence*, pages 211–218. Elsevier Science Publishers, 2001.

[JZ99]   Jens H. Jahnke and A. Zündorf. Applying graph transformations to
            database re-engineering. *Handbook of graph grammars and computing
            by graph transformation: applications, languages, and tools*, 2:267–286,
            1999.

[KETF07]   Adam Kiezun, Michael Dean Ernst, Frank Tip, and Robert Mack Fuhrer.
            Refactoring for parameterizing java classes. In *ICSE '07: Proceedings
            of the 29th international conference on Software Engineering*, pages 437–
            446, Washington, DC, USA, 2007. IEEE Computer Society.

[KG98]   Walter Fred Korman and William G. Griswold. Elbereth: Tool support
              for refactoring java programs. Technical Report CS98-576, University of
              California, San Diego, Computer Science and Engineering, April 3, 1998.

[KHH+01]   Gregor Kiczales, Eric Hilsdale, Jim Hugunin, Mik Kersten, Jeffrey Palm,
              and William G. Griswold. An overview of AspectJ. *Lecture Notes in
              Computer Science*, 2072:327–355, 2001.

[KHR07]   Güter Kniesel, Jan Hannemann, and Tobias Rho. A comparison of logic-
              based infrastructures for concern detection and extraction. In *Workshop on
              Linking Aspect Technology and Evolution (LATE'07) March 12-16, 2007,
              Vancouver, British Columbia*, Vancouver, British Columbia, March 2007.

[KK04]   Günter Kniesel and Helge Koch. Static composition of refactorings. *Sci-
              ence of Computer Programming*, 52(1-3):9–51, 2004. Special issue on
              Program Transformation, edited by Ralf Lämmel, ISSN: 0167-6423, digi-
              tal object identifier http://dx.doi.org/10.1016/j.scico.2004.03.002.

[KL03]   Jan Kort and Ralf Lämmel. Parse-tree annotations meet re-engineering
              concerns. In *Proc. Source Code Analysis and Manipulation (SCAM'03)*,
              pages 161–170. IEEE Computer Society Press, September 2003. 10 pages.

[Kle07]   Meike Klettke. *Modellierung, Bewertung und Evolution von XML-
              Dokumentkollektionen*. Number ISBN 978-3-8325-1790-8. Logos Verlag
              Berlin, decembre 2007. (in german).

[Kli93]   Paul Klint. A meta-environment for generating programming environ-
              ments. *ACM Transactions on Software Engineering and Methodology*,
              2(2):176–201, April 1993.

[KLM+97a]   Gregor Kiczales, John Lamping, Anurag Mendhekar, Chris Maeda,
              Cristina Lopes, Jean-Marc Loingtier, and John Irwin. Aspect-oriented
              programming. In Mehmet Akşit and Satoshi Matsuoka, editors, *11th
              Europeen Conference on Object-Oriented Programming*, volume 1241
              of *Lecture Notes in Computer Science*, pages 220–242. Springer Verlag,
              1997.

[KLM+97b]   Gregor Kiczales, John Lamping, Anurag Menhdhekar, Chris. Maeda,
              Cristina Lopes, Jean-Marc Loingtier, and John Irwin. Aspect-Oriented
              Programming. In Mehmet Akşit and Satoshi Matsuoka, editors, *Proc.
              of the ECOOP'97*, volume 1241 of *Lecture Notes in Computer Science*,
              pages 220–242, Jyvaskyla, Finnland, June 1997. Springer-Verlag.

[KLV02]   Jan Kort, Ralf Lämmel, and Chris Verhoef. The grammar deployment kit.
              In Mark G.J. van den Brand and Ralf Lämmel, editors, *LDTA 2002, Sec-
              ond Workshop on Language Descriptions, Tools and Applications (Satel-
              lite Event of ETAPS 2002), 13 April 2002, Grenoble, France*, volume 65

of *Electronic Notes in Theoretical Computer Science*, pages 117–123. Elsevier Science Publishers, July 2002.

[KLV05a]   Paul Klint, Ralf Lämmel, and Chris Verhoef. Toward an engineering discipline for grammarware. *ACM Trans. Softw. Eng. Methodol.*, 14(3):331–380, 2005.

[KLV05b]   Steven Klusener, Ralf Lämmel, and Chris Verhoef. Architectural Modifications to Deployed Software. *Science of Computer Programming*, 54:143–211, 2005.

[KM00]   Meike Klettke and Holger Meyer. Managing XML documents in object-relational databases. In *Info XML 2000*, May 2000.

[KMBG06]   Andy Kellens, Kim Mens, Johan Birchau, and Kris Gybels. Managing the Evolution of Aspect-Oriented Software with Model-based Pointcuts. In D. Thomas, editor, *Proc. of the ECOOP 2006*, volume 4067 of *LNCS*, pages 501–525. Springer Verlag, 2006.

[KMS96]   Marc Kirschenbaum, Spiro Michaylov, and Leon S. Sterling. Skeletons and Techniques as a Normative Approach to Program Development in Logic-Based Languages. In *Proceedings ACSC'96, Australian Computer Science Communications, 18(1)*, pages 516–524, 1996.

[KMS00]   Nils Klarlund, Anders Mœller, and Michael I. Schwartzbach. *DSD 1.0 Specification*, 2000. Available at http://www.brics.dk/DSD/index1.html.

[Knu68]   Donald E. Knuth. Semantics of context-free languages. *Mathematical Systems Theory*, 2:127–145, 1968.

[KO05]   Karl Klose and Klaus Ostermann. Back to the future: Pointcuts as predicates over traces. In G. T. Leavens, C. Clifton, and R. Lämmel, editors, *Foundations of Aspect-Oriented Languages*. March 2005.

[Kob86]   Isamu Kobayashi. Losslessness and semantic correctness of database schema transformation: another look at schema equivalence. *Inf. Syst.*, 11(1):41–59, 1986.

[KSJ93]   Marc Kirschenbaum, Leon S. Sterling, and Ashish Jain. Relating logic programs via program maps. *Annals in Mathematics and Artificial Intelligence*, 8(III–IV):229–246, 1993.

[Kul99a]   Marija Kulaš. Annotations for Prolog – A Concept and Runtime Handling. In Bossi [Bos99], pages 234–254.

[Kul99b]   Marija Kulaš. Debugging Prolog Using Annotations. In M. Ducassé, A. J. Kusalik, and G. Puebla, editors, *Proc. of the 10th Workshop on Logic Programming Environments (WLPE'99)*, volume 30(4) of *Electronic Notes in Computer Science*, Las Cruces, NM, USA, November 1999. Elsevier.

[KV98]   Paul Klint and Chris Verhoef. Evolutionary software engineering: a component-based approach. In *Proceedings of the IFIP TC2 WG2.4 working conference on Systems implementation 2000 : languages, methods and tools*, pages 1–18, London, UK, UK, 1998. Chapman & Hall, Ltd.

[KV01]   Tobias Kuipers and Joost Visser. Object-oriented tree traversal with JJ-Forester. *Electr. Notes Theor. Comput. Sci.*, 44(2), 2001.

[Lak89]   Arun Lakhotia. *A Workbench for Developing Logic Programs by Stepwise Enhancement.* PhD thesis, Case Western Reserve University, 1989.

[Läm99a]   Ralf Lämmel. Declarative Aspect-Oriented Programming. In Olivier Danvy, editor, *Proc. of the ACM SIGPLAN Workshop on Partial Evaluation and Semantics-Based Program Manipulation (PEPM'99), San Antonio, TX, USA*, number NS-99-1 in BRICS NOTES Series, pages 131–146, January 1999.

[Läm99b]   Ralf Lämmel. *Functional meta-programs towards reusability in the declarative paradigm.* PhD thesis, University of Rostock, Department of Computer Science, 1999.

[Läm00]   Ralf Lämmel. Reuse by Program Transformation. In Greg Michaelson and Phil Trinder, editors, *Functional Programming Trends 1999.* Intellect, 2000. Selected papers from the 1st Scottish Functional Programming Workshop.

[Läm01]   Ralf Lämmel. Grammar Adaptation. In *Proc. Formal Methods Europe (FME) 2001*, volume 2021 of *LNCS*, pages 550–570. Springer-Verlag, 2001.

[Läm02]   Ralf Lämmel. Towards generic refactoring. In *Proc. of Third ACM SIGPLAN Workshop on Rule-Based Programming RULE'02*, Pittsburgh, USA, October5 2002. ACM Press. 14 pages.

[Läm04a]   Ralf Lämmel. Editorial: transformations everywhere. *Science of Computer Programming*, 52(1-3):1–8, 2004.

[Läm04b]   Ralf Lämmel. Evolution of Rule-Based Programs. *Journal of Logic and Algebraic Programming*, 2004. Special Issue on Structural Operational Semantics.

[Läm05]   Ralf Lämmel. Evolution of language interpreters. *Electronic Notes in Theoretical Computer Science*, 127(3):49–54, 2005.

[LdM01]   David Lacey and Oege de Moor. Imperative program transformation by rewriting. *Lecture Notes in Computer Science*, 2027:52–70, 2001.

Bibliography

[Leh74]   Meir Manny Lehman. Programs, cities, students - limits to growth? In *Imperial College of Science and Technology Inaugural Lecture Series*, volume 9, pages 211–229. 1970-1974.

[Leh97]   Meir Manny Lehman. Laws of software evolution revisited. In *EWSPT '96: Proceedings of the 5th European Workshop on Software Process Technology*, number 1149 in LNCS, pages 108–124, London, UK, 1997. Springer-Verlag.

[Les03]   Uwe Lesta. C# Interface to SWI-Prolog. `http://gollem.science.uva.nl/twiki/pl/bin/view/Foreign/CSharpInterface/`, 2003.

[LL01]   Ralf Lämmel and Wolfgang Lohmann. Format Evolution. In *Proc. 7th International Conference on Reverse Engineering for Information Systems RETIS 2001*, volume 155, pages 113–134. OCG, July 2001.

[Loh99]   Wolfgang Lohmann. Ein Rahmenwerk für höher-funktionale Meta-Programmierung. Master's thesis, University of Rostock, Department of Computer Science, 1999.

[Lou97]   Kenneth C. Louden. *Compiler construction: principles and practice*. International Thomson Publishing, 1997.

[LR99]   Ralf Lämmel and Günter Riedewald. Reconstruction of paradigm shifts. In *Second Workshop on Attribute Grammars and their Applications, WAGA 99*, pages 37–56, March 1999. INRIA, ISBN 2-7261-1138-6.

[LR01]   Ralf Lämmel and Günter Riedewald. Prological Language Processing. In Mark van den Brand and Didier Parigot, editors, *Proceedings of the First Workshop on Language Descriptions, Tools and Applications (LDTA'01), Genova, Italy, April 7, 2001, Satellite event of ETAPS'2001*, volume 44 of *ENTCS*. Elsevier Science, April 2001.

[LR03a]   Wolfgang Lohmann and Günter Riedewald. Layout preservation for nontrivial traversal schemes in declarative first order rewriting. Rostocker Informatik-Berichte 28, Universität Rostock, Fachbereich Informatik, August 2003. 14p.

[LR03b]   Wolfgang Lohmann and Günter Riedewald. Towards automatical migration of transformation rules after grammar extension. In *Proceedings of 7th European Conference on Software Maintenance and Reengineering (CSMR 2003)*, pages 30–39. IEEE Computer Society Press, March 2003.

[LRL99]   Ralf Lämmel, Günter Riedewald, and Wolfgang Lohmann. Projections of Programs Revisited. In Bossi [Bos99].

[LRL00]   Ralf Lämmel, Günter Riedewald, and Wolfgang Lohmann. Roles of pro-
            gram extension. In *LOPSTR'99: Selected papers from the 9th Interna-
            tional Workshop on Logic Programming Synthesis and Transformation*,
            pages 136–155, London, UK, 2000. Springer-Verlag.

[LRS04]   Wolfgang Lohmann, Günter Riedewald, and Markus Stoy. Semantics-
            preserving migration of semantic rules during left recursion removal in
            attribute grammars. *Electronic Notes in Theoretical Computer Science*,
            110 C:133–148, Dezember 2004.

[LRW08]   Wolfgang Lohmann, Günter Riedewald, and Guido Wachsmuth. Aspect-
            oriented prolog in a language processing context. *IET Software, Special
            Issue on Software Language Engineering*, 2008.

[LRZ06]   Wolfgang Lohmann, Günter Riedewald, and Thomas Zühlke. A lightweigt
            infrastructure to support experimenting with heterogeneous transforma-
            tions. In *Proceedings of the International Conference on .NET Technolo-
            gies*, May 2006.

[LV01a]   Ralf Lämmel and Chris Verhoef. Cracking the 500-language problem.
            IEEE Software, 18(6):78–88, November/December 2001.

[LV01b]   Ralf Lämmel and Chris Verhoef. Semi-automatic Grammar Recovery.
            Software—Practice & Experience, 31(15):1395–1438, December 2001.

[LW01]   Ralf Lämmel and Guido Wachsmuth. Transformation of SDF syntax def-
            initions in the ASF+SDF meta-Environment. In Mark van den Brand and
            Didier Parigot, editors, *Proceedings of the First Workshop on Language
            Descriptions, Tools and Applications (LDTA'01), Genova, Italy, April 7,
            2001, Satellite event of ETAPS'2001*, volume 44 of *Electronic Notes in
            Theoretical Computer Science*. Elsevier Science, April 2001.

[MDDB⁺03]   Tom Mens, Serge Demeyer, Bart Du Bois, Hans Stenten, and Pieter
            Van Gorp. Refactoring: Current research and future trends. *Electronic
            Notes in Theoretical Computer Science*, 82(3):483–499, December 2003.

[Mic06]   Microsoft   Research,   http://www.research.microsoft.com/fsharp/.
            F#   Homepage,   (februar   2006)   edition,   2006.
            http://www.research.microsoft.com/fsharp/.

[MJ95]   Erik Meijer and Johan Jeuring. Merging monads and folds for functional
            programming. In J. Jeuring and E. Meijer, editors, *Tutorial Text 1st Int.
            Spring School on Advanced Functional Programming Techniques, Bås-
            tad, Sweden, 24–30 May 1995*, volume 925, pages 228–266, Berlin, 1995.
            Springer-Verlag.

Bibliography

[Mog91]   Eugenio Moggi. Notions of computation and monads. *Inf. Comput.*, 93(1):55–92, July 1991.

[Moo01]   Leon Moonen. Generating robust parsers using island grammars. In *Proceedings of the 8th Working Conference on Reverse Engineering*, pages 13–22. IEEE Computer Society Press, October 2001.

[Moo02]   Leon Moonen. Lightweight impact analysis using island grammars. In *Proceedings of the 10th International Workshop on Program Comprehension (IWPC 2002)*. IEEE Computer Society Press, June 2002.

[Mos99]   Peter D. Mosses. Foundations of modular sos. In Miroslaw Kutylowski, Leszek Pacholski, and Tomasz Wierzbicki, editors, *Mathematical Foundations of Computer Science 1999, 24th International Symposium, MFCS'99, Szklarska Poreba, Poland, September 6-10, 1999, Proceedings*, volume 1672 of *Lecture Notes in Computer Science*, pages 70–80. Springer, 1999.

[Mos02]   Peter D. Mosses. Pragmatics of modular sos. In *AMAST '02: Proceedings of the 9th International Conference on Algebraic Methodology and Software Technology*, pages 21–40, London, UK, 2002. Springer-Verlag.

[MP97]   Peter McBrien and Alexandra Poulovassilis. A formal framework for er schema transformation. In D. W. Embley and R. C. Goldstein, editors, *ER '97: Proceedings of the 16th International Conference on Conceptual Modeling*, volume 1331 of *Lecture Notes in Computer Science*, pages 408–421, London, UK, November 3-5 1997. Springer-Verlag.

[MS99]   Erik Meijer and Mark Shields. XMΛ: A functional language for constructing and manipulating XML documents. Technical report, IBM, 1999. Draft, available at http://www.cartesianclosed.com/pub/xmlambda/.

[MSV00]   Tova Milo, Dan Suciu, and Victor Vianu. Typechecking for XML transformers. In *PODS '00: Proceedings of the nineteenth ACM SIGMOD-SIGACT-SIGART symposium on Principles of database systems, May 15-17 Dallas, Texas, USA*, pages 11–22, New York, NY, USA, 2000. ACM Press.

[MvLA99]   Marjan Mernik, Viljem Žumer, Mitja Lenič, and Enis Avdičaušević. Implementation of multiple attribute grammar inheritance in the tool lisa. *SIGPLAN Not.*, 34(6):68–75, 1999.

[MWD+05]   Tom Mens, Michel Wermelinger, Stéphane Ducasse, Serge Demeyer, Robert Hirschfeld, and Mehdi Jazayeri. Challenges in software evolution. In *IWPSE '05: Proceedings of the Eighth International Workshop on Principles of Software Evolution*, pages 13–22, Washington, DC, USA, 2005. IEEE Computer Society.

[Nai96]   Lee Naish. Higher order logic programming in Prolog. In M. Chakravarty, Y. Guo, and T. Ida, editors, *JICSLP'96 Post Conference Workshop on Multi-Paradigm Logic Programming*, Bonn, June 1996.

[NS98]   Lee Naish and Leon Sterling. A Higher Order Reconstruction of Stepwise Enhancement. In Fuchs [Fuc98], pages 245–262.

[NS00]   Lee Naish and Leon S. Sterling. Stepwise Enhancement and Higher-Order Programming in Prolog. *The Journal of Functional and Logic Programming*, 2000(4):34–58, March 2000.

[OJ90]   W. F. Opdyke and R. J. Johnson. Refactoring: An Aid in Designing Application Frameworks. In *Proceedings of the Symposium on Object-Oriented Programming emphasizing Practical Applications*, pages 145–160. ACM-SIGPLAN, September 1990.

[O'K84]   Richard A. O'Keefe. advice.pl – Interlisp-like advice package. In *DEC-10 Prolog Library*. August 1984.

[OMG]   OMG. UML specification, table with formally released versions of UML. read 2008-06-16.

[OMG08]   OMG. Xml metadata interface, September 2008. http://www.omg.org/spec/XMI/.

[Opd92]   William F. Opdyke. *Refactoring Object-Oriented Frameworks*. PhD thesis, University of Illinois at Urbana-Champaign, 1992.

[Paa91]   Jukka Paakki. Prolog in Practical Compiler Writing. *Computer Journal*, 34(1):64–72, February 1991.

[Paa95]   Jukka Paakki. Attribute grammar paradigms — A high-level methodology in language implementation. *ACM Comput. Surv.*, 27(2):196–255, 1995.

[Par90]   Helmut A. Partsch. *Specification and transformation of programs: a formal approach to software development*. Springer-Verlag New York, Inc., New York, NY, USA, 1990.

[Pep99]   Peter Pepper. LR Parsing = Grammar Transformation + LL Parsing. Technical Report CS-99-05, TU Berlin, April 1999.

[Pig96]   Thomas M. Pigoski. *Practical Software Maintenance: Best Practices for Managing Your Software Investment*. John Wiley & Sons, Inc., New York, NY, USA, 1996.

[PJ07]   Markus Pizka and Elmar Jürgens. Automated language evolution. In *First IEEE/IFIP International Symposium on Theoretical Aspects of Software Engineering*, pages 305–315, Shanghai, China, June 2007. IEEE/IFIP, IEEE Computer Society.

[Pla]   Plato. Republic. Socratic dialog.

[PP96]   Alberto Pettorossi and Maurizio Proietti. Rules and strategies for trans-
            forming functional and logic programs. *ACM Computing Surveys*,
            28(2):360–414, June 1996.

[PS90]   A. John Power and Leon Sterling. A Notion of Map between Logic Pro-
            grams. In Peter Warren, David H.D.; Szerdei, editor, *Proceedings of the
            7th International Conference on Logic Programming (ICLP '90)*, pages
            390–404, Jerusalem, June 1990. MIT Press.

[PW80]   Fernando C. N. Pereira and David H. D. Warren. Definite Clause Gram-
            mars for Language Analysis - A Survey of the Formalism and a Com-
            parison with Augmented Transition Networks. *Artificial Intelligence*,
            13(3):231–278, 1980.

[RBJ97]   Don Roberts, John Brant, and Ralph E. Johnson. A refactoring tool for
            Smalltalk. *Theory and Practice of Object Systems (TAPOS)*, 3(4):253–
            263, 1997.

[RC06]   Chanchal Kumar Roy and James R. Cordy. Evaluating the evolution of
            small scale open source software systems. In *Special issue on CIC 2006,
            15th International Conference on Computing*, Research in Computing Sci-
            ence 23, 2006.

[RF98]   Julian Richardson and Norbert Fuchs. Development of Correct Transfor-
            mation Schemata for Prolog Programs. In Fuchs [Fuc98].

[Rie91]   Günter Riedewald. Prototyping by Using an Attribute Grammar as a Logic
            Program. In Henk Alblas and Borivoj Melichar, editors, *Proceedings of the
            International Summer School on Attribute Grammars, Applications and
            Systems (SAGA'91)*, volume 545 of *LNCS*, pages 401–437, Prag, Tsche-
            choslowakei, June 1991. Springer-Verlag.

[Rie92]   Günter Riedewald. The LDL - Language Development Laboratory. In
            Compiler Construction, 4th Int. Conf., CC'92, Proceedings, volume 641
            of *Electronic Notes in Computer Science*, pages 88–94, 1992.

[RK04]   Tobias Rho and Günter Kniesel. Uniform Genericity for Aspect Lan-
            guages. Technical Report IAI-TR-2004-4, CS Dep. III, University of
            Bonn, 2004.

[RL88]   Günter Riedewald and Uwe Lämmel. Using an Attribute Grammar as a
            Logic Program. In Pierre Deransart, Bernard Lorho, and Jan Małuszyński,
            editors, *Proceedings of the 1st International Workshop on Programming
            Language Implementation and Logic Programming (PLILP'88)*, volume
            348 of *Lecture Notes in Computer Science*, pages 161–179, Orléans,
            Frankreich, May 1988. Springer-Verlag.

[RM85]   Peter Rechenberg and Hanspeter Mössenböck. *Ein Compiler - Generator für Mikrocomputer*. Carl Hanser Verlag, 1985. in german.

[RMHVP06]   Damijan Rebernak, Marjan Mernik, Pedro Rangel Henriques, and Maria Joao Varando Pereira. Domain-Specific Aspect Languages for Modularizing Crosscutting Concerns in Grammar. In *Proceedings of DSAL 2006, Portland, OR*, Oct 2006.

[Rob92]   David Stuart Robertson. A Simple Prolog Techniques Editor for Novice Users. In Geraint A. Wiggins, Chris Mellish, and Tim Duncan, editors, *Proceedings of the 3rd UK Conference on Logic Programming, Edinburgh, 10-12 April 1991. Workshops in Computing*, pages 190–205. Springer, 1992.

[Rob96]   David Stuart Robertson. An Empirical Study of the LSS Specification Toolkit in Use. In *8th International Conference on Software Engineering and Knowledge Engineering, SEKE '96, June 10-12, 1996, Lake Tahoe, Nevada, USA*, pages 153–160. Knowledge Systems Institute, June 1996.

[Rob00]   C. Moore Roberts. Removing left recursion from context-free grammars. In *Proceedings of the first conference on North American chapter of the Association for Computational Linguistics*, pages 249–255. Morgan Kaufmann Publishers Inc., 2000.

[SB95]   James P. Schmeiser and David T. Barnard. Producing a Top-Down Parse Order with Bottom-up Parsing. *Information Processing Letters*, 54(6):323–326, 1995.

[Sch06]   Daniel C. Schmidt. Model-driven engineering. *IEEE Computer*, 39(2):25–31, February 2006. Guest Editor's Introduction.

[SdM01]   Ganesh Sittampalam and Oege de Moor. Higher-order pattern matching for automatically applying fusion transformations. *Lecture Notes in Computer Science*, 2053:218–237, 2001.

[SdPL99]   M. Sant'Anna and J. C. S. do Prado Leite. An architectural framework for software transformation. In *Proceedings of the International Workshop on Software Transformations STS'99, ICSE'99*, 1999.

[SGM86]   Information processing – text and office systems – standard generalized markup language (SGML), 1986.

[Sie99]   Siemens AG Österreich, Wien. *IF/Prolog V5.3 Reference Manual*, 1999.

[SJK93a]   Leon Sterling, Ashish Jain, and Marc Kirschenbaum. Composition Based on Skeletons and Techniques. In *ILPS '93 post conference workshop on Methodologies for Composing Logic Programs, Vancouver*, October 1993.

Bibliography

[SJK93b]   Leon S. Sterling, Ashish Jain, and Marc Kirschenbaum. Composition Based on Skeletons and Techniques. In *ILPS'93 Post Conference Workshop on Methodologies for Composing Logic Programs*, Vancouver, Canada, October 1993.

[SK93]   Leon S. Sterling and Marc Kirschenbaum. Applying Techniques to Skeletons. In Jean-Marie Jacquet, editor, *Constructing Logic Programs*, chapter 6, pages 127–140. John Wiley & Sons Ltd, 1993.

[SK94]   Ken Slonneger and Barry L. Kurtz. *Formal Syntax and Semantics of Programming Languages: A Laboratory Based Approach*. Addison-Wesley, 1994.

[Spi02]   Diomidis Spinellis. Unix tools as visual programming components in a GUI-builder environment. *Software Practice and Experience*, 32(1):57–71, 2002.

[SS97]   Leon Sterling and Ehud Shapiro. *The Art of Prolog*. MIT Press, Cambridge, USA, second edition, 1997.

[SS04]   Tom Schrijvers and Alexander Serebrenik. Improving prolog programs: Refactoring for prolog. In *Logic Programming, Proc. of the 20th International Conference, ICLP 2004*, volume 3132 of *LNCS*, pages 58–72, Saint-Malo, France, September 6-10, 2004. Springer Berlin/Heidelberg.

[SSB+00]   Jayavel Shanmugasundaram, Eugene J. Shekita, Rimon Barr, Michael J. Carey, Bruce G. Lindsay, Hamid Pirahesh, and Berthold Reinwald. Efficiently publishing relational data as xml documents. In *VLDB '00: Proceedings of the 26th International Conference on Very Large Data Bases*, pages 65–76, San Francisco, CA, USA, 2000. Morgan Kaufmann Publishers Inc.

[Ste03]   Dirk Steinke. Refactoring für logische Programme. Master's thesis, University of Rostock, 2003. (in german).

[Ste07]   Perdita Stevens. Bidirectional model transformations in qvt: Semantic issues and open questions. In *Proceedings of 10th International Conference on Model Driven Engineering Languages and Systems, MODELS 2007, Nashville October 5, 2007*, volume 4735 of *Lecture Notes in Computer Science*, pages 1–15. Springer, 2007.

[SV99]   Alex Sellink and Chris Verhoef. An architecture for automated software maintenance. In *IWPC '99: Proceedings of the 7th International Workshop on Program Comprehension*, page 38, Washington, DC, USA, 1999. IEEE Computer Society.

[SV00] Alex Sellink and Chris Verhoef. Scaffolding for software renovation. In *CSMR '00: Proceedings of the Conference on Software Maintenance and Reengineering*, page 161, Washington, DC, USA, 2000. IEEE Computer Society.

[TM03] Tom Tourwé and Tom Mens. Identifying refactoring opportunities using logic meta programming. In *Proceeings of 7th European Conference on Software Maintenance and Reengineering (CSMR 2003)*, pages 91–100. IEEE Computer Society Press, March 2003.

[Tou02] Tom Tourwé. *Automated Support For Framework-Based Software Evolution*. PhD thesis, Departement Informatica, Vrije Universiteit Brussel, 2002.

[TS97] Walid Taha and Tim Sheard. Multi-stage programming with explicit annotations. In *Symposium on Partial Evaluation and Semantics-Based Program Manipulation, Amsterdam, The Netherlands, June 1997*, volume 32(12) of *ACM SIGPLAN Notices*, pages 203–217. New York: ACM Press, 1997.

[Van01] Michael L. Van De Vanter. Preserving the documentary structure of source code in language-based transformation tools. In *IEEE International Workshop on Source Code Analysis and Manipulation (SCAM2001)*, Nov 2001.

[Vas93] Wamberto Weber Vasconcelos. Designing Prolog Programming Techniques. In *Logic Program Synthesis and Transformation'93*, pages 85–99, 1993.

[vdBdJKO00] Mark G. J. van den Brand, Hayco A. de Jong, Paul Klint, and Pieter A. Olivier. Efficient annotated terms. *Software, Practice and Experience*, 30(3):259–291, 2000.

[vdBSV98] Mark G. J. van den Brand, A. Sellink, and C. Verhoef. Control flow normalization for cobol/cics legacy system. In *CSMR '98: Proceedings of the 2nd Euromicro Conference on Software Maintenance and Reengineering (CSMR'98)*, page 11, Washington, DC, USA, 1998. IEEE Computer Society.

[vdBvDH+01] Marc van den Brand, Arie van Deursen, Jan Heering, Hayco de Jong, Merijn de Jonge, Tobias Kuipers, Paul Klint, Leon Moonen, Pieter A. Olivier, Jeroen Scheerder, Jurgen J. Vinju, Eelco Visser, and Joost Visser. The ASF+SDF Meta-Environment: a component-based language development environment. In Reinhard Wilhelm, editor, *Proceedings of the 10th International Conference on Compiler Construction (CC'01)*, volume 2027 of *LNCS*, pages 365–370, Genua, Italien, April 2001. Springer-Verlag.

Bibliography

[Vin05]   Jurgen J. Vinju. *Analysis and Transformation of Source Code by Parsing and Rewriting*. PhD thesis, University of Amsterdam, november 2005.

[Vis97a]   Eelco Visser. Scannerless generalized-LR parsing. Technical report, University of Amsterdam, 1997. Technical Report P9707, Programming Research Group, University of Amsterdam.

[Vis97b]   Eelco Visser. *Syntax Definition for Language Prototyping*. PhD thesis, University of Amsterdam, 1997.

[Vis01]   Eelco Visser. Stratego: A language for program transformation based on rewriting strategies. System description of Stratego 0.5. In A. Middeldorp, editor, *Rewriting Techniques and Applications (RTA'01)*, volume 2051 of *Lecture Notes in Computer Science*, pages 357–361. Springer-Verlag, May 2001.

[Vis02]   Eelco Visser. Meta-programming with concrete object syntax. In *Generative Programming and Component Engineering (GPCE'02)*, Lecture Notes in Computer Science. Springer-Verlag, Oct 2002.

[Vis04]   Eelco Visser. Program transformation with Stratego/XT: Rules, strategies, tools, and systems in StrategoXT-0.9. In C. Lengauer et al., editors, *Domain-Specific Program Generation*, volume 3016 of *Lecture Notes in Computer Science*, pages 216–238. Spinger-Verlag, June 2004.

[VV08]   Sander Vermolen and Eelco Visser. Heterogeneous coupled evolution of software languages. In K. Czarnecki, editor, *International Conference on Model Driven Engineering Languages and Systems (MODELS'08)*, Lecture Notes in Computer Science. Springer, October 2008.

[W3C99a]   W3C. XML Path Language (XPath) version 1.0, November 1999. http://www.w3.org/TR/xpath/.

[W3C99b]   W3C. XSL Transformations (XSLT) version 1.0, November 1999. http://www.w3.org/TR/xslt/.

[W3C00a]   W3C. Extensible Markup Language (XML) 1.0 (second edition), October 2000. http://www.w3.org/TR/REC-xml.

[W3C00b]   W3C. XML Schema Part 0: Primer, October 2000. http://www.w3.org/TR/xmlschema-0/.

[W3C01a]   W3C. XML Schema Part 1: Structures, May 2001. http://www.w3.org/TR/xmlschema-1/.

[W3C01b]   W3C. XML Schema Part 2: Datatypes, May 2001. http://www.w3.org/TR/xmlschema-2/.

[Wad92]   Philip Wadler. The essence of functional programming. In *Conference Record of the Nineteenth Annual ACM SIGPLAN-SIGACT Symposium on Principles of Programming Languages*, pages 1–14, Albequerque, New Mexico, January 1992.

[Wag98]   Tim A. Wagner. *Practical Algorithms for Incremental Software Development Environments*. PhD thesis, "Department of Electrical Engineering and Computer Science, Computer Science Division, University of California, Berkeley", March 1998.

[Wal07]   Robert Waltemath. Einfluss des Programmierstils auf Layouterhaltung bei Quelle-zu-Quelle Transformationen. Studienarbeit, in german, 2007.

[War80]   David H. D. Warren. Logic programming and compiler writing. *Software — Practice and Experience*, 10(2):97–125, February 1980.

[WB00]   David Watt and Deryck Brown. *Programming Language Processors in Java*. Prentice Hall, February 2000.

[WBBL99]   Jon Whittle, Alan Bundy, Richard Boulton, and Helen Lowe. An ML editor based on proofs-as-programs. In *ASE '99: Proceedings of the 14th IEEE international conference on Automated software engineering*, page 166, Washington, DC, USA, 1999. IEEE Computer Society.

[Wes01]   Hedzer Westra. Cobolx: Transformations for Improving COBOL Programs. In Eelco Visser, editor, *Proceedings of the Second Stratego Users Day (SUD'01)*, Utrecht, The Netherlands, February 2001. Institute for Information and Computing Sciences, Utrecht University.

[WGRM05]   Hui Wu, Jeff Gray, Suman Roychoudhury, and Marjan Mernik. Weaving a Debugging Aspect into Domain-Specific Language Grammars. In *SAC '05: Proceedings of the 2005 ACM symposium on Applied computing*, pages 1370–1374, New York, NY, USA, 2005. ACM Press.

[Wie03]   Jan Wielemaker. An overview of the SWI-Prolog programming environment. In A. Serebenik F. Mesnard, editor, *Proceedings of the 13th International Workshop on Logic Programming Environments*, volume cW 371., pages 1–16,, Heverlee, Belgium,, 2003. Katholieke Universiteit Leuven,.

[Wie06]   Jan Wielemaker. *SWI Prolog 5.6 Reference Manual*. Department of Social Science Informatics, University of Amsterdam, Amsterdam, March 2006.

[Wie07]   Jan Wielemaker. SWI-Prolog Home Page. http://www.swi-prolog.org/, 2007.

[Wil97]   David S. Wile. Abstract syntax from concrete syntax. In *Proceedings of International Conference on Software Engineering (ICSE'97)*, pages 472–480. ACM Press, May 1997.

Bibliography

[WM77]   David A. Watt and Ole Lehrmann Madsen. Extended attribute grammars. Technical Report no. 10, University of Glasgow, July 1977.

[WP94]   Paul G. Whiting and Robert S. V. Pascoe. A history of data-flow languages. *IEEE Ann. Hist. Comput.*, 16(4):38–59, 1994.

[WR99]   Malcolm Wallace and Colin Runciman. Haskell and XML: generic combinators or type-based translation? In *ICFP '99: Proceedings of the fourth ACM SIGPLAN international conference on Functional programming*, pages 148–159, New York, NY, USA, 1999. ACM Press.

[WWWa]   WWW.   Data   base   of   rewriting   systems. http://rewriting.loria.fr/systems.html.

[WWWb]   WWW. Eclipse. 2008-06-13.

[WWWc]   WWW. Intellij idea. 2008-06-13.

[WWWd]   WWW. Transmogrify. 2008-06-13.

[WWW08]   WWW. Monodevelop, September 2008.

[XP99]   Hongwei Xi and Frank Pfenning. Dependent types in practical programming. In *POPL '99: Proceedings of the 26th ACM SIGPLAN-SIGACT symposium on Principles of programming languages*, pages 214–227, New York, NY, USA, 1999. ACM Press.

[YAK95]   Mark Young, Danielle Argiro, and Steven Kubica. Cantata: visual programming environment for the Khoros system. *SIGGRAPH Comput. Graph.*, 29(2):22–24, 1995.

Index

.NET, 146

abstract syntax, 88
abstract syntax tree, *see* AST
advice, 114, **129**
    around, 130
    port, 130
    term, 130
AOP, **114**, 113–144
around advice, 115, 130
aspect, 114, **130**
    generic, 116, 131, **134**
aspect library, 133
aspect-oriented programming, *see* AOP
AspectG, 140
AspectLISA, 140
AST, 118
    construction, 118, 119
attributed grammar, 64
    i-attributed, 72
    multi pass, 74
    notion, 64
    s-attributed, 68

box, 150–152

co-evolution, 7–9
computation
    backward, 151
    forward, 151
concern, 114, 117
    crosscutting, 114
consequence
    grammar evolution, 162
context, *see* pointcut context
converter, 150
core calculus, 30–35
crosscutting, 114

crosscutting expression, 114

disciplined meta-programming, 21, 163
DTD, 41–61

effect space, 24
evolution, 3–9
    DTD, 41
    format, 41–61
    grammar
        consequence, 162
    language description, 9
    maintenance tool, 13
    XML, 41

format evolution, 41–61

generalised technique, 134
grammar
    aspect, 117–123, 140
    extension, 84
    logic, *see* logic grammar
grammar adaptation, 64, 78, 87
grammar engineering, 9, 63
grammar extension, 79–96
grammarware agenda, 9

heuristics, 93

IF/Prolog, 125

join point, 114, **125**, 126
join point model, 114
join point shadow, 114

language description
    aspect, 164
language processing
    crosscutting, 114
language processor, 11

aspect, 117–123
language technology, 2
Laola, 115, 117, 125
  DSL, 136
Laptob, 117
layout, 80
layout preservation, 79–111
layout preserving
  conditional strongly, 101
  strongly, 101
  weakly, 101
left recursion removal, 63–78
Lisa, 152
LLL grammar, 87
Logic aspect-oriented language, *see* Laola
logic grammar, 12, 88, 113, 117
  modularisation, 113–115

maintenance, 3–9
  language description, 9
  maintenance tool, 81
  tool, 1
    usability, 164
  tools
    improvement, 163
maintenance factory, 10–11, 161
meta-programming framework, 23
migration
  document, 41
  semantic rule, 63–78
  transformation rule, 79–96
migration relation, 91

object-oriented combination model, 145,
    148, 164

pointcut, 114, **126**
  use, 129
pointcut context, 116, **127, 129**
  left, 128
  parallel, 127
  parent, 128
pointcut description, 114, **126**
port advice, 115, 130
port model, 115, 116, **125**

Prolog, 12, 113–144
  control flow, 125
  port model, *see* port model
  programming techniques, 116

refactoring, 5, 49
research question, 13–16

scanner integration, 118
semantics-preservation, 29
skeleton, 133
SMF, *see* maintenance factory
software co-evolution, *see* co-evolution
software evolution, *see* evolution
software language engineering, 1
software maintenance, *see* maintenance
software maintenance factory, *see* main-
    tenance factory
stepwise enhancement, 21, 115, 133
sumlist
  aspect-oriented description, 123
Swell, 117, 136

technique, 123, 133
  calculate, **134**
  generalised, 134
techniques, 35
term advice, 115, 130
trace, 89, 90, 92, 93
Trane, 145–159
  box, 150–152
    comand line tools, 155
    DLL import, 152
    hierachy box, 152
    native libraries, 152
    web service, 152
    XSLT, 154
  concept, 147
  converter, 150
  dynamic compilation, 156
  object-oriented model, 148
  web service, 152
transformation
  semantics-preserving, 21
  two-level, 58

transformation net, 147
two-level transformation, 58

usability, 16, 164

weave, 93
weaver, 92, 93, 114, 116, **131**
web service, 152

XML, 41–61
XSLT, 154